PURSUING CHINA

Pursuing
C·H·I·N·A

Memoir of a Beaver Liaison Officer

BRIAN L. EVANS

THE UNIVERSITY
of ALBERTA PRESS

Published by
The University of Alberta Press
Ring House 2
Edmonton, Alberta, Canada
T6G 2E1
www.uap.ualberta.ca

LIBRARY AND ARCHIVES CANADA
CATALOGUING IN PUBLICATION

Evans, Brian L., 1932–
   Pursuing China : memoir of a beaver
liason officer / Brian L.Evans.

Includes index.
Also issued in electronic format.
ISBN 978-0-88864-600-2

   1. China–History–1976-2002.
   2. China–History–2002-.
   3. China–Foreign relations–Canada.
   4. Canada–Foreign relations–China.
   5. Diplomatic and consular service,
      Canadian–Biography.
   6. College teachers–Canada–Biography.
   I. Title.

DS779.29.E93A3 2012   951.05092
C2011-907315-3

First edition, first printing, 2012.
Printed and bound in Canada by
Houghton Boston Printers, Saskatoon,
Saskatchewan.
Copyediting and Proofreading by Kirsten
Craven.
Indexing by Adrian Mather.

The University of Alberta Press is committed to protecting our natural environment.
As part of our efforts, this book is printed
on Enviro Paper: it contains 100% post-
consumer recycled fibres and is acid- and
chlorine-free.

The University of Alberta Press gratefully
acknowledges the support received for
its publishing program from The Canada
Council for the Arts. The University of Alberta Press also gratefully acknowledges
the financial support of the Government
of Canada through the Canada Book Fund
(CBF) and the Government of Alberta
through the Alberta Multimedia Development Fund (AMDF) for its publishing
activities.

Canada   Canada Council   Conseil des Arts   Government
          for the Arts   du Canada   of Alberta ■

To my parents Dora Evelyn Lines and Evan Evans,
who went without so I might prosper.

CONTENTS

★ ★ ★ ★

ACKNOWLEDGEMENTS

What sparks an interest in a youngster's mind? How long-lasting is an interest once sparked? In my case, it was China, an interest sparked by a childhood friendship with a young Chinese Canadian boy named Herbert How. This memoir is an attempt to illustrate the consequences of that interest sparked over seven decades ago.

Were it not for the persistence of Patricia Fong, the following pages would have been unlikely to have seen print. Patricia, a fellow Taberite, but much younger, thought my life experiences worthy of an audience. To prove otherwise, I prepared a draft memoir for her to read. To my genuine surprise, this only whetted her appetite and she insisted that I add more detail. I did so in the spring and early summer of 2009 while I was undergoing radiation treatment for prostate cancer. This second draft took on the guise of a confession. I decided to ask the advice of another friend, Merrill Distad, as to what to do with it. He generously read the manuscript and became an enthusiast. He suggested some changes and advised me to try the University of Alberta Press as a possible publisher. Linda Cameron, the director of the press, agreed to have a look at the text, which now included Distad's suggestions, and ultimately she and her colleagues decided to send it to outside readers. Meanwhile, I circulated the manuscript to Debbie Forsyth and Ginette Lamontagne, both close friends, for their reactions. They shared Distad's enthusiasm with one or two small caveats. The anonymous, outside readers were more muted in their opinions but raised no insurmountable obstacles or objections to publication. Throughout this time, the various drafts always included the subtitle, Memoir.

In the spring of 2010, the editorial board of the press suggested that the manuscript should be revised to make it less of a memoir and more of a history of China–Canada relations. I reworked the manuscript in the summer, but I was not happy with it—I was wedded to the original chronology. I solicited the opinions of two more friends, Pat Prestwich and Jane Haslett. Each independently rejected the new formulation in favour of a memoir, while Prestwich made substantive editorial suggestions, most of which I incorporated before resubmitting the manuscript to the press. In September 2010, Cameron and University of Alberta Press Managing Editor Peter Midgley sent it off to freelance editors at Craven Editorial for an opinion. To my great joy, after reading it through, Meaghan Craven opined that the manuscript should be reworked to transform it back into a chronological memoir. The University of Alberta Press accepted this view and placed me in the hands of Kirsten Craven, with the result that you now hold in your hands. Nearly all of the photos were taken by me or by members of my family, with some enhanced by my friend Gordon Elbrond. Alan Brownoff has made them fit for publication.

To each of the individuals mentioned above, I owe debts of gratitude for their encouragement, suggestions, and efforts to make the manuscript better. In addition, I have been urged on in this endeavour by friends on both sides of the Pacific: Brian Harris, Josh Bilyk, Murray Douglas, Gordon Houlden, Terry Mackey, Sharon Mah, Victor Rajudko, Lynn Ogden, Wang Bing, Liu Guangtai, Chen Qineng, and Jiang Peng. Throughout, I have relied upon my constant companion, MOOKIE. I, of course, accept full responsibility for the content and opinions contained between these covers.

Finally, I will add this note on the text. In China, family names appear first. Thus, for example, Wang Qijiang's surname is Wang. Throughout the text, the system known as *pinyin* is used for Chinese words and names, with the exception of Sun Yat-sen, Chiang Kai-shek, and Peking duck, whose names became popular in the West through an earlier system of transliteration.

BRIAN L. EVANS
Edmonton, Alberta
The Year of the Rabbit

ONE ★ ★ ★ ★

Prairie Roots

A WHITE ASH YOUTH

In 1932, when I was born, my father was already broke. A Welshman, miner, insurance salesman, and World War I veteran who was mustard gassed twice, Evan Evans was advised by his doctor to find a climate drier than Britain's. In 1920 he married Dora Lines, an Englishwoman who was also a war veteran, and sailed for Canada, settling on the arid prairie of southern Alberta. The climate was certainly drier than that of Britain, but much colder. Evan nearly died each winter when his mustard-scalded lungs filled with phlegm. Dora, raised in the brilliant green lands of Suffolk, found herself surrounded by brown grass, cacti, and Russian thistle that provided shelter for gophers, rattlesnakes, and all manner of bugs and beetles. Moreover, the westerly wind that blew daily from dawn to dusk annoyed her ears. She was deaf, the result of a childhood illness.

I was the youngest of four children born at three- to four-year intervals. Evan, born in 1921 in Lethbridge, and I, born in Taber, bracketed our two sisters, Gwen and Mary, born in 1924 and 1928 in Cardston. Taber, Alberta, where the family moved in the fall of 1928, was the family's final stop in our father's search to find prosperity in the mining business. Once a thriving mining town with eleven active coal mines, Taber had passed its peak when Evan invested his remaining cash in the Bay mine located directly north of the town.[1] Along with two farmers, who invested a couple thousand each, my father invested around a thousand dollars in the mine, only to find that it flooded and was unworkable. His partners then quit, leaving my father "low and wet," so to speak. Added to this, the expansion of the Drumheller coal fields, the onslaught of the Great Depression, and the discovery of sufficient natural gas in the area to enable the town to heat homes and businesses pretty well put paid to the coal business, at least as far as my father was concerned. He turned to farming in the spring of 1932, moving the family to a house and a quarter section of farm land four miles north of Taber. This move would leave my parents with no visible means of support. The land was no prize with its barren soil, and the "house" was actually one of three buildings that remained from the Regal Colliery, a large mining enterprise on a site called White Ash, so named because of the colour of the residue from the burned coal. I was born in that house with the assistance of a Belgian midwife.

Along with the buildings were other trappings from the abandoned mine. There was a railway spur and a 200-foot-deep shaft, beside which stood a concrete foundation in the shape of a large arch that anchored a steel tipple[2] used to raise (and lower) the coal wagons and the miners from the coal face below. Behind the tipple was a large slag heap that had burned itself out to form a red mass that looked very much like a prone lion in profile. There was also a large steel scoop that was used to fill railcars with coal and an extensive area of compressors and pumps affixed to a concrete pad. A pipeline, connecting the pumps with the river, ran at a depth of six feet over the bluffs that mark the eastern edge of the Belly River (the name given to that section of the Oldman River), across the river flats to a pumping station at the river's edge. On its way to the river, it passed by a small concrete building half-buried in the hillside. It was at a distance from the main mine site because it had been used to store dynamite. There was one other structure of note: red brick and square, it was the mine office. It had a slight upward oriental tilt to its eaves, where bats and large spiders found homes. Although the telephone and power lines, which once connected it to the town of Taber, were long gone, the mine office retained its wires and light switches.

Mrs. Angel LeLoup, the Belgian midwife, lived in the third building that remained in White Ash. There were no other habitations within a mile radius. My earliest memories, when I was three years old, are of the house in which I was born. I remember looking out the west window to see the midwife's house being dismantled, and I remember when our cow wandered into the house and broke her leg. She had to be put down and from then on we were dependent upon Dan and Emma Hein, our German neighbours who lived a mile away, for milk, cream, and butter. From my point of view, the cow's demise was not such a disaster. Soon after my birth, my parents discovered I could not digest cow's milk, except as provided in condensed form in cans. I also remember looking out the front window of our house at the herds of antelope that leapt and flowed over the prairies, uninhibited by fences. It was through that same front window that I saw a horse-drawn wagon arrive on my fourth birthday.

Family home, 1948, before new windows and doors.

In it were two friends of my father's, one of whom handed me a brown and white puppy. Nip, as she was called, was to be my companion and confessor until I was eighteen, when one night she took herself off to a quiet coulee to die. Terry, one of her puppies that we kept, lacked her character and spirit. He died from poisoned meat not long after his mother. The trauma of their loss has remained with me and I have not wanted a dog since.

I have one other vivid memory of the house in which I was born: leaving it and moving one-quarter of a mile north to the brick mine office building. I recall the excitement surrounding the preparations for the move. The walls and ceiling of our home-to-be had to be papered, the woodwork painted, and linoleum laid. My parents, brother, and sisters did most of the work, but I remember helping to mix the flour paste that was used to affix the wallpaper and standing on top of a chair, placed on top of a table, helping to paper the ten-foot ceilings and to adjust the borders. I was not yet five on the night we moved to the office building, aglow in the night from kerosene lamps, their light glinting off the abandoned wall switches. (Wick and later Coleman kerosene lamps were to be our only source of light for over two decades before electricity was restored.)

Shortly thereafter, our old house was knocked down, leaving an unobstructed view of the prairie and the town to the south. Our old house had two storeys and a root cellar. Our new home had neither of these, but it did have a crawl space where Nip would go to have her puppies and through which the

Home: White Ash looking north to the family house, summer 1952.

wind flowed freely, lifting the linoleum on the floor above—a problem my father sought to solve each year by banking the foundation with fresh earth and ashes. The problem persisted and my father reclad the brick walls of the building with layers of wood and finally with asphalt shingles made to look like brick. Over the years, the walls of the house grew thicker and thicker. Many years later, in 1969 when the house was bulldozed, the new landowners were surprised to find it was made of real brick.

A negative aspect of the move to the new house was that the well, on which we relied for water, was still at the old site, as was the garden. During our first winter and spring at the new house, we had to make the half-mile trek to and from the old well to carry buckets of water back to the house. When the time came to dig a well closer to the new house, I was the one who was lowered into the excavation to shovel away the dirt and sand as the wooden casing was eased lower and lower until the water pooled at a depth sufficient to fill a bucket with room to spare. In the coldest winters, the bucket was weighted and dropped at speed to break through the ice that formed on the water. In summer, it was lowered gingerly, filled with Sunday desserts of Jell-O and whipped cream. Having no icebox or fridge, we sunk a steel drum on the north side of the house, out of the sun, where butter and other items could be kept cool. In 1944, when my father decided to add on to the house, we dug a small basement, which functioned as a cellar for storing vegetables and jars of pickles and fruit.

In its isolated splendour on the prairie, the house was prey to the elements. Generally speaking, although summer temperatures in late July and early August could exceed 100°F, the house remained cool, particularly as the walls grew thicker. The real problem was heating it during the winter. For cooking, my mother had a large wood/coal stove called a range, with a warming oven above it and a small cistern on the side to heat water. The other part of the house was heated by a pot-bellied stove around which we huddled on winter evenings before going to bed. In the early morning, when we children prepared to go to school, it was the kitchen stove on which we relied, each of us taking a turn sitting on the open oven door to warm up, because the temperature in our bedrooms was below freezing. The kitchen stove was also responsible for heating the water for our Saturday night baths, which we took in a round metal tub. In the winter, the tub was filled with snow and placed on top of the stove until the water and tub were hot.

During my childhood and youth, the provision of wood and coal for the stoves was a major chore. On the Prairies, during the Great Depression, wood was hard to come by, unless it took the form of a rotting or rotten fencepost or some other scrap. Our land was too dry to grow trees. Indeed, the nearest tree visible was nearly a mile away and not on our property. The poplars that grew on the banks of the Belly River below our house were unusable. Apple boxes provided useful kindling for starting fires, but one had to be rich enough to buy apples by the box, or else place a grocery order large enough for Hayworth and Patterson, the store my mother favoured, to deliver it in a wooden apple box. This did not happen often, since we usually hand-carried groceries home from town.

While wood was scarce, coal was readily available. The problem lay in getting at it. Luckily, my father was able to put his mining skills to work, tunnelling in at the base of the bluffs that formed the high banks of the river to dig the coal with a pick and a shovel, and occasionally blast it with dynamite. He would then have to haul the sacks of coal up the steep bluffs to the house. Already perspiring profusely from the exertion of mining, he would be chilled to the bone by the time he reached home. A bout of bronchial flu inevitably ensued each winter. Our dry-land farm was not mechanized, although at times before World War II we had horses for drawing a wagon or sleigh back and forth to town and for pulling ploughs, harrows, and seeding machinery in the spring. To transport coal by horse up from the river flats required a road, a road that my father set us to building over the course of two summers in 1943 and 1944.

Harvesting at White Ash in the 1930s.

Once the road was completed, loads of coal could be brought up to be stored against the winter. But by then we were down to one horse, a fellow called Bob, who liked to stop at the most precarious parts of the road, risking being carried over the side by the load he was pulling.

Regardless of his chosen coal mining method, my father was actually bootlegging and he was not averse to inviting other economically challenged citizens to do the same. He named his mine Little Rascal and applied for a mining licence in 1937. He had received permission from Regal Collieries, the bankrupt owners of the coal rights, to dig their coal. As was the custom, he began mining while waiting for the licence, but due to bureaucratic delay he did not receive the answer—no—until the warm days of spring arrived. Although technically bootlegging, the harsh times had even the RCMP ordering coal from my father during the winter for local welfare families. As such, the constabulary looked the other way, unless someone lodged a specific complaint. After 1937, my father mined coal for the use of his family, until 1944 when, with the assistance of my godfather, he acquired the mineral rights from Regal Coal agents in Chicago and was able to freely dig his own coal.

Once World War II started, my father took steps to improve the family's economic status by using the resources at hand. Wartime shortages of materials for munitions brought a market for bones, which provided much needed phosphorous, and for metal. We scoured the prairie around us for what bones there were and sold a pile of them to a dealer in Lethbridge (especially rich sources of bones on the prairie were the bases of old buffalo jumps). However, there was more money to be made from scrap iron from all the machinery left behind at the old mine. Slowly, we dismantled the old mine's compressors and pumps, pouring kerosene over the rusted bolts to loosen the nuts. If they proved to be stubborn, I held a cold chisel while my father swung an eight-pound hammer to cut the nuts free. He never missed, but I was not always that confident. We broke up the larger pieces of cast iron using dynamite. As a former miner, my father was a dab hand with dynamite. He was cool with it, also largely because in World War I he had been a member of a bomb disposal unit. Being small, he was the one they would lower into craters to remove the detonators from unexploded bombs and shells.

In addition to bones and scrap iron, my father found a market for the red ash that formed the large slag heap north of our house. It was made up of the overburden of the coal seams and rock dug from under the seams. Like the coal, it was brought to the top in cars but stacked in a heap. During the course of the mine's life, this heap became substantial and was also subject to spontaneous combustion, leaving a pile of reddish material, also called ash. When the coal itself was burned it left a white ash. For a short while, the red ash was used to alleviate the quagmire created on Taber's clay-rich streets during the heavy rains in June. Later, it fell out of favour when the town was rich enough to actually pave its streets. We also sold a bit of gravel from a pit located near our house, but the gravel was not clean enough to find a steady market. All of these items provided small amounts of found money but not a steady income. Later, as the war drew to a close, my father took a job as pit boss with a newly opened coal mine. He was already over sixty and the work, underground and damp, presented conditions that aggravated his burnt-out lungs, but he persisted until he had a falling out with the mine owner who failed to maintain safety standards. Nevertheless, my father made close friendships with many of the miners who worked with him. They were from Italian and East European families and were great gardeners. Because the land they lived on was irrigated and ours was not, they regularly had good crops and they shared their potatoes, carrots, cucumbers, tomatoes, onions, and melons with us.

Money in the late thirties and during the war was in short supply, but what little there was went further. Those were the days before rampant consumerism, before the transistor radio and television, and before planned obsolescence. It was a time when the word "durable" was used frequently in sales pitches. Some items were ridiculously cheap back then, such as canned red sockeye salmon,

Nip, the author, and sisters Mary and Gwen with puppies on the steps of the family house, 1938.

which became a staple along with wieners, bologna, and cheese. Peanut butter or bologna sandwiches were standard items in our lunch pails. The land around us provided some supplements in the form of chokecherries, picked by the bucketful from the bushes on the river flat that my mother transformed into delicious jam and jelly; Saskatoon berries, which made their way into pies and into jars as cooked fruit; gooseberries that were turned into jam; and red and orange currants, from bushes planted by an earlier generation of miners, delicious to eat fresh or in the form of jelly. In September there were bright orange bull berries that made a tart jelly to be served with meat, and succulently sweet cactus berries, from the pie-shaped cactus that produced brilliant pink blooms in the spring. The berries made a wonderful jam if they were not all eaten beforehand! In the winter, there were the bright red hips from the wild rose, the skins of which were very tasty and rich in vitamin C. In addition, in the days before synthetic pesticides like DDT, dandelions and other wild greens provided variety, as did the mushrooms that appeared magically along the abandoned railway spur after the heavy rains in spring.

Along with the flora, our section of the prairies was home to a variety of fauna, most of them considered to be inedible. There were beavers, badgers, coyotes, porcupines, skunks, rattlesnakes, bull snakes, and weasels, all to which one gave wide berth when encountered. Nip, on the other hand, had regular run-ins with porcupines and skunks and had to have quills pulled from her head or have her coat washed with tomato juice. She developed a technique for tackling rattlesnakes and weasels, leaping into the air each time they struck at her. More challenging for her were the tiny rock rabbits that lived on the bluffs, as well as the jackrabbits, and gophers. She never caught a rabbit, but gophers were another matter. She chased the prairie chickens and partridges, again without success. She stayed well away from coyotes. And like the rest of the household, she was in awe of the antelope that seemed to float across the prairie on their way to the river. Although it was widely rumoured that our Greek neighbour made an excellent gopher and rattlesnake stew, the only member of the previously listed fauna that our family tasted—and only once— was antelope provided by a hunter in exchange for hunting on our land during the Depression. My parents were not great meat eaters, preferring fish. The Belly River produced little in the way of edible fish, but in the winter fishermen came by the house, selling frozen fish that we stored in snowbanks.

Although my family did not regard the local fauna as suitable food, we had other options. My mother was an excellent cook, particularly of pastries and cakes. She was the daughter of a baker in Ipswich and had trained as a candy and sweet maker. She was a great cook but a noisy one. Because she was hard of hearing, she had no idea of the clang, clack, and clatter she made with pots, pans, and dishes. My father had lost his sense of smell and taste when he was gassed, and was not in the best position to appreciate her cooking, but his keen sense of hearing, developed during his teenage years in the mines of South Wales, was mightily assailed by the anvil chorus from the kitchen. This continued for the first twenty-five years or more of their marriage until they could afford to buy her a hearing aid shortly after World War II, after which she heard what my father had been complaining about.

I realize now that my mother's was a lonely, isolated life. She was unable to clearly hear her husband or her children, or the radio, except with her head pressed closely to the speaker. Occasional trips to Lethbridge were a treat because the cinema there was equipped with aids for the hard of hearing. But otherwise she listened to conversations with her right hand cupped over her ear while reading the lips of those talking to her. Her closest women friends were an hour's walk away in the town. At least once a month, in all seasons and in all types of weather, she walked into town to visit them, returning in the early evening carrying bags of groceries, often to be met by my father, angry that she had been away so long. From time to time her frustrations grew too much and she threatened to leave for good, to join her sister in Winnipeg, but the lack of money, which was at the root of her frustrations, made it impossible for her to leave. She maintained a regular correspondence with her sisters in England and during the war she became a star knitter for the war effort. Her skills were much in demand in the district because she could follow the most intricate patterns and produce bed jackets and sweaters in record time. Her cake-making was also famous and she prepared wedding cakes for many in the area. She could also play the piano, but neither we, nor anyone in the immediate district, owned one.

My mother was able to make only one trip back to her native England in 1956 when my wife and I were living in London. She travelled on her own by Greyhound bus from Taber to Montreal to catch a ship to Southampton. She spent six weeks visiting the scenes of her childhood and youth, comparing the reality with what they had become in her imagination, and visiting places she had never seen before. Although her oldest, and favourite, sister had passed away, she was able to visit with the three remaining ones, not so much to catch up on gossip, because they were regular correspondents, but to see their circumstances and to meet her nieces and nephews. Reluctantly, she returned to the burned-brown prairies north of Taber, where she found my father, gaunt from eating his own cooking.

My mother was less gregarious than my father, who loved to talk, particularly politics. He had been active in Liberal-Labour politics when he was in Britain, but once in Canada, he found the Liberal Party to best suit his views and interests. He was particularly devoted to Mackenzie King, and when my godfather, local lawyer Brian Cooke, was chosen to run for the Liberals in a local by-election in 1934, my father volunteered to be his agent. They travelled about the district in my godfather's car, speaking to gatherings of rural and townsfolk, but the timing was wrong. The days of the Liberals, at least provincially, were over and my godfather was but another casualty in the run up to the William Aberhart sweep in the general election the following year. My father's efforts then, and later, on behalf of the party, brought him some minor patronage jobs. For example, he was a census-taker for the 1941 Dominion census and was also engaged to prepare voters' lists and lists for plebiscites. Once, or perhaps twice, our house was used as a district polling station. I remember the paper-wrapped grease pencils that I was allowed to have once the voting was over.

During the war, my father got me entangled in his admiration for Prime Minister Mackenzie King. I do not remember the precise issue that inspired him but he had me draw a few panels of cartoons depicting Mr. King and his opponents, whom he bested. I was doing well in drawing and art at school, but I laboured long and hard over this task. The cartoons were sent off to the prime minister, much to my embarrassment. The response came from the prime minister the following week. I have kept it and the signed photograph, because it was perhaps the most gentle and generous way of telling my father that I lacked talent. Dated January 13, 1945, it reads:

Dear Mr. Evans:

It was kind of you to write to me on January 5th and to send me the interesting drawings done by your twelve-year-old son. I am sure that his talent will continue to develop with practice and experience. I thought he might like to have a signed photograph, which is perhaps a better likeness than those he has thus far collected.

With all good wishes to your son and yourself,
Yours sincerely,
W.L. Mackenzie King,
(signed)

Needless to say, my career as a cartoonist ended at that point.

In 1935, the federal government introduced the Prairie Farm Rehabilitation Act (PFRA) and the Prairie Farm Assistance Act (PFAA). After World War II, in 1947, my father was selected to be one of the inspectors to visit farms to report on the extent of environmental damage and the impact of drought on grain yields. Based upon these reports, farmers could receive financial assistance from the government to compensate for their losses. This brought about a major change in our style of life. To carry out the job, my father needed a car, so he invested what little money he had in a 1933 Chevy that he drove over the narrow dirt and gravel roads of the vast district that was his jurisdiction. He had never driven a car before, although as a youth in Wales he owned a motorcycle with a sidecar. He was sixty-three or sixty-four when he got his licence to drive. Fortunately, most of the country roads back then were lightly trafficked and did not encourage speeding. If anything, my father drove below the speed limit. By this time he was slightly deaf and, to be sure that the car was running, he would rev the motor to a high pitch and then, in a style much favoured later by hot rodders but mocked during his time, he released the brake, taking off

Evan Evans (father) and Dora Lines (mother) prior to marriage and
sailing for Canada from the United Kingdom, 1920.

at speed with dust and gravel spraying behind him. My father's driving skills
were the subject of jest among my friends. I could not avoid the joking comments, nor could I dodge their hectoring about when I would learn to drive.[3]

Although I recall times of great tension and crisis in my parents' marriage,
overall their union was blessed by a sense of harmony. Perhaps an unlikely pair
because of my mother's deafness and my father's Welsh accent, which could
be difficult to understand at the best of times, she and my father met one night
in 1917 in a cinema in Gillingham, Kent, when she was serving as a clerk in the
Army Pay Corps. I think she won his heart when she told him he was not getting
the rate of pay that the army owed him for his dangerous work. As a result, my
father appealed to his commanding officer and the matter was resolved in his
favour. He carried a large portrait of my mother in his knapsack for the rest of
the war. After they had settled in Canada, they were never happier than when
they were working together. In all of his government jobs, from the census to
the PFAA, my father and mother worked as a team. My father would gather
all of the required information, which he would then record in pencil on the
appropriate forms. Afterward, my mother would transcribe it in ink using
her superior penmanship to best advantage, questioning any inconsistencies

that might appear on the forms as completed by my father. She enjoyed the car travel these jobs required because she could usually visit with the farmers' wives and put her new eyeglasses, equipped with a built-in hearing aid, to good use. The districts to be covered were so large that they would sometimes stay overnight in a far-off town. It was like a mini-holiday.

Actually, the word "holiday" was not one used much in our house during the nineteen years I lived there. There was no such thing as a family holiday, save for day trips to Lethbridge, taken in the early days by train and then by car once my father had acquired the 1933 Chevy. These trips were infrequent, perhaps two or three times a year, and the ritual was always the same. They began with an early start and an arrival in Lethbridge well before the stores opened. We would occupy ourselves by walking the streets, looking in windows. Once the stores opened, my mother and I would go inside, but my father stayed out on the street hoping to meet someone he knew with whom to talk politics, or he would seek out the publisher of the *Lethbridge Herald*, or a well-known judge, both of them Liberals. Just before noon, we would gather at a Chinese restaurant to eat soup, halibut with mashed potatoes, and coleslaw, ending with pie and ice cream. I drank water and my parents sometimes had tea. After lunch we waited until the cinema opened for its Saturday matinee performance. In the early years, we went to the Capitol Cinema, but later the Paramount opened with hearing aids for the deaf in certain aisle seats. After the movie, we would catch the evening train, or drive in a sedate manner back to Taber and White Ash. By the time I was in my final year of high school, my father had sold the Chevy and purchased a 1939 Ford. It was a beautiful automobile with a swept-back contour and a glowing, caramel-coloured paint job that looked to be an inch thick. While we had had the temerity to carry out repairs on the Chevy, changing axles, brakes, tires, and transmission gears, the Ford had to be serviced in town. Much later, when my father had graduated to a brand new Chevrolet, he took to parking on the outskirts of Lethbridge, afraid of the city traffic. He was the ultimate defensive driver.

Like the family trips to Lethbridge, my summer holidays growing up were rather routine. Had I belonged to the Scouts, or later, to the Air Cadets, I might have gone to summer camps in the mountains, but I belonged to neither of these groups, largely for the same reason I did not play organized winter sports: the difficulty in getting to town in winter evenings made any regular attendance impossible. In fact, holidays simply meant that time from the final day of school in June to the first day of school in September, the highlight being the first of

July parade and celebrations. When I was not yet in my teens, we went to the fairgrounds, which consisted of a wooden grandstand and a sort of racetrack. There was a small fee for admission, but children in turn were given tickets for free ice cream and pop. When money was really short at home, there was often tension as to whether or not we children could go, but somehow we always did. We were driven into town by our neighbour Dan Hein and we dressed in our finest—actually the new clothes that we would wear in September when school resumed—and behaved properly. There were usually some sideshows and games, and a feature baseball contest in the afternoon. I do not remember my father or mother ever attending these events.

Sometimes, during the summer, we children and my mother would go down to the Belly River to dog-paddle in the backwater, disturb the fresh-water clams on the muddy shore, and sometimes go fishing using a bent pin on the end of a piece of string tied to a stick. We caught tiny sardine-sized fish that we threw back into the water. The Oldman, or Belly, River had formed two islands, one to the south of our property and one to the north. Crossing the river to get to them was a little hazardous and something that I was absolutely forbidden to do after my brother left home. The relative purity of the river did not last long beyond the installation of the town's sewer system in 1950, which dumped raw sewage into the water just upstream from our property. The next year, the new Rogers beet sugar factory opened, discharging its waste water into the river as well. In 1970, the Belly River, that section of the Oldman River that flowed past our former property, was declared one of the most polluted in North America.

Our summers were further leavened by our neighbours the Hein family. Mrs. Hein was very good to us, inviting us to summer picnics where we were fed sandwiches, hotdogs, roast corn, watermelon, cake, ice cream, and Jell-O. The angel food cake always contained silver symbols shaped like horseshoes, slippers, and shamrocks and our futures were judged by which one was in our slice. My two sisters were classmates of the Hein daughters, Isobel and Sybil, and were friends, but my parents, my father most particularly, did not participate in these picnics. He did not approve of our neighbour, partly as a hangover from the Great War and partly because of the brutal manner in which Dan Hein treated his animals. I believe also the fact that Hein, a man with little or no education or sophistication, was prospering and my father was not played a role. My father did not like it that he had found himself dependent on our neighbour through the wages paid to my brother Evan, who worked on Hein's farm. During World War II, German prisoners of war were held in camps near Lethbridge and Medicine Hat. Some of them were employed by local farmers. Dan Hein employed several. They wore blue dungarees with large red circles painted on the back. Whenever there was a break from a camp, my father was certain that the escapees would be found in Hein's cellar or barn. After the war, however, during his PFAA work, if my father had to call on Dan Hein, he was a model of civility.

If our family had a credo, it was the one laid down early on by my father: money isn't everything, be generous with what you have, never give anyone reason to call you a slacker, and, above all, see the funny side of life. A good sense of humour was absolutely essential to him and fortunately he possessed one, as did my mother. His went to political jokes, irony, and absurd situations, while my mother's was gentler and less personal. If my father could not share a laugh with someone, he wrote them off as difficult and of minimal interest. If he had to deal with such people, usually government bureaucrats, particularly members of the Department of Veterans Affairs (DVA), he was beside himself.

My father's efforts, ultimately successful, to get a disability pension because of his damaged lungs took a great deal of time and patience on his part. The DVA's argument was basically this: if you were disabled by what happened to you during the Great War, why are you still alive? Even though the department's own doctors from the Colonel Belcher Hospital in Calgary confirmed the seriousness of my father's condition, the DVA dragged its feet. Once the pension of $90 per month was granted, effective September 16, 1953, when my father was nearly seventy, the DVA would send inspectors on surprise visits to check whether or not he was fitter than he said and whether or not he was more prosperous than he was supposed to be. By then, and by dint of saving and abstemious living, my father had put enough aside to purchase a new Chevrolet, which he put under my name. Sure enough, an inspector asked how he could afford such a car and perhaps his pension should be reduced accordingly, but my father replied brightly, "Oh the car belongs to my son, but he lets me drive it." In the end, my father had the last laugh—he lived well past his ninety-ninth birthday. On his deathbed he made me promise that I would make sure that the DVA paid the costs of his funeral and headstone as they were duty bound to do. Even though I have never learned how to drive or possess a driver's licence, I have still owned two cars courtesy of my father. One was the Chevrolet mentioned above, and the other was his last car, the delight of his life, an Oldsmobile.

In those days, none of my peers had their own car. They borrowed the family car if it was available. Like most of my contemporaries, apart from my Chinese friends who had motorcycles, a bicycle was our mode of transport. Even so, I was late in getting one. I was given my first bicycle early in 1945. It was a gift from my godparents who were always generous with me. They also gave me small amounts of money on my birthday and presents at Christmas and Easter. The money went toward the purchase of war bonds. As much as these gifts were appreciated, I dreaded having to write a suitable thank-you note, largely because I really did not know what was suitable. The bicycle was a secret, kept from me until it was actually delivered. It was no secret that I wanted a bicycle, but my family simply could not afford it.

The bike was both a joy and a disappointment. It was brand new, of course, but it was a wartime bike, which meant it had no chrome. The handlebars were painted taupe and the body maroon. It was what CCM had to offer at the time. Braking was done by reverse pedalling; hand-operated brakes were unknown in the town in those days. The bicycle transformed my life. I could leave home a little later in the morning and come home later after school. Instead of carrying groceries and gallon jars of kerosene home, I could put them on the back of the bicycle or in a basket in front. The road between our place and town was by then much improved, but there was still the gully to be crossed and a steep hill to climb. Even with these obstacles, I became speedy enough to get to town in twenty minutes or so and to return a little quicker, because the hill and wind were in my favour. The wind was always my enemy going to town during the day, and there were some days when the wind was too strong. Of course, cycling was nearly impossible between mid-December and early March, or during the heavy rains of May and June. And there were some days when it suited my mood to walk rather than ride. On hot days in the summer, when the temperature was in the high nineties, heading for 100°F, my father would suggest that I ride into town for some ice cream. This meant riding to the Cameo Café for the best brand of ice cream, which was made by Crystal Dairies of Lethbridge.

I remember one such ride in particular, early in August 1945. The streets of town were nearly empty as people waited for the cool of the evening. At the Cameo, my friend Herbert How was working behind the counter on his own. The ice cream freezer was a deep freeze with rubber-lined trap doors over its four compartments. When a trap door was opened, the cold air from the freezer was a welcome breath of winter. As I waited for the ice cream to be wrapped in several layers of the previous day's *Lethbridge Herald*, a news bulletin on the radio broke into the conversation I was having with Herbert. A new type of bomb called an atomic bomb had been dropped on Hiroshima in Japan. World War II would soon be over.

During the course of the war, our part of Alberta changed from an economy dependent upon animal power to one entirely dominated by the internal combustion engine. This was a mark of the prosperity that the war had brought to the district, as well as to the whole of the country. The war also brought a sense of togetherness. We all knew our side was in the right and that the enemy was completely in the wrong. We listened to FDR like he was our father, Churchill like an older brother, and Stalin like an uncle. We were urged to accept shortages as part of our contribution to the war effort and to be on the look out for spies and for people who attempted to subvert the rationing system by hoarding restricted items. As kids, we collected and traded airplane cards that were found in boxes of Cracker Jack. We learned to identify airplanes and we longed to see some other than the Harvard and Cessna training planes that criss-crossed the district daily as part of the Commonwealth Air Training Scheme. We listened to radio programs like *L for Lanky*, the continuing story of a Lancaster bomber crew, and pored over the maps in the weekend papers that documented the war zones and cheered the newsreels that showed our victories and the enemy fleeing or being bombed. We were too young to even begin to think that we might ultimately have to join up.

As part of our wartime education, we were constantly made aware of the hateful nature of the Germans and the Japanese. I remember the night of May 8, 1945, Victory in Europe Day (V-E Day), when we were part of the gathering at the fairgrounds to watch while the effigies of Hitler and Mussolini were consumed by flames from a stack of used tires. We were excited and joyful, thinking about all the wonderful things that would now happen according to the many promises, which always began with the phrase: "After the war there will be..." The continuing war with Japan seemed to be an annoying obstacle in the way of their fulfillment, but we were assured that it would only be a matter of time. Apart from the cartoon images of Tojo, with his enormous buck teeth, we knew little of the Japanese leaders, yet we were reasonably convinced that it was the Japanese military and not the people who were the most to be feared and hated. By now we had numerous Japanese Canadian friends and we could not think of them as evil. Moreover, we were unaware of Canada's role in the Pacific and we looked on that theatre of war as an American affair, just as it was portrayed in the movies, although there was talk that Canadians might be sent there.

Thus, we were very excited over the news of the atomic bomb. The brief description of its destructive capacities was so awe-inspiring that we saw it as the ultimate harbinger of peace to the world. This may seem ironic now, but within the context of the war's end, Russia and the United States were still seen as allies and the Cold War had not yet begun. We were convinced by the Allied wartime propaganda of making the world safe for democracy, just as the propaganda of World War I had been that it was to be the war to end all wars. I am afraid we did not consider the thousands of civilians whose lives were wiped out by the blast. By now we had become hardened to the view that whatever our side might do, it could and would not be worse than what the enemy did. On that stifling hot day in early August 1945, after I heard the news of the bomb on the radio, I grabbed my ice cream and pedalled home like the wind. I was on a high while I sailed home, thinking of the perfect future that awaited us all.

My bicycle meant increased freedom and speed, but it had not always been my mode of transport to and from school. White Ash was once a school district and had a one-room school located just north of our house beyond the red slag heap. My brother Evan, eleven years my senior, attended this school, but by the time I was ready to start school the building had been abandoned for some years, the White Ash district having been subsumed within the Taber School Division. This meant a distance of 4.25 miles lay between our house and the local seat of learning in Taber. During my first two years of school from 1939 to 1940, my sisters and I were taken to and from the handsome four-storey brick building, constructed in 1910, by horse-drawn wagon or sleigh. No longer in school and having taken work as a farm labourer, my brother Evan would drive us. Once my brother joined the army in the fall of 1941, we had to walk to and from school, in rain or shine, snow or sleet, wind and dust.

Although a bit of a trek, the walk to school was not without interest. About a half a mile south of our house was a deep gully that ran down to the river. The town had chosen its northern cliff for a garbage dump or "nuisance grounds" as it was politely called. Our route skirted this site and took us along the Hein farm's barbed wire fence, decorated with loose papers, bits of cloth, and other items carried from the dump by the wind. There was a shortcut down through the gully. Although the road made a detour to cross the gully further up at a shallower part, we followed a trail worn through Hein's property, emerging just below a little rise that led to his house, before rejoining the main road, which by now was straight and level for the remaining three miles to town. Hein kept a large black dog called Touser who watched the road for cars. Wheels annoyed him. He did not bother pedestrians, but later, when I rode a bicycle, I had to dismount or attempt to outrace him.

Half a mile south of Hein's house was the Taber cemetery. The original plan for the town had been for a cemetery site north of its current location. Thus, the graveyard was not as close to its main source of supply as originally intended. During the day, passing the graveyard was simple, but in the dark, with our overactive imaginations and heightened senses of hearing, it was quite another matter, particularly in late October. Even as a teenager on a bike, I sped by the graveyard at night, full moon or not. About a mile and a half south of the graveyard was a slaughterhouse, a postwar addition, and finally, a little further on, the town water tower, which in those days marked the northern limits of Taber and whose resident watchman kept pigeons—lots of them. A further three-quarters of a mile brought us to the schoolhouse, which sat a few blocks to the east of the road we came in on.

Despite the man-made obstructions, a wonderful part of the walk in the spring was the joyous call of the prairie meadowlarks, perched upon fence posts en route, and the appearance, like magic, of deep blue lupins, bright yellow buffalo beans, delicate pinkish-red Canterbury bells, and bright yellow and pink cactus flowers. There was also the possibility of a chance meeting with a skunk, porcupine, badger, snake, or Richardson's ground squirrel making their way through the prairie grass. In June, the air was full of the delicate scent of wild roses and fresh grass, while the town reeked of lilacs. However, by July, when a south wind began to blow, the odours from the town dump and the stench from Hein's pigpens overrode anything the Prairies had to offer.

As children we made the walk to school at least two hundred times a year, each school day morning and late afternoon, not to mention Saturday and Sunday afternoons and the occasional evening. It was never dull. We allowed an hour for the walk from home to school and, depending upon the weather, we were either early or just on time. Winter storms presented the biggest challenge with ground blizzards and winds biting our faces. In the spring, heavy rain turned the roads into layers of sticky clay, which we called "gumbo." The gumbo may have increased our height, but it slowed our pace. During the spring runoff, the shortcut over the gully was made impassable because of the raging torrent that ran through it. In my first two years of schooling, the wagon

Brother Evan and Nip, 1940.

and sleigh rides, courtesy of my brother Evan, inured me to the chilly winter walks to come.

My brother Evan remains a shadowy figure to me—my memories of him are relatively few. I remember, prior to my enrolment in school, going with him and my father in our horse-drawn wagon to the railway station to get two boxes of apples—one green, one red—that formed part of a large rail shipment that was sent from Nova Scotia and distributed free to the needy families on the Prairies. And I remember rides on the back of his bay mare, which he rode without a saddle (at that time, who could afford one?). I remember clinging onto the back of his coat for dear life as I bounced in the air behind him, experiencing a rudimentary form of weightlessness. Not long after I turned eight, I also remember seeing him white as a sheet one chill December morning as he dropped us at the school the day of the Christmas party. I did what I had been frequently told not to do. I jumped from the wagon before it came to a halt. I slipped on the frosty wooden sidewalk and fell beneath the back right wheel, which ran over my head from hairline to chin. Fortunately, the wagon had rubber tires and was not a great weight. I escaped with a swollen head and puffed lips that made speech nigh impossible.

After my fall, my brother was beside himself with concern for me and for what our parents would say about his stewardship. He had been severely criticized the previous year when I had gone to the local cinema after school to attend a patriotic review, which included members of the Chinese community who, although Canada was not yet at war with Japan, had received a sympathetic response to their campaign to raise funds to alleviate suffering in China at the hands of Japanese troops. The event was put on by the local Legion branch to raise funds for the war. I had told no one in my family that I was going, because I did not know about it until I was swept along by my friends, who thought it was the thing to do. I came out of the performance into the evening darkness to find that my brother had been up and down the streets of the town, frantic with worry over my safety and bracing himself for the avalanche of criticism that would be his fate on our return home. To make matters worse, at the review I had pledged the family to provide twenty-five cents a week toward the cumulative purchase of a war bond. Apart from these incidents, I remember that he teased me a lot and that he tried to teach me to identify the constellations that, with the sparkling belt of the Milky Way, pressed down upon us on pitch-black prairie nights. Once in the army, he sent me little souvenirs of where he was stationed: Petawawa, Grande Prairie, and Prince Rupert.

Of course, I will always remember receiving news of Evan's death at age twenty-one. At that time, our main source of home entertainment was a radio, a floor model that ran on very large batteries, two As and a B, the latter having to be topped up with water from time to time. To get reception, we strung a long aerial outside the house, high up between two metal pipes sunk in the ground. It provided high-quality reception from stations in Alberta, Saskatchewan, and the United States. The radio was the purveyor of news, hockey, and baseball games, as well as variety shows from comedies to horror, plus western tales. One of my favourite shows was *The Shadow*. I remember listening to an episode in the early evening of March 11, 1942, and noticing, out the front window, the approach of a car, a coupe of dark bottle-green, owned and driven by my godfather Brian Cooke, who I have previously mentioned was a town lawyer, who had befriended my father on his arrival in Taber in 1928. It was after my godfather that I was named, given the un-Welsh but very Irish name of Brian. It was usual for my godfather and my godmother, Agnes Kennedy Cooke, a trained nurse whom I thought rather severe, to make visits on Sunday afternoons. Because I found them intimidating in their kindly way, I would slip out the back door and over the hills with Nip. An evening visit by my godfather unaccompanied by my godmother was unusual, but then, the next day was my father's birthday and they were very good friends.

As I listened to Orson Welles as Lamont Cranston, along with his faithful Margo Lane, begin to solve another mystery, I noticed my father was acting strangely and that his face had turned ashen. After a few moments, my godfather drove off and my mother, now sensing something was the matter, waited inside the door. My father entered and said with a quavering voice: "Evan has been killed—drowned when the army truck he was in slid off a log bridge in the rain in Prince Rupert." They both stood stunned. The last letter from my brother had been posted from Petawawa and they knew nothing of his move to Prince Rupert. They briefly clung to a hope that it was a mistake, but it was not—the news was confirmed in the newspaper.

My family never recovered, either emotionally or economically, from Evan's death. My brother had been the family breadwinner. In August 1938, my father had written to Alberta Premier William Aberhart, describing the family's circumstances. Aberhart was elected on a platform promising a grant of twenty-five dollars per month for each citizen, a social credit, according to his economic philosophy. He argued that the province should have control over its money supply, which would enable it to print money to give increased purchasing power to each citizen and thus prime the economy. It was a very appealing promise to people facing extremely hard times. The government also pledged to supply seed grain for farmers in the spring with a lien placed against the harvest to recover the cost of the seed. In his letter, my father explained that once he had paid for harvesting the crop and with wheat worth forty-nine cents a bushel (at best), he would have exactly $31.85 left after the seed liens were paid. He asked the premier how a family of six could live for a year on $31.85, when the premier had defined twenty-five dollars per month per adult as basic subsistence? When there was no response from the premier, my father took a shorter version of his letter to the *Lethbridge Herald*, which printed it on the front page on Saturday, September 3, 1938, with heavy black edging. Shortly thereafter, the government lifted the seed liens. Just before this, my brother Evan had quit school to work on the family farm. Later, when he took a job with Hein as a farm labourer at a dollar a day, he turned his wages over to our mother.

As work dried up in the fall of 1941, Evan, without telling our parents, joined the army, the first recruit for the newly formed 112th Light Anti-aircraft Battery R.C.A being raised in Lethbridge. He arranged for most of his monthly pay to be sent to our mother. Because he died without a will, the army divided his estate between my parents. Each received a cheque for $14.15—their share of his remaining pay, and three five-dollar war bonds that were redeemed before maturity. The army paid the seventy dollars needed to ship Evan's body from Prince Rupert to Taber, including seven dollars for the local United Church minister (the minister was originally promised fifteen). The costs of the military funeral were met by the local branch of the Canadian Legion. A bill for thirty-five dollars, totalling the costs of the undertaking and cemetery expenses, was presented to my father. However, this was included in an account rendered to the army on behalf of the local Canadian Legion by my godfather, who in

To the Next of Kin of:

M. 68502, Gunner Evan Victor Evans
This commemorates the gratitude of
the Government and people of Canada for the life of
a brave man freely given in the service of his Country.
His name will ever be held in proud
remembrance.

Minister of National Defence

Card from Minister of Defence Ralston, received after Evan's death.

addition to being a lawyer was also a World War I veteran. Evan's commanding officer appealed for a pension for my mother, based on the family's dire need. The Reverend W.J. Collett, who presided over the funeral, wrote a letter in support of the request:

> The Evans family is in great need financially. The lad was their main source of support since the father is crippled with one complaint and another and is unable to work. Evan did most of the farm work and also hired out to the neighbours turning over practically all his wages to the Mother. As you know, he has signed over a portion of his own Army pay to his folks. Just what the future holds for the family, two children still being in school, I do not know. One thing is very certain and that is the Father will not be in a position to work and, I might add, the farm is in one of our dried out sandy areas and would produce only meagrely if worked efficiently. Hence I have no hesitation in saying that, if some form of assistance can be provided, I am sure the need is very great.

Despite the opinion of the commandant that "this is a very worthy case," no assistance was forthcoming. Three years later, under provision of a newly passed federal wartime service gratuity act that provided twenty-five cents for each day a person served in the forces, to be awarded at the rate of $7.50 for complete blocks of thirty days only, my parents received—after filling in many forms—a cheque for thirty dollars to cover Evan's 135 days in the army.

I did not attend my brother's funeral on March 17, 1942. I was asked to stay home to make sure the water was boiling for tea to serve to those who came back to the house after the burial. I am ashamed to say that when I returned to school the next day, I rather enjoyed the sympathy and notoriety my brother's death brought me. Looking back, I am not quite sure that I can forgive my nine-year-old self for that yet.

After my brother joined the army in the fall of 1941, my older sister Gwen quit high school at seventeen, never having liked it all that much anyway, to work on our farm. After Evan's death, she took a job as a waitress at the Rex Café in town to help provide for the family. She rented a room in town and was consequently placed in the way of temptations. My own mother and father neither smoked nor drank. Each had had a father who loved the bottle and they reacted accordingly. Neither was inclined to smoke, my father because above all he did not have the lungs for it, and my mother because it was not something that women did in those days and in any case she despised the habit. It was all for the best anyway, since my family had little or no money for such vices. While she did not think it necessary to caution my sisters, my mother exacted a promise from me to neither smoke nor drink until I was twenty-one, and I made good on that promise. Never tempted to smoke, I did not taste alcohol until I was thirty-two.

But my sister Gwen was young when she started working in town. She was petite, dark, and feisty, and, like my father, she had paper-thin skin and took umbrage at the smallest slight. Quick of temper, she was equally quick to forgive. She believed in honesty and hard work. She was also a sucker for a dare. One day, in the spring of 1943, my parents received an anonymous note in the mail. That makes it sound too grand. We did not receive mail in those days but instead begged for it at a small wicket behind which stood Mrs. Munro, a most unfriendly woman who fixed us with a scowl as she thumbed through the *D*s to the *F*s. Never once did we leave the post office without the sense that she had held something back. She was particularly intimidating to youngsters like me. On this particular day, I picked up the anonymous letter and carried it home to my parents. I remember it saying something like, "I think you should know that your daughter Gwen has been seen smoking and drinking." I do not know whether it was signed "well wisher" or not, but it was as though a bomb had exploded in our house. My father was particularly angry, while my mother was greatly disappointed. After weathering the storm, Gwen promised to mend her ways but, although she gave up drink, she did continue to smoke for some years.

I particularly liked it when Gwen worked at the Rex. The café stood next door to the Rex Theatre, where most Saturday afternoons I attended a matinee, usually made up of coming attractions, a cartoon, an episode of a serial, a newsreel giving accounts of the war on all fronts, and a main film, most often a musical or adventure story set in some far off place. After the matinee had ended, I would exit the theatre into the blinding afternoon sun and quickly enter the café, where my sister would give me, for the cut-rate price of a nickel, a huge ice cream cone, made up of three large scoops. "That's my smart kid brother," she would say in way of explanation, as she deposited an extra dime in the cash.

THE ALLURE OF CHINA

During my childhood, I was raised in relative isolation, with no contact with any children of my own sex and age. The first day of school was traumatic, and yet, school was to become everything to me. I remember one scene from my first day. The class was seated in desks set in rows on two-by-four skids. I looked to my left across the aisle and saw the smiling face of a Chinese boy. He was smiling despite the fact that he had fallen and knocked out his two upper front teeth that morning. In a matter of days, we were the closest of friends. Herbert How, known then as "Git," became my first real friend.[4] Prior to this, I had relied on imaginary ones named Inky, Pinky, and Blinky, who, I contended, lived in a well beside a house that was barely visible across the river on the western horizon. Although by grade ten Herbert and I were to go our separate ways, we have remained friends. His impact on me was greater than mine on him. He was the town-dwelling son of the owner of the Cameo Café and a member of a large family—unlike myself, he was surrounded by friends his own age from his earliest days. More importantly, it was Herbert How's disproportionate impact on me from our very first meeting that led to my interest in China and the desire to know more about its culture and people.

Cameo Café, 2003. [Photo Robert How]

In our first few years, Herbert and I bonded closely for at least a couple of external reasons. Both our families were caught up in the developing world war, his because of the Japanese invasion of China and the consequent horrors, and mine because of the growing threat to Britain and what it meant to my mother's family (my father had lost contact with his own). As Herbert and I marched around the schoolyard as part of an exercise class, we worried about which side of the war our families would end up on, a matter that the attack on Pearl Harbor decided for us, much to our relief. Our bond was also strengthened by the fact that we had each lost an older brother. Herbert's had died suddenly from scarlet fever in 1939 at the age of sixteen.

The isolated circumstances of my life gave me an advantage at school. Blessed with a good memory (although not as good as my father's, which was photographic), I spent the time going to and from school recalling everything I had been taught that day or the day before. With no distractions, save small farm chores and the radio, I was able to concentrate on homework assignments, completing them always on time, if not before. I soon became every teacher's pet, as well as the object of snide remarks and derision from some of my classmates who had too many things other than homework to occupy their time outside of school. I was nicknamed "the Pirate" for stealing all the high marks. In the early grades, Herbert and I surfaced at the top of the class and we enjoyed the friendly competition, but later he was distracted by other activities and hobbies and what proved to be an abortive attempt by the Chinese families in town to teach their children Chinese after school. Besides, every member of Herbert's family had to pitch in, putting in long hours at the Cameo. Git taught himself to type using the hunt-and-peck method and knew the rudiments of bookkeeping by the time he was six. He eventually dropped out of school in grade ten and later joined the Royal Canadian Air Force. (He and I both yearned to fly, but he was the first to do anything about it.)

Because of our friendship, the Cameo became the focal point of my existence when I was in town. In time, I became friends with other members of the How family, which included Herbert's three brothers and three sisters. Mrs. How joined her husband "Charlie" (his English name was Charles) in Taber in 1923, the year the Exclusion Act went into force, banning any further immigration of Chinese women (and Chinese men who were not merchants) to Canada. She was a Christian but spoke little English. Nonetheless, she taught me how to use chopsticks and fed me authentic Chinese food. Midmornings, when she was not busy cooking, she could be seen sitting alongside the local Chinese laundryman Sing Lee at the Cameo lunch counter, chatting in their local South China dialect. Sing Lee knew very little English. Conversations with him consisted of asking, "How are you Sing Lee?" To which he replied, "Me sick, all time sick." And this, I believe, was probably true. Herbert's father did not distinguish me from the swarms of youngsters coming into the Cameo each day for chocolate bars, gum, pop, and ice cream. He suffered from some illness and I did not get to know him before he died. When I was in high school, Herbert's sisters Alice and Irene and I used to sit in a back booth of the café offering, for free, to read the leaves of those who ordered Chinese tea. Our interpretations were quite fanciful, but then, as now, you get what you pay for.

With World War II came new friends. The Canadian government's decision to move inland all Japanese Canadian residents living within 350 miles of the Pacific coast was to visit great hardship and stress upon these most loyal of Canada's citizens. Their property was seized and confiscated and they were given little choice: either live in flimsy camps in the interior of British Columbia, or venture across the Rockies to work in other parts of Canada. A number of families opted for southern Alberta, where there was a shortage of workers in the sugar beet fields. Forbidden to live in the cities or towns, they were housed in shacks, or secondary dwellings, on farmers' properties.

Alberta does not have a history of legislated racism as is the case in British Columbia and Saskatchewan. At that time, the number of Asian immigrants in Alberta was small and was never considered to be a serious "threat" to white society. Before the outbreak of war, Chinese and Japanese families[5] resident in southern Alberta (outside the cities of Lethbridge and Calgary) were generally well integrated and were highly regarded fellow citizens. However, anti-Japanese feeling ran high after Pearl Harbor and many people were suspicious of all Japanese. Even the few Japanese Canadian families that had settled in the town and district well before the outbreak of war felt some of the heat. Taber was the centre of one of the host areas for displaced Japanese Canadians during the war. Labour-hungry beet farmers were anxious to get whatever help they could, but townsfolk, led by prejudiced members of the Canadian Legion and the local newspaper editor, rejected the idea of having "such traitors" living in our midst. Indeed, my brother's funeral, which took place just after the government made the announcement that Japanese would be accepted as beet workers, became the occasion for the Legion to demonstrate its strength and to emphasize the need to protect the country from both internal and external threat. Extremists were calmed somewhat when E.C. Manning pledged that at war's end the Japanese would be sent out of Alberta, to which was added the federal government's pledge to send the Japanese back to Japan.

As far as our school was concerned, the influx of Japanese families meant an influx of new students. Our grade four teacher announced one morning that the next day we would be having some new class members and that we should treat them well. My recollection, confirmed later in life by Japanese Canadian friends and former classmates, is that there was little or no overt prejudice in the school, contrary to what other Japanese Canadians might have felt in other parts of the province. Rather, our new classmates were the source of endless fascination. Not only had they come from the exotic and largely unexperienced (by us) Pacific coast but they brought new skills ranging from origami to baseball. During the school day, these kids did not refer to their hard life—few of us realized that they began and ended their days working in the fields. Because they came and went to school by bus (often with the sons and daughters of the farmers for whom they worked), they were not exposed to the prejudices held by some diehard townspeople.

Not all of the townsfolk were prejudiced. The bulk of prejudice seemed to be harboured by people with English heritage, what with all that the Empire

Taber High School graduating class, June 1951. The author is third from right, back row. From *Dawn*, Taber High School yearbook, 1951, edited by the author. [Photo Luehr Studio]

had taught them about the "Yellow Peril" and Rudyard Kipling's "The White Man's Burden." In town, these people were the veterans at the Canadian Legion and the publisher of the *Taber Times*. Most people in town, particularly the women, were more open-minded, especially when it became known that there had been no documentable threat from Japanese Canadians and people began to learn how the Japanese had been treated. Some of the merchants catered to the newcomers. Cecil Johnson, a druggist and a leader in the Lions Club, was but one of the local businessmen who differentiated between Japan the enemy and Canadian citizens of Japanese ethnicity. Through their hard work, and calm quiet behaviour, Japanese Canadian evacuees put the lie to unreasoned prejudice. By Victory in Japan Day (V-J Day) on August 15, 1945, there were few people in the district who sincerely believed their Japanese friends should be sent packing, although the federal and provincial governments were taking steps to keep their pledges. A picture in the *Lethbridge Herald*, published before V-J Day, showed Charlie How and two Japanese customers in the Cameo, smiling happily in anticipation of the end of hostilities.

Integration within the school was achieved because of a couple of factors. First, our teachers, who were likely progressive for their time and drawn from different ethnic groups (Scots, Welsh, Italian, Polish, Japanese, Dutch), were on the alert for any signs of unfair treatment of anyone, because the classes contained children from a whole range of ethnic groups. In school we were learning how racism was at the root of the war, and how the postwar world was to be free of it through the much-anticipated United Nations organization. As a result, we wanted to be better than our elders, those who took a narrow view of race. Second, and most of all, we liked each other. We played together, undertook school projects together, and we co-operated in school student organizations. Despite their hard lives, the Japanese Canadian students were always ranked among the top of the class, working and studying hard. Among the graduates from Taber High School in the spring of 1951, I was the only non-Japanese student in the academic stream. Perhaps, a further index of the degree of harmony that was achieved is the fact that my friend Herbert How married a Japanese Canadian from the district; intermarriage became increasingly common. In fact, in Taber the main source of friction was religion, not race.

As I mentioned earlier, school was my life and from the first few days it provided me with more than I needed to know, officially and unofficially. One of these latter founts of knowledge was sex. Sex education was not a subject mentioned in the classroom and children picked up knowledge as they could from local lore. Farm children were likely to know more, having observed animal life and asked questions. In my family, which was not unique, the question never arose and there were no "birds and bees" conversations. I remember I had entered grade two when, one morning at recess, I encountered a slightly older student, who had failed to advance to grade three, surrounded by my male classmates. He described to us the differences between the sexes and how people copulated. We were enthralled and only later did we learn that his information was faulty at best. In grade three one of the pretty girls drew a few pictures on the blackboard one noon hour to straighten us out. After that there was little else to know—except not to practice what we had learned until we were married. These admonitions were not always followed because Taber was regularly cited in provincial newspapers as having one of the highest rates of social disease. Our school was mixed, but it had separate entrances for boys and girls, with the girls playing on one side of the building during breaks and the boys on the other. Later, this idea was abandoned and we lined up in classes before entering the school in the morning. There were indeed battles between and among the sexes, and between various religious groups. We were such a mix of ethnic groups and religions that everyone at one time or another was teased or bullied.

When I began school, there were still students from the country who boarded in town during the winter. Others arrived each morning on horseback, putting their horses in the school barn for the day. As prosperity returned to the district during the war and with the end of the Depression, more and more students were brought to school by family car or truck and, ultimately, transported by one of several district school buses. But no bus came out to White Ash in my day. Instead, my family received a small allowance to compensate for this fact. It was based upon the distance we lived from the school and the number of days I attended each year. I became infamous for perfect attendance, year after year. Even on days when wintry weather had closed the school down, I was there. We had no telephone and there was no way to know for certain if the school was closed. Not only did I always attend school, but I was never late. Looking back now, I realize I was insufferable.

During the Depression and the war, school was quite egalitarian. There were no great signs of wealth because no one was really wealthy. Some of the town kids dressed a little better, but not that you would notice. Our family was heavily dependent upon World War I surplus and on hand-me-downs from our only relatives in Canada, my mother's sister in Winnipeg, and briefly, before the war, from her sisters in England (I say briefly, because soon the war had us attempting to send parcels to them). In my early years I could be seen in a grey jacket with an English school crest on it, courtesy of a cousin in Suffolk, but more generally I had two costumes. One, which I wore between Easter and Thanksgiving, was fairly universal among boys and consisted of a shirt, bib overalls, and high-topped canvas running shoes. The latter were called Fleet Foot and a round rubber medallion on the side of them protected one's anklebones. In winter, I was a little more mysterious, wearing knee-high leather boots, well dubbined to keep out the wet, riding britches, and a fighter pilot's leather jacket and cap. As I hiked to school, I looked less like a student and more like a pilot whose Sopwith Camel had crashed somewhere on the prairie. My family relied on catalogues for shopping, sending to Eaton's in Winnipeg, or to the Army and Navy in Vancouver. One cut-rate catalogue from a firm called Gowdy's became the source of a family joke. My father, who one winter during the Depression walked to town with gunny sacks wrapped around his stocking feet, ordered a twenty-nine-cent pair of shoes from Gowdy's. They arrived and were the correct size, only the right one was made in India and the left in Brazil.

From the foregoing, one might correctly conclude that I did not participate in sports. This is almost entirely true. Winter sports such as hockey and basketball were out because there was no way that I could return to town in the evening to attend practices, nor could our family afford the equipment as rudimentary as it was in those days. The only organized sport I engaged in was baseball, and this was because of the insistence and ingenuity of an extraordinary fellow student called Elmer (otherwise known as "Moe") Haynes. Moe had only one good eye, but he appeared to live for sports. He was a natural and was the main organizing force behind our baseball team. There were a number of Japanese students who had played baseball on the west coast prior to evacuation and they generously supplemented the talents of the rest of us. Moe decided I was a centre-fielder and when I could not get to practices, he would come to collect me in his father's three-ton truck. When he came to pick me up, all I could see was a pith helmet resting on a steering wheel, for at the time, Moe was only twelve years old. Nowadays, any twelve year old trying this would be guaranteed front-page headlines and a visit to juvenile court. Despite my indifferent skills and nervousness, Moe had faith in me and eventually I was part of the Taber Juvenile team that won the Juvenile Championship of Southern Alberta in 1950. As grand as that sounds, we never had a large enough lead for the coach, a gruff Hungarian called Casey, to chance putting me out in centre field. Ah yes, well it is written that "some are born great, some achieve greatness, and some have greatness thrust upon them." The only other game I played was badminton at noon hour in the school auditorium. I got quite good at it, but I later quit the game when I was in England when I hit a beautiful Chinese girl from Malaya in the head with a bird, making her cry.

Throughout my school years I was favoured with exceptional teachers. Taber was not a large town, but the town school did offer more amenities than did the average rural school, even though there was no indoor plumbing until 1947. A majority of the teachers were women, dedicated to their tasks. Discipline was from time to time a problem—in grade six we literally drove one teacher to a nervous breakdown with our behaviour. But this was, thankfully, the exception. I encountered my first male teachers when I was in grade eight. They proved to be equal in quality to the female teachers and they taught us well. As a testament to my teachers' skills, after writing the province-wide

Southern Alberta Juvenile Baseball Champions, 1950. From *Dawn*,
Taber High School yearbook, 1951. [Photo Luehr Studio]

examinations in grade nine, I won the Governor General's Bronze Medal for
the highest marks in the district.

Winning the medal raised my teachers' expectations for my performance in
high school. In the meantime, I got caught up in other things, such as editing
the school paper and yearbook and running for president of the students' union.
Still, I regularly won awards for these activities and for academic standing. One
award even proclaimed me All Round Boy, but in truth I was not giving my
studies their full attention. Despite claims to being "all round," I was foolhardy
enough to think that I could do all that I was doing and still perform well when
it came to the grade twelve provincial departmental examinations in 1951. I did
well, but not *well* enough. I lacked (and still do) one basic skill: the ability to
read quickly. While some are able to read like a searchlight, taking in a page
at a glance, my style has always been that of the clothesline, examining each
item before moving on to the next.

When it comes to skilled educators, two teachers stand out for me from
my high school years. Frank Semaka was the most memorable of my teachers
and remains high in the affections of all who were fortunate to have him as an

instructor. Not only was he completely in command of the subject matter of his courses—chemistry and trigonometry—but, just as important, he was in command of the classroom. Teenage males are notoriously difficult to make behave, but Semaka had the knack. Whether he was comparing our intellectual capacity to a nearby fence post or uttering some other insult, we revelled in his imaginative and caustic comments. To have been singled out by Semaka was a badge of honour. He did not lose his capacity to please us. In his nineties, when some of my old classmates called to see him, his first comment was: "My, my...imagine them letting you all out of jail at the same time!"

The second memorable instructor for me was Ted Aoki. He was a dynamic educator at the school and the advisor to the students' union. He was also the first Japanese Canadian teacher in southern Alberta. He won friends, affection, and admiration wherever he taught, although he was no stranger to racism. When attending a teachers' convention in Lethbridge in 1946, he was thrown out of the lounge of the Marquis Hotel where he had gone with friends for a drink because the hotel would not serve "a Japanese." He would later move to Lethbridge to teach. Still later, he was appointed as a professor at the University of Alberta, where we were colleagues, and remains an internationally acclaimed educational theorist. During his time at my school in Taber, he was active in the Japanese Canadian Citizenship Association (JCCA), which was working toward proper recognition by Canada of the contributions of Japanese Canadians. He fought to have the term "Jap" expunged from textbooks and newspapers. As a student advisor, he taught me about the benefits and joys gained through co-operative efforts. Aoki is now ninety years old and lives in Victoria.

Looking back, there are many reasons why I would not change anything about my early life and high school years. It was a turbulent time on both the world and home front, with the continuing economic hardships of the Depression and the upheaval of the war. Yet it was precisely these tensions and the new and exciting cultural influences occasioned by Canadian immigration policies, the Japanese invasion of China, and the evacuation and internment of Japanese Canadians from the Pacific coast of Canada that predisposed me to a curiosity about Asia, and led to a life devoted to the study of China. My childhood friends and early education were essential to my aspiring to become a sinologist. At the same time, my family's straitened circumstances prepared me to get by with few resources—and this I found, as I headed off to university, was essential to achieving that goal.

TWO ★ ★ ★ ★

Seeking a Path to China

By 1951, Asia was almost constantly in the news. The Chinese Communists under Mao proclaimed the People's Republic on October 1, 1949, followed in June 1950 by the outbreak of war on the Korean peninsula. Through the United Nations, Canada joined in the war on the side of South Korea against the North Korean invaders. The war almost won, then almost lost, by General MacArthur, continued until a truce was signed on July 27, 1953. The Communist victory in China and the Korean War were to have a major impact on the study of China in North America, stunting it for a quarter of a century or more.

When I enrolled in the honours history program at the University of Alberta starting in the fall of 1951, I had little idea of what the university had to offer. I wanted to study the history of China, an ambition that had grown stronger within me in the years since first meeting my friend Herbert How. In general I was attracted to Asia. I was very impressed with Mahatma Gandhi, reading whatever I could find about him, and my Japanese friends aroused in me an interest in Japan. I even tried to learn some Japanese from Ted Aoki's father who was a great scholar and teacher. The Communist victory in China in 1949 and the outbreak of the Korean War in June 1950 made Asia ever more present in my life. It seemed logical to me that I would be able to study the history of China at U of A. However, the first-year honours program contained only one history course, on Europe, taught by Don Blackley. I went to the acting head of the department, Ross Collins, a fine scholar who specialized in Medieval and Renaissance Europe. When I told him I wanted to study the history of China, he responded, "Why? There isn't a future in it." (I did not have the wit to say, "But oh, what a past.") There was little hope of Chinese history being taught in the department, nor was it likely to be taught in the near future. I was destined to study the history of France and Europe. As much as I enjoyed these courses, I grew restless about China.

Despite dreaming about studying China at university, the reality of my dreams was less concrete. Prior to attending U of A, I had very little money beyond the bare minimum for fees, room and board in a university residence, and transportation to Edmonton—a 13.5-hour journey over narrow gravel roads in a smoke-filled Greyhound bus containing, from time to time, a drunk or two. From the age of fifteen I had taken summer jobs to help out at home and to save for my future education. My first job was on the night shift at Broder's vegetable cannery, monitoring the machines that washed and sieved the peas, corn, and beans. Dressed in rubber boots and a rubber apron, I directed jets of live steam at the machines to clean them at the end of the shift. The job called for cleaning out the residue from huge metal drawers positioned under the rotating drum sieves. The noise and heat were terrific and quite disorienting. I rode home utterly exhausted at dawn and slept until evening when it was time for me to head back to town for the next shift. The next summer I took a job at the Dyson's Pickles salting station. Farmers brought in truckloads of pickling cucumbers that were put into large wooden vats and covered with salt and water. Later, the salted cucumbers were loaded, by the wheelbarrow-full, into rail tanker cars. The tanker cars had to be scrubbed clean inside to accept the cukes. If lucky, one managed to do this in the cool of the morning, but on occasion, the work had to be done in the heat of the afternoon when the temperature inside the tankers rose to 120°F and beyond.

The following two summers I worked at Taber Furniture, the local furniture store. It paid less, but it was inside and it was regular work—not dependent upon the cucumber harvest. The store was run by a couple of elderly English-men, Mr. James Hussey, who owned the store, and Mr. Jimmy Milne, who was a salesman and furniture assembler. Time had passed by Taber Furniture. As Taber grew and the district prospered after the war, the road to Lethbridge, thirty miles away, was widened and paved by October 1947. With this, Taber merchants, among them Hussey, were exposed to "big city" competition. A survey taken a few years after the highway was further improved and twinned showed that 70 per cent of Taberites regularly shopped in Lethbridge, while over 20 per cent of those who did not would if they could. Only about 10 per cent of Taber's residents felt that loyalty to local merchants was important.

Yet, despite the new competition, Taber Furniture carried on in its old ways. Hussey and Milne were fixtures in the town and only slightly noticed the changes that threatened their business. Sales at the store were cash only.

Hussey was nearing retirement, as was Milne, an alcoholic who punctuated his workday with trips across the back alley to the beer parlour of the Palace Hotel. Hussey, a very kind man, looked the other way. Hussey's kindness meant he went so far as to hire two students—myself and a fellow student named Leon Nielson—for the summer when there was barely work for one of us. Hussey had actually been roped into hiring me—he had promised my father he would give me a job. Unfortunately, at the same time Milne had offered the job to Leon. Hussey honoured both promises, absorbing the additional cost. The second summer Leon and I were both invited back, but by now Hussey had sold his business. The new owner, Walt Nielsen, was a modern salesman who introduced "buy now, pay later" financing. He also introduced new lines of furniture, particularly a wider range of chrome kitchen sets, which were all the rage at the time. He also purchased a delivery truck for the store, which was now called Nielsen's Furniture, with smart lettering on the side. Nielsen was dynamic, enthusiastic, and fun to work for. Leon had a driver's licence, so he and I delivered furniture throughout the district. But there were slow patches during the summer months, so we worked doing gardening around the Nielsen house. I used to regularly grab my lunch at the Cameo Café.

With the savings from these summer jobs, the war bonds I purchased with money given to me over the years by my godparents, a $150 Roger's Sugar Factory Scholarship, and a contribution of clothes from my parents, I prepared for university. I had one new suit, one new jacket and trousers, a portable Remington typewriter, a small electric powered radio, a couple of pairs of shoes, three sports shirts, one dress shirt and tie, socks and underwear, and a towel and soap, all of which I packed into a metal steamer trunk.

When I left for Edmonton in mid-September 1951, I was very much a country boy, wet behind the ears. I was thin, with a brush cut, and one or two chips on my shoulder. I was anti-American, somewhat anti-British, and perhaps a bit pro-Russian. I was anti-privilege and I generally took the side of the underdog. I was convinced, perhaps by all the radio shows and movies I had absorbed in my youth, that good would conquer evil and that it was my duty to speak up if I witnessed any wrongdoing. At the same time, I was trained by my mother to wait my turn and to be respectful of the needs of others. I was an odd mix of my father's temerity and my mother's timidity. I was alert to the funny and the absurd, I loved irony.

My high school self was also a bit of a prude and lacking in social skills. As I mentioned in the previous chapter, I neither smoked nor drank and I thought less of those who did. Although not a Mormon, I avoided tea, coffee, and Coke. And I disliked foul language. These traits may have pegged me as religious, but I had little interest in religion. Perhaps indulging in one or two of the above vices would have helped me cover up the fact that simple small talk was beyond me. What I lacked in social skills I did not make up for with physical grace. In high school I had attended Saturday night dances but only as a spectator. Before leading off the graduation prom as president of the Taber High School Students' Union, I had taken a couple of waltz lessons, but to no avail. My date for the night, Aiko Morahira, a beautiful Japanese Canadian girl, probably still has sore feet from the experience. Despite my position as a student leader, I was also not comfortable speaking in public. I trembled, something that acting in one or two high school plays did little to cure. My valedictory speech was probably the shortest one on record. I envied my Mormon friends who, through their church, received valuable experience in public speaking. If anything, I had perhaps one saving grace: I could make people laugh, a trait picked up early in my schooldays to ward off threats of physical violence from school bullies.

As inexperienced as I may have been, I had also fallen in love, and during the summer of 1951, as I prepared for university, I became determined to find out how she felt about me. In high school I had excellent teachers, but I only fell in love with one of them. Margo Burwash was my high school French teacher, a beautiful woman fifteen years my senior. She was born in Toronto but raised in Edmonton, where she obtained her BA, BEd, and MEd from the University of Alberta. She began teaching in the late 1930s and resumed the profession after a stint in the Women's Royal Naval Service—the Wrens—during World War II. Until she arrived in Taber in the fall of 1949, she taught in smaller towns in rural Alberta. She taught English, French, and social studies and sometimes music, but at Taber High School she was the French teacher. She was also my home room teacher, not that this meant much since we students moved around the school a lot taking different subjects.

From her first appearance in our class in September 1949, I thought Margo was someone special, and I was not alone. She was open, approachable, and had a gentle teasing sense of humour. She was also serious about her subject and displayed an inexhaustible understanding of French grammar. Because she played the piano well, she was asked by the school principal, Harry B. Myers, to accompany the boys' chorus he conducted. I was not a member of that group because I had sworn off singing when I was eight, following a ter-

Margaret (Margo) Jean Burwash, 1950.

rifying experience I had when rendering a solo performance of "Little Doggie Rover" at a music festival held in the Mormon Church across the street from the school. But Margo was asked to do one more extra task by the principal. She was to be the advisor for the school yearbook, of which I was the editor for the next two years. During those two years we developed an easygoing and bantering friendship. After a chance meeting between her and my parents in town one Saturday afternoon she was invited, if ever she took one of her long weekend walks, for which she was becoming known, in our direction, to drop in for tea. On a few occasions she did, much to the delight of my parents, who, like everyone else, enjoyed her company. My father particularly liked the opportunity to discuss the English classics, which he had read since childhood, and the works of Arthur Conan Doyle, whom he had met at spiritual séances in London years before. My mother was delighted to have the company of a younger woman interested in her life, her knitting, and how she found life on the dry prairie.

During my final two years of high school, I was in contact with Margo as a matter of course, but in the summers she returned to Edmonton before taking her mother on tours of Britain and the continent. She would send me a post-card, and it is well said that absence makes the heart grow fonder. I realized that my regard for Margo went beyond friendship, but I also knew that under the circumstances there was a bridge that I could not cross until I graduated.

During the summer of 1951, Margo travelled to Bermuda, but once she got back I was able to see her at the beginning of her school year because my first university term at U of A did not begin until the third week of September. I put my case before her, and she did not reject me. Margo was clearly intrigued by my precociousness, and in fact it became clear we had love for each other. Thus began two years of discussions between us about whether such a match was possible and would be strong enough to go against the prejudices of the day. It was not until I graduated from the University of Alberta at twenty-one years old that she agreed to marry me. By today's standards, our courtship was perhaps strange, inhibited to the point of being weird, but marriage was a step that required much examination, and we were living at a time when moral standards were very strict and conservative.

Having let Margo know how I felt about her, it was now time for me to travel to Edmonton. When I first arrived in the city, it was small and predominantly white, comfortable with its British heritage. This sounds quaint and charming, but the early 1950s was a time when women were routinely objectified; homosexuals were called "fruit"; crepe-soled shoes, referred to as "fruit boots," and wedge-shaped fur hats were a sure sign that the wearer was pro-Russian, or at the very least communist; many ethnic groups were looked down on; and Aboriginal people were shown little respect. Although I was placed in a good single residence room on the third floor of Assiniboia Hall on campus, I immediately felt lonely. Before then, I had never slept away from home for more than one night. I felt overwhelmed. Luckily, I was not alone in this feeling. The residence was full of young men drawn from farms and small towns. I became good friends with Thomas Peacocke, a dynamic young scholar from Barons, Alberta. He shared a room on the first floor and we sat at the same table for meals. Each morning I woke him up for breakfast, so now I tease him, saying that I take full credit for his outstanding career as an award-winning director and actor in theatre and film—because otherwise he would have slept through his career. There were others in residence as well from outside Canada, from India, Nigeria, and England. I became friends with a student from England. Philip Heath, a former British merchant seaman, was studying for a degree in education and was a budding writer. Our friendship continued in later years when we were both in England, or when he was teaching in France.

Residence, especially eating in residence, turned out to be a civilizing experience. We had a regular eating schedule, and were assigned, apart from breakfast, to specific tables of twelve each. All of the meals were taken in the large dining hall attached to Athabasca Hall, the oldest of the three residences. Dinner and Sunday lunch began with grace, usually said by Provost Aylmer Ryan, or some other guest at his head table. The tables were covered with white linen, the utensils were silver and silver plate, and the china was heavy and white, imprinted with the U of A's green crest. At each table sat a mix of newcomers and second- or third-year residents. At the head and foot of each table sat a senior student who was expected to set an example of good behaviour. The food was, overall, excellent, with the menus prepared by the university's dietician. However, sometimes a table would barbarically rebel at what they thought was an inferior or too repetitive a meal and overturn their serving bowls on the table. Breakfasts were a free-for-all with residents coming and going, or not at all. While Assiniboia and Athabasca Halls were for men, the third, Pembina Hall, with its own dining room, was for women. In my second or third year it was decided to mix the sexes for breakfast at least. Other times for mixing were the Saturday nights when the Athabasca dining hall was cleared and dances were held, a tradition going back to the days of Henry Marshall Tory, the university's first president. I remember these events less for the dances than for the table-moving at the end of the evening when those of us who helped were provided with a midnight "lunch."

During this time at university, I missed Margo terribly, but our contact was fragile and intermittent. Neither of us had access to a private phone, so we relied on letters and the long holiday weekends when Margo would spend hours on the bus to come to Edmonton to visit her family. I met her parents on Thanksgiving weekend in 1951, and she and I managed to take a long walk one afternoon.[1] We exchanged gifts at Christmas, but we had little time together because as I headed south to Taber for the holiday, she was headed north to Edmonton, with the reverse happening after New Year.

Otherwise, in residence I continued to make more new friends and got used to indoor plumbing and general-use showers. I was, however, thrown by the amount of free time I had. High school life seemed highly regulated in comparison. I was assigned five full-year courses in history, English literature, political science, economics, and French, accompanied by a course in physical education. I think I studied enough and read the textbooks, but doing the research for my essays proved challenging. The university had just opened a new library (now known as Rutherford South), but the stacks were closed to undergraduates, leaving one to be a supplicant at the attending librarian's desk. The French class was accompanied by sessions with a native speaker. Our native speaker was a visiting French student named Roland DeLagerie. Sessions with DeLagerie were held in the high-ceilinged seminar rooms on the third floor of the library. For someone in love with his high school French teacher, I did not keep my end up. My final mark was not high enough to gain me automatic entrance into a senior-level course. I had to petition Professor E.J.H. Greene for permission to attend the next year. I am glad I did because he made French literature exciting, although oddly enough, he likened my accent to that found somewhere near Marseille.

With so much free time on my hands, I had to find something to do to fill it. As a former high school newspaper editor, I found that something in the offices of the *Gateway*, located on the top floor of the newly opened (1950) Students' Union Building (now known as University Hall). I found myself immediately among friends of a similar iconoclastic outlook. We were generally against censorship and control from outside groups like the Student Union Executive; and we did not like fraternities, both men's and women's,[2] because they were "controlled" from the United States and were, in a number of cases, founded by segregationists who wrote a colour bar into their constitutions. To their credit, University of Alberta's fraternities lobbied against such restrictions but with limited initial success.

Like all newspapers, the *Gateway* worked to deadlines and the final preparations for a new edition were always hectic. The paper was set by a linotype operator at the University Print Shop. Copy was sent to the print shop and the proofs were returned to us. We then arranged the stories into columns on a dummy page, with suitable headlines of various sizes indicated. Partly because this process appealed to me, and partly because I lived in residence and could work later and slip the results under the door of the print shop in the wee small hours of the morning, I was appointed to the position of makeup editor.

The paper came out once a week on Thursdays, but in my later years, a supplement called the *Fencepost* was issued on Tuesdays. I became its editor late in 1953 and gained some national attention early in 1954 for some of the short editorials I wrote. On Friday, January 22, 1954, Mr. George Drew, leader of the Conservative Party of Canada spoke on campus. In sharp contrast to the treatment afforded controversial speaker Jim Endicott the year before, the university administration cancelled classes to ensure Drew of a good audience. Students reacted negatively to the cancellation and to the speech. I published an editorial in a rushed edition of the *Fencepost* the following Monday. Entitled "Drew," it read: "Anyone who had fears that the Rt. Hon. George Drew would expound the philosophy of the second party in Canada at the meeting Friday morning in Convocation hall was no doubt relieved. Instead, Mr. Drew gave a very pleasant address emphasizing the need for greater stress on political education. Mr. Drew had [a] very pleasant platform manner. Mr. Drew had a pleasant voice. Mr. Drew was pleasant." A few days later, the *Ottawa Citizen* was particularly complimentary about what I wrote, saying it showed how editorials should be written. I had another minor scoop when two students from England managed to fly the Russian flag atop the Arts Building on the first anniversary of the day Joseph Stalin died.

The *Gateway* also put out a comic issue each year, poking fun at the *Edmonton Journal* (dubbed the *Joynil*), which was the only daily paper in Edmonton at the time, and which, in our eyes, was too full of itself. One of the perks of working on the *Gateway* was free passes to movies and concerts in return for writing a review. Along with Philip Heath, I became a movie and concert reviewer, but my brand of criticism was clearly the type described by the wit who said: Critics are people who observe a battle and when it is over come down from the hilltop to shoot the wounded.

In addition to writing for the *Gateway*, I joined two campus clubs. The History Club was almost required and was one of the oldest clubs on campus, while the Political Science Club was inspired by a dynamic new professor named Grant Davy. The History Club drew its members from the professors in the department, honours students, masters students, and one or two others. The club met on a Saturday night, once a month during term. Members would meet at the home of a professor where one of the student members would give a paper. The evening concluded with snacks and desserts provided by the wife of the host for the evening. It was always a pleasant experience, except for the night when I was the one giving the paper. The club provided an opportunity for students and professors to get to know one another outside the classroom.

The Political Science Club was less formal and more dynamic. It met when and where it was felt necessary. It was active in bringing speakers to campus to engage in political discussion and debate. The leaders of all the political parties, including Tim Buck of the Communist Party of Canada, were invited to speak at public meetings, usually in Convocation Hall. These various events went well until we invited the Rev. James Endicott to speak in February 1953. As I mentioned earlier, Endicott was very controversial. He was born in China in 1898. In 1952, he returned from a trip to China, where he had worked in the 1930s and 40s as a missionary and political activist. While in China, he charged the Americans with using germ warfare in Korea, a charge he repeated on his return home. He said he had seen evidence of this in Manchuria across the border from North Korea. In addition to the ruckus stirred up by his words, he had enraged many people by accepting the Stalin Peace Prize that same year. He was arrested and held for one day on his return to Canada, but External Affairs Minister Lester Pearson, a fellow student of Endicott's from Victoria College, University of Toronto, thought it best not to make him a martyr. Naturally, with the Korean War going on, the debate raging in America over who "lost China," Senator McCarthy's communist witch hunt progressing in Washington, DC, and China becoming less visible behind a bamboo curtain, Endicott was just the person we students wanted to hear speak. Members of the club were called in by university President Andrew Stewart, who, to everyone's surprise insisted that no speaker could be brought on campus without his permission. When it had come to previous speakers, the club had neither sought, nor been told of the need for, such permission. (Also, as mentioned earlier, this was in sharp contrast to the way George Drew was received one year later). Endicott was effectively barred from campus and so we went to the Corona Hotel across the river on Jasper Avenue to hear him speak. Endicott was a big man and a dynamic speaker. He lost none of his lustre, but Andrew Stewart did. His actions touched off a student call for free speech and for a new policy on visiting speakers, He was also taken to task in an editorial by the *Calgary Herald*. Later, in 1963 and 1974, Endicott spoke on campus without incident.[3] Even in his eighties, he had lost none of his fire and determination to prove that his charge of germ warfare was accurate, a cause taken up after his death in 1993 by his son Stephen.

Endicott was not the only missionary returning from China to speak at the university. The previous year at a campus gathering, Kathleen Hockin, a returned United Church missionary, in explaining that China had not gone completely communist just because of Mao's victory in 1949, remarked, "When we left China, God did not follow us like a little dog." Many of us students signed a petition for the People's Republic of China (PRC) to be admitted to the United Nations, something that took twenty years to accomplish. By the end of my second year I was determined to go somewhere else so I could study

China. With the friendly assistance of Dean Walter H. Johns, I switched to a three-year general degree. The following spring, in 1954, I had been accepted at Cambridge University and at the School of Oriental and African Studies (SOAS) at the University of London. The latter appealed to me more and I looked forward to exploring the London my father had spoken so much about.

HOW DO YOU GET TO LONDON?
WORK, WORK, WORK...

Getting accepted at SOAS was all very exciting, but, as always, there was the question of money. Just as I had in high school, I continued to work different jobs during the summers to pay for my university education. After my first year at U of A, I had returned to Taber in May to work at a coal mine. The mine was on our land and was run as a partnership between my father and Omer Malo, the owner of a local lumberyard. My father provided the surface and sub-surface rights along with his mining skills. Malo provided the money to launch the project, to lay the tracks down the hillside, and to build a tipple for drawing the mine cars from the river valley and to empty them through a sloping chute into trucks waiting below.

Despite my father having a good reputation as a coal miner with his customers, some of whom drove up to fifty miles to fill their trucks, the mine lasted only three years. My father, already in his late sixties at the time, found the work very stressful. In addition, friction developed between him and Malo over mine safety. In the end, my father quit the mine and eventually it closed down. Working at the mine had at least a couple of advantages for me: I was able to stay with my parents, help them, and save some money; and I was able to see Margo at regular intervals to press my proposal for a future life together. We tried to be as discreet as possible. I visited her on Friday nights after work at her small apartment in the teacherage where most of the teachers lived on the top floor of the elementary school. On Sunday afternoons we went for walks, but Taber was a small town where to be seen twice with the same person was a cause for gossip and three times the making of a scandal. Margo, whose life as a single teacher in a small town prior to her coming to Taber had made her "a great catch" for any lonely local bachelor, had felt the stress caused by idle gossip. We knew that the pop psychologists of the day would conclude that she was looking for a son, while I was searching for a mother, and some "well-wishers" would accuse her of robbing the cradle. For her part, she was uncertain about my determination, particularly for the long term. She repeatedly argued that eventually I would meet someone my own age and regret our marriage, but I held my ground.

Regardless of its perks for my personal life, working at the mine made me very little money. Had I not won the Hudson's Bay Company Prize in history, life during second year at U of A would have been very austere. Indeed, the following April I was anxiously looking for a well-paying summer job, and I found it with the Canadian Pacific Railway (CPR). The CPR and the Canadian National Railway (CNR) were major employers of students during the summer tourist season. There were jobs in their hotels, restaurants, and on their trains. The trains offered employment as conductors, dining car stewards, waiters, and sleeping car porters. I was accepted as a sleeping car porter—it was one of the better things to happen to me. In early May 1953, after reporting for work in Calgary, I was sent with a group of other new porters to Vancouver for training. Up to this time in my life, I had spent all of one and a half days in the mountains, although we lived within two hours' drive of them. From an early age I knew what they were like, because of mirages. Under the right conditions, from our house in White Ash we could get a view of the mountains at Waterton Lakes to the southwest, or the mountains at Sweet Grass, Montana, to the southeast of us. Mirages also produced views of the town of Vauxhall, across the river northwest of our farm. But now, courtesy of the CPR, I was to have close, prolonged, and frequent views of them.

To me, even now, nothing can compare with that first morning after we left Calgary on our way to Vancouver. We awoke surrounded by a wonderland of mountains. I had never seen so many shades of green. Then came the exhilaration of arriving in Vancouver to smell the salty air off the Pacific. We stayed in the CPR bunkhouse at False Creek and attended training lessons given by Harold Ramsay, who taught us the finer points of portering. He was one of the best instructors I have ever had, for any of the subjects I have ever been taught. Black, and a former porter, he had risen about as high as he could in the CPR of those days.

When in Calgary during my stint with the CPR, I shared a room in Mount Royal with two other porters, or rather two of us paid rent to another porter who had previously rented the room in the upper part of a large three-and-one-half-storey house. Our porter-landlord, Roger Jowett, was an Englishman of some pretensions, and a friend of the famous Mitford family. A professional photographer, and a self-proclaimed ladies' man, Jowett had run into financial and social trouble in Hong Kong where he had gone from England following the war in 1949. He claimed that his romantic entanglements with married women became too complicated to sustain. It also damaged his efforts to establish himself as a professional photographer. He claimed his life to be the basis of a character in Han Suyin's 1952 novel, *A Many-Splendored Thing*.[4] Early in 1953, he had fled to San Francisco, then to Vancouver, and finally to Calgary, where he had hocked his camera equipment. With no prospects, he had signed on as a porter, a job for which he had neither the knack nor the enthusiasm. Although he was broke, Jowett's accent and suave English manner enabled him to rent a room, small kitchen, and bath at the top of a house owned by a lady from one of Calgary's best families. He smuggled the two of us in as paying guests and because we were very rarely all three in the city at the same time, he was able to dupe his landlady, passing us off as friends who had just stopped by.[5] Roger was very embarrassed to be a porter, but he adapted. He learned very quickly, as did the rest of us, how to earn and to receive good tips. He was excited about my plan to travel to England, giving me addresses of his friends, among them Irmgart Siefried, the famous Swedish opera diva with whom he claimed a very close ("nudge, nudge, wink, wink") relationship. He also gave me the name and address of his barber. Under no circumstances was I to say what he was doing for a living in Canada. As far as his friends in England were concerned, he was touring the Empire, taking exciting and beautiful pictures. Apart from his barber, I contacted none of them.

As the first of the Calgary-based summer porters to be assigned a trip, I had an advantage. The system of being assigned trips worked in favour of those who were away from their home base. For example, a porter on a one-way trip to Winnipeg on arrival was placed ahead of any of the local Winnipeg porters waiting for a trip out. The same held true for outsiders in Calgary. If a trip ended in your home depot—in this case, Calgary—then you fell to the bottom of the list. Thanks to this system, I stayed on the road continuously for nearly one month, never being assigned to a trip ending in Calgary. My friends, waiting patiently on stand-by duty in Calgary, brought me mail and laundry as I passed through.

Despite the long hours of work and the constant feeling that one needed a nap, portering had its compensations in the form of opportunities to spend time in places like Vancouver. The company supplied us with uniforms that included a starched white jacket to be worn inside the train and a tunic jacket to be worn outside. We were paid on the basis of a 20.5-hour workday, with 3.5 hours of sleep. With so little sleep afforded us, it is no wonder that passengers often commented about "lazy" porters who napped during the afternoon. Porters were given a discount on the meals served in the dining car, but even so, the food was expensive, served on fine china and crystal, with linen tablecloths and silver cutlery. It was cheaper to buy one's own food and prepare it in the kitchens of the so-called Colonist cars, which were designed to accommodate parties of immigrants to enable them to cook their own style of cuisine. Portering could be tedious, but the changing scenery and the passengers, drawn from all parts of the world, more than made up for it. With luck, one could live off tips and save one's pay for the next university year. These benefits made it easier to put up with shining shoes, cleaning spittoons and toilets, scrubbing floors, polishing mirrors, and carrying heavy luggage.

Most of my fellow porters were Canadians of African descent. Some of these men had made portering a career, while others were hired for the summer. Unlike the situation in the United States, where companies using the sleeping car developed by George Pullman were obliged to hire only black porters, railways in Canada were not so obliged. Some of the younger porters hired for the summer were African Americans. This was my first contact with Americans my own age. They were lively, frequently loquacious, and some used foul language of a quality I had never before heard. The ones I encountered were students from Texas, who were inclined to comment negatively on life in the cold North and the "crazy Canadian accent." Their language and behaviour often shocked the older Canadian porters, who were generally soft-spoken and courtly in their manner and who treated their work as a profession.

I worked a second summer as a CPR sleeping car porter in 1954 in the months before leaving for England. During that summer, I shared a room in Calgary with my good friend Cameron Wordie,[6] a business student specializing in accounting who had a summer job in an oil company office, in a house full of girls of unknown occupations. Wordie, who was more regularly in Calgary, noticed that the girls always seemed to be at home and entertaining many male friends. The girls were friendly enough to us and took amusement in watching us do our own laundry and ironing. As for seeing the woman in my life, during the two summers I worked on the trains, Margo and I had minimal contact save through letters. We saw each other in late April after I finished examinations and again in early September before university term began.

Financially, that last summer with the CPR was not as profitable as the first because I signed on to the job later on in May than I had the first year and I was lower down on the priority list. However, the company offered me one final perk, a pass to travel free to Montreal where I boarded the *Empress of Scotland*, bound for England and marriage to Margo. When I boarded the ship to England, I did not expect to return to Edmonton ever again.

BECOMING A SOASian

My parents spoke many times about the old country and what it was like when they left in 1920, but what I saw was not what I expected. I arrived in Liverpool late in September 1954 after a rough crossing. (In May, Margo and I had agreed to marry in September in London. She and her mother toured Scotland and England in August and September, and afterwards met up with me in London.) Rows and rows of dark brick houses met me on my arrival, their tile and slate roofs seeming to stretch to the horizon. Everything appeared greatly in need of cleaning. The train I then took to King's Cross in London was made up of small, cramped carriages with dirty, torn upholstery. After only a few days in the city, I saw extensive war damage and began to appreciate how far the London and England I had imagined were from the reality. Adding to the overall bleakness, coal was still the fuel of choice or necessity in London, blackening the exteriors of buildings and contributing to the killer fogs that plagued the city.

Nevertheless, I had opted to study in London and that was that.[7] At that time, London was an inexpensive place to live, and the university fees were low. My fees at SOAS for seven years ended up being less than C$300 in total, partly offset by a $100 research grant the university gave me to do research in Paris. I quickly became a Londonphile and did not regret choosing the University of London over Cambridge—I came to regard Cambridge as just a nice place to visit.

Studying in the United States, rather than in England, had never been an option for me—even then, the cost was prohibitive. But it was not just the money—my reasons were also political. The United States was in the throes of McCarthyism, the "who lost China" debate, and the Pat McCarran Un-American Activities Committee hearings. A casualty of this political activity was the study of China. The United States refused to recognize the People's Republic and urged its friends to place a trade embargo on China. The US treated anything coming from the new People's Republic as incurably red and dangerous. Even a panda was refused entry into the States in 1958 on the order of the Secretary of State John Foster Dulles because it was Chinese and Communist.[8] Moreover, famous and distinguished China scholars, like Owen Lattimore of Johns Hopkins University and John King Fairbank of Harvard, were under a cloud of suspicion. William Hinton, an agriculturalist living in rural China, on returning to the United States in 1953 with a study of the Communist revolution's impact on a Chinese village, had his manuscript seized—it was not to be returned or published for years to come. Hinton's work, *Fanshen*, published at last in 1966, is now considered a classic. Graham Peck's memoir, *Two Kinds of Time*, a brilliant depiction in words and drawings of wartime China, was seized within a week of publication in 1950 and the plates destroyed. A Canadian account of life under the new Chinese regime, called *Five Stars over China* by Mary Endicott, wife of James Endicott, was not allowed into the United States.[9] In this atmosphere, serious study of China was next to impossible. The American academic community was divided on the subject of China. Effectively, it turned to the study of Taiwan and closed itself off from the New China.

Consequently, these events in the US further fuelled my anti-Americanism and turned me toward London. Britain recognized Beijing in January 1950, continued to trade with China, and academic exchanges took place. Britain was more balanced in its reporting on China, although the events there, such as the Hundred Flowers and the anti-Rightist movement against Mao's critics, caused forebodings of a Stalinist approach by the new Chinese government. In 1958, Mao launched the Great Leap Forward in industry and the People's Communes in agriculture in defiance of Soviet advice and experience. Mao was convinced that if properly ideologically motivated, the Chinese people could do anything, no matter how gigantic the task set before them. He boasted that with the Great Leap Forward, China would overtake Britain in steel production within fifteen years, by setting up thousands of backyard furnaces. The Great Leap would modernize China at one fell swoop, while the People's Communes would, through collectivized peasant efforts, provide bountiful harvests. Initial statistics proved him correct until it was discovered that the statistics were a fiction provided by zealous ideologues wanting to please the Chairman. Economic collapse and famine, in which an estimated twenty million people starved to death, followed, along with an ideological dispute and a break with Moscow. In three years, the Leap was over and China sought wheat from Canada to help feed its people. All this only proved to America that it was correct in turning its back on China and embargoing its trade. Meanwhile, the British kept their relations open with China—they were more preoccupied with the Soviet Union and the number of Englishmen who were its spies.

. Brian and Margo Evans on the steps of Friern Barnet church, wedding day, October 8, 1954.

A final reason for my going to England related to family. At the time it did not particularly matter to me, because I had never met my relatives, but my parents felt better about my going so far away from home knowing that I would be close to family. Only later, when I got to know my cousin Reg and his wife Betty, did I appreciate how important this family factor was.

I registered at SOAS at the University of London on my birthday, Wednesday, October 5, 1954, and was assigned a tutor, Dr. Cyril Birch. He and I met the next day to outline my course of studies. As I was leaving his office, I asked if it was all right if I could take that Friday off from class, since I was going to get married. His jaw dropped as he said yes. I learned later that he assumed I would be away for a couple of weeks. He was very surprised when I appeared in class the next Monday.

Although our original plan was to marry in September, Margaret (Margo) Jean Burwash and I were married on the morning of October 8, 1954, in a Congregational Church in Friern Barnet on the northern outskirts of London. It was a cold morning and even colder inside the church. Only three other people were present apart from the minister: Margo's mother, and my cousin and his wife. After the service, we had some soup and cake in our flat, at 24 Petworth Road not far from the church. Margo and I had told our parents of our intention to marry back in Canada, prior to our coming to England. At that time, I was not sure how my parents would receive the news. I expected warnings about how I was still very young, but to my joy and surprise, both of my parents quite approved of the match. In fact, they were enthusiastic about the prospect. Margo received perhaps a slightly less enthusiastic endorsement from her parents, but approval nonetheless.

Margo and her mother, after completing their tour of Scotland and England in the weeks before our marriage, had found us a flat. It consisted of a large sunny front bedroom with bay windows and a back room overlooking the garden, in which a sink and stove had been installed to make a combined kitchen and living room. We shared the bathroom on the landing with the homeowners, Mr. and Mrs. Bond, who had a newborn son called Simon. Our rent was three pounds per week, roughly ten dollars Canadian. Friern Barnet was of higher elevation than central London and was far away from the smog and killer fogs, but it was also a long way from SOAS. The journey on the Number 134 red double-decker bus took about an hour and a quarter on good days, but much longer when the weather was bad. I got used to the commute, passing the time, as did Londoners, by reading, or, in my case, studying Chinese characters.

Once married and back at school, I soon learned that SOAS, fondly known as the "School of Ornamental and Accidental Studies," was a product of the Empire. Most of the histories, languages, and cultures of the countries touched by the British colonial overseas expansion were represented within the program. SOAS attracted many visitors, from troupes of African drummers and dancers to distinguished scholars like Professor Owen Lattimore, following his political persecution in the United States. We students were few in number and the academic staff outnumbered us. A large round table in the student common room provided seating for nearly all of us. Needless to say, our classes were small. Because of our mixed backgrounds, cultural, occupational, and socio-economic (Tibetan to Bostonian, military officers to elderly economists, children of workers to sons and daughters of Pashas), we lacked cohesion as a group. But in the fall of 1956, the Suez Crisis united us against Britain and France. Ironically, SOAS, the product of British imperialism, was dead set against its final disastrous fling.

Early on, I did become friends with two of the full-time SOAS students, both of them Englishmen. One of them, David Barnikel (Barny), became interested in China following his stint of national service in the Royal Navy aboard a warship on patrol in the Yellow Sea. The other was the son of a London newspaper shop owner. He was younger and had no intention of doing his two years of national service. He managed, through various poses and stratagems, to avoid it until it was abolished. He was an accomplished organist and used to keep a dog collar in his briefcase, using it to pose as a priest to gain access to churches to play their organs. He became known to us as "Father Payne." His full name was John Philip Henry David Lambert Barrack Payne. He never explained why he was interested in China, but I suspect he had distant Chinese relatives.

On admission to SOAS, I was advised to study classical Chinese, but my tutor Cyril Birch, a specialist in Chinese literature, made it clear that the path to classical Chinese began with the study of modern Chinese. I was assigned to a first-year class in Chinese where my fellow students included people from the Colonial Office, the Foreign Office, the British Air Force, and the Army. Some were on leave from Chinese-speaking parts of the Empire, while others were preparing to go to Beijing and Hong Kong as part of official diplomatic missions. Still others were young men fulfilling their national military service obligations by studying an Oriental language. Of the twenty or so members of the class, less than a handful were full-time students enrolled in regular degree programs. We were to learn later that among us there was at least one spy.

The SOAS method of teaching Chinese, while interesting, was confusing. The head of the department, Walter Simon, was a famous senior scholar. Jewish, he had left Germany before the war to become a professor at SOAS. He published introductory teaching materials and a Chinese dictionary using a system of transliteration of Chinese sounds called *Guoyu Romantzh*, adopted by the Chinese Nationalists, who, after 1949, were no longer in control of China. The other and older system of transliteration was known as Wade-Giles. It was devised in the nineteenth century by a British ambassador to China (Thomas Wade) and modified by an Oxford scholar of classical Chinese (Herbert Giles). This latter system was well established and widely used. It was, however, misleading and confusing with its use of apostrophes. For example *T'ao* was to be pronounced *tow* and *Tao* as *dow*. The casual reader, however, was most likely to pronounce *T'ao* as *te-ow* and *Tao* as *tayo*. The system also used small numbers above each word to indicate one of the four tones of the standard (Mandarin) dialect. Nonetheless, it was for many years the only system around and was deeply rooted in a range of publications.

SOAS linguists generally went for the *Guoyu* system, which got rid of the apostrophes and numbers, the tones being indicated through the spellings. For example, the sound *Ma*, meaning horse, was rendered in Wade-Giles as *Ma* with a 3 over the *a*, indicating a third tone. In the *Guoyu* system, *Ma* became *Maa*, the double *a* indicating the third tone. The *Guoyu* system was not accepted by all sections of the SOAS—historians and others continued to use Wade-Giles because the majority of texts and dictionaries used it. As students, we had to be aware of and use both. To add to this confusion, the new Communist Government in China was developing an entirely new system called *pinyin*, using Cyrillic and Latin letters, which has since become the standard.

Introductory Chinese was taught for three or more hours, Monday to Friday, beginning at 9:30 or 10 a.m. Each hour during the day was taught by a different instructor (Cyril Birch, Patrick Hanan, John Chinnery, James C.Y. Liu, D.C. Lao, G. Malmquist, and Harry Simon),[10] each with a different approach to teaching and to Chinese in general. Some of the instructors emphasized writing, some speaking, and some reading, while some took a purely cultural or political approach. The instructors covered various aspects of Chinese from grammar to writing and speaking. A set of phonograph records available in a room upstairs enabled us to hear the language as spoken by native speakers. We could refer our questions to Miss Bao, a charming and beautiful Chinese assistant. There were, however, too many of us for the resources available and the records crackled and popped as they were played. Learning Chinese was an intense, if sometimes bewildering, experience. After a year, we faced a set of examinations, the results of which were posted on a board on a wall across the street from SOAS, outside Senate House, the administrative hub of the University of London. The top student in the class, who had marks never seen before in the history of the program, was named Evans, but it was not *this* Evans. It was Richard Evans from the Foreign Office, who much later in his career in 1984 was British ambassador to China and the person designated to negotiate the agreement to return Hong Kong to China. We sat side by side in class. He was known as "Evans FO," and I, as "the other Evans."

After the introductory year, I went on to take more specialized courses in classical Chinese, which was used in historical records and government documents. Meanwhile, the head of the History Department, who was also chair of the committee of all historians in the many colleges that made up the University of London, put me forward for entry into the doctoral program. At that time, a masters degree was considered a terminal degree and something that was awarded to those who did not make it through the PhD. Because of this, I do not hold a master's degree, but my rate of progress toward a doctorate in Chinese history was directly related to money and my ability to make it. Seven years after I enrolled at SOAS, I received my degree. It would not have been accomplished without Margo's hard work and dedicated support.

While we both worked, Margo's jobs were tedious and lacked the intellectual stimulation that I enjoyed during the academic year. On our marriage, Margo and I pooled our resources. Her contribution was greater than mine and consisted of her remaining savings after paying for the costs of the summer tour with her mother, but together we did not have much. Fortunately, the Canadian dollar was strong—worth slightly more than the American. In the first few months, we established a pattern that we were able to follow for most of our time in England. Once a week we went to a play and or a concert, purchasing the cheapest seats. On the weekends we tried to see parts of London, such as the beautiful squares and gardens, particularly Kew Gardens. We also visited art galleries and churches, and took day trips to nearby places such as St. Alban's or Canterbury. None of these activities cost a great deal of money, but it soon became clear that Margo would have to look for a job and I would have to seek summertime employment. Among the students at SOAS, I was unique in that I had neither grants nor scholarships, in other words no visible means of support. British students were each given grants from their home counties, grants that were large enough to pay for their tuition, room and board, entertainment, and some travel, particularly if they were able to save money by living at home. Other foreign students were on scholarships of varying richness. When I chose to study in England, there were only two scholarships I could apply for: the Rhodes and the IODE (Imperial Order of the Daughters of the Empire). Even if I had the necessary credentials for one of these, I was immediately disqualified because they were for single white males only.

Shortly after our marriage, Margo began to look for work. Just after Christmas, she found employment with the Canadian Embassy Immigration section located on Greene Street. While this was good news, it was also bad news. She was paid the wage of a locally engaged staff and so made barely enough to cover our bus fares, food, and cheap weekly theatre tickets. My opportunity to contribute did not come until the next May, in 1955, when I went in search of a job. I think I was the only student looking for a job, judging by the surprised looks on prospective employers' faces. I am sure they were thinking: Why doesn't he have a grant? Doesn't that say something about his abilities? Besides, we're looking for full-time workers not summer time wonders. In despair, I went for an interview at a house that was once the home of Lord Nelson's mistress, Lady Emma Hamilton, but was now the office of the Finchley North London Municipal Works Authority, or some such grand name. I was accepted as a summer time gardener at the North Finchley municipal swimming pool, a job I did for two summers. As a gardener, I received three pounds a week, precisely our rent. Each Friday afternoon I lined up with the rest of the workers to sign for my pay packet, a small buff envelope containing three pounds exactly, in cash. Each Monday morning, I turned it over to Mrs. Bond.[11]

My tasks as a gardener at the swimming pool were fairly simple. The pool was set back from a main road behind a high hedge. Trimming that hedge was one of my jobs. The pool was surrounded by a high fence and people entered through the front buildings that included changing rooms and snack bars. Smoking was allowed everywhere. My other main job was to pick up chocolate bar and ice cream bar wrappers and cigarette butts that littered the open areas between the edge of the pool and the fence. It was not the pleasantest of tasks, but what could one expect when earning three pounds a week? Inside the fence, around the pool, patrons attempted to wear as little clothing as possible. Public morality accepted this, but this acceptance did not extend outside the fence where several times a week men in dirty raincoats flashed and exposed themselves. These fellows were subject to arrest, fine, or imprisonment. The gardens around the pool included lawn bowling greens, but I was never allowed to operate the mowers that kept them in billiard-table condition. Instead, I pushed a hand mower on the less prized lawns.

My half-dozen fellow workers at the pool were older men, each of whom had suffered a nervous breakdown or had been invalided out of the services at the end of the war. They were fine and decent people and each had a compelling story. For example, a fellow worker named Cyril had one of his lungs full of special sponges to stop it from collapsing. He had been in a bomber shot down during the war. He gasped as he worked, but was never at a loss for a broad smile. Another worker, John, had been a theatre stage manager in a West End musical theatre but the stress had got to him and he had had a nervous breakdown. He told stories of performers and performances he had been involved with. As well as working at the pool, he did iron work as a hobby and provided me with the iron struts to mount a window box at our flat. George, the boss, was a pleasant man, set in his ways and credited at times with nearly driving those under him to a second nervous breakdown.

These older men made a pet out of me, looking after my interests, and giving me good advice on how to get along in London. Most of them accepted that the swimming pool was to be the rest of their working lives, but at least one fellow, much younger than the rest, was determined to recover and get back into the mainstream. Len had owned his own business, which had gotten the best of him, but he worked like a person possessed. The older workers at the pool took bets as to whether or not he would make it. Those who bet against him, lost. As far as we knew, he disappeared back into the world of commerce. There was one other younger person working at the pool named Freddie. He was not there because of any physical ailment or nervous breakdown. He was short-tempered and mentally challenged. Cutting the high hedge with him as my partner made for long days. Each of us took a side, staring at each other as we clipped. Conversation was limited to the weather and the sharpness of the shears. Other subjects made him angry, so we lapsed into silence. After a couple of months, he was recommended for work at another garden. He was pleased and so were we.

One day, after a long day at the pool, I returned home to our flat and smelled gas. It had been a lovely warm day and the windows were open to circulate air. I thought the smell was because the small gas heater in the bathroom had been slow to ignite. Shortly after, when I was making myself a cup of tea and preparing supper, our landlord Mr. Bond knocked at the door. He was trembling and holding baby Simon. He was white as a sheet. "My wife has gassed herself," he said, and he went downstairs to wait for the coroner and the police. It turned out that Mrs. Bond, who had always appeared cheerful and busy, suffered from post-partum depression. It was such a sad situation and a great shock to Margo when she returned home from work. Soon after, Mr. Bond decided to sell the house and move. We attempted later to get in touch with him, but he did not respond.

Before Mr. Bond sold the house, we began flat-hunting, viewing an amazing range of spaces converted for student tenants. One of them I remember was later taken by a Pakistani friend who invited us to dinner served on a sheet of plywood that covered the bathtub when it was not in use. After what appeared to be a hopeless search, we found a cold-water, two-room attic flat at Muswell Hill across the road from Highgate Wood on a street called Onslow Gardens. The rooms were originally meant for maids, but that time had passed. The flat was to be our home for the remainder of our time in London. It was only half the distance to SOAS, and just a little more expensive. Our new landlord was an instructor in economics at the City of London College and he liked the sound of the word "guineas" more than "pounds." Our rent had gone up 10 per cent and now was eleven dollars Canadian. Mr. Bernard Moore and his wife Nina were delightful and they, their three children, and particularly their cat Tulip, made us feel at home, and, at times, even special by inviting us for tea; recommending plays, exhibitions, and movies we should see; and treating us like members of the family. Tulip was a mix of Abyssinian and Burmese, with the most remarkable ability to speak loudly. Like all cats, creature comforts were at the top of his agenda. Once he found that we kept the gas heater on upstairs, when we were home and the landlord was absent, he was at our door asking for an opportunity to tend our fire. He was a remarkable animal and I found it very difficult to leave him when we eventually returned to Canada. Subsequently, I visited him whenever I was in London.

It did not take us long to settle into our new digs and explore the district, in particular Highgate Wood and the village of Highgate. The two rooms of our attic flat at 6 Onslow Gardens had sloped ceilings. One could walk upright in the middle of the room, but one had to stoop when approaching the sides. Small hinged windows looked out back at the garden and out front at the street. On the landing, a few steps lower than our flat, was a small kitchen stove and a sink for washing. Above the kitchen was a skylight. Level with the kitchen landing, but out of sight, was an attic with a storage tank full of water. The water was supplied through lead pipes that ran up the outside of the brick wall of the house. A few steps down from the kitchen landing was the bathroom on the second floor, the same floor as the Moore family's bedrooms. We shared the bathroom in which there was a "geyser gas water heater" operated by plugging a meter with shillings. Other meters controlling electricity and gas supplies to our flat were located in a small cupboard on the ground floor under the stairs. They could be filled with enough money to last for a week or so. Energy costs were high and in the damp, dark, and cold months from November to March, the meters whirled at high speed. There was an inefficient gas heater in the study/sitting/dining room, but the bedroom had no such advantage. We used porcelain pigs to warm the bed. When I was writing my thesis during our final two years in London (1959–1961), I sat in the bed typing with fingerless gloves, waiting for the study to warm up.

Some winters in London were more exciting than others. In February 1956, London suffered a heavy snowfall and a cold snap; all the water pipes in Onslow Gardens froze. The city set up a standpipe in the street and we carried water in buckets up to our flat. It took me back to my childhood and Margo back to her days living in teacherages in rural Alberta. Neither Margo nor I found it much of a trial. Ten days later came the thaw, very early one morning, at about 3 a.m. The street filled with noise and shouting, which I took to be delight at the end of the cold weather. Nothing was further from the truth. With the thaw came burst pipes and flooding. At 6 Onslow Gardens, Margo and I were high and dry, but on the next floor down the leaking water caused a major disaster. The water tank overflowed and the ceiling on which it rested gave way. Down with it came a stack of books that Mr. Moore had squirrelled away out of the sight of Nina who objected to his buying so many.

DEATH AND LIFE AT LONDON UNIVERSITY

Our former landlady Mrs. Bond's was not the only suicide to alter my life in my second year at the University of London. Students at soas were drawn from every part of the globe. A high percentage of those who came from the Middle East and Asia were children of very well-to-do families, sons and daughters of merchants and government officials. One of these students was a stunningly beautiful Eurasian girl from Malaya. Her beauty gave everyone pause, but none more than an equally handsome and beautiful young man from Nigeria. Victor Ogarigbe was utterly fascinated by her. He began to follow her around just to look at her. In the library stacks she would look up to find Victor staring at her. This unnerved her, and she reported matters to the soas authorities. Victor was summoned before the school secretary, who just happened to be a former officer in the East African Rifles. Victor was dressed down in military fashion and ordered not to go within eyeshot of the young woman or else face expulsion. According to Victor, he had just come back to soas to return a book when he saw the young woman again. Regardless of his excuse, he suffered the consequences. Shortly thereafter, he jumped in front of a tube train at Russell Square Station, a block from soas. Of the students at soas, my friend "Father Payne" was the closest to Victor, although my other friend David Barnikel and I were on friendly terms with him. Father Payne noticed that Victor had not been seen for several days and he began to enquire after him. He discovered what had happened and that Victor's body, which had not been claimed, was about to be given a pauper's funeral in a north London cemetery. In haste, the three of us went to the funeral. It was a cold, raw, January day.

The three of us were very upset by Victor's fate and the insensitivity shown him by soas. So, we decided to do something about it. We made an appointment to see the foreign student advisor for the University of London. Her office was in Birkbeck College, next door to SOAS. Miss Mary Trevelyan was the daughter of a very famous historian and was herself much more interested in her research than "babysitting" foreign students. She saw her role as being there for students to consult should they have a problem, and should they know that her office existed. She completely supported SOAS's actions regarding Victor. We left her office knowing that if something should be done, we would have to be the ones to do it. The University of London had a students' union, but SOAS did not, so we formed one, of which I became the secretary.

As part of our new students' union, we introduced a system of modest student mentoring. Each new foreign student registered at SOAS would be assigned to a second- or third-year student who would meet the newcomer on their arrival in London, assist them in finding a place to stay, help them settle in, and remain a point of contact should they have any questions in the future. SOAS co-operated with us, sending out our information to new students to let them know that if they provided us with the when and where of their arrivals, one of us would meet them. The system worked extremely well and a number of lasting friendships were formed in this way. In only one case was our offer rejected and that by a Bostonian who felt our efforts represented an invasion of his privacy. But John Spellman was different. He used to kick Englishmen in the shins in order to hear *them* say: "Oh, I am terribly sorry!" He later redeemed himself when he, almost single-handedly, revived student interest in the moribund Royal Asiatic Society that was founded in 1823, primarily to promote the study of India. He helped them to increase their membership and to improve their finances. The society was so grateful that he was given a nearly private office from which to work, with free tea and a newspaper delivered each day. John, whom I regarded as a deliberately rough diamond, was nevertheless a friend. He was later appointed a professor of Indian Religion and History at the University of Windsor, Ontario.

In my second and third years at SOAS, I took Chinese, Japanese, and European history courses. The history of modern China was taught by a Dutchman, Otto Van Der Sprenkel, an expert on Ming bureaucrats. He was very generous to his students, taking us to lunch and having us to his home at Tanza Way on the edge of Hampstead Heath for parties. He adored the Marx Brothers and used to pepper his conversation with Chinese translations of Groucho's bon mots, such as *Shangdi ai yi ge yatz* ("Lord Love a Duck"). He wore broad-brimmed hats and was usually seen with a crocodile of students in pursuit.

Early Chinese History was taught by Denis Twitchett, a brilliant scholar of the history of the Tang, who was lured away to Cambridge, not long after Otto accepted a position at Canberra, Australia. The history of Japan was taught by the only professor I was to study with, William G. Beasley. He was in the Navy during the war and learned Japanese, taking a degree in history after the war ended. He was well published and was appointed professor of history prior to my arrival at SOAS. Under the British system, there were very few professors (or chairs). The next rank down was reader, followed by lecturer. The situation was such that if a young scholar was named professor, there was little hope of advancement to that rank for years to come for those below him and little opportunity elsewhere, particularly in so-called esoteric fields. Some relief came in the 1960s when a major government report led to the establishment of centres of Asian Studies in provincial universities, and with the Vietnam War and the ensuing expansion of Asian Studies in the United States, which absorbed many of the scholars from SOAS. But that was to happen after my SOAS days. In 1957, two other historians were hired at SOAS: Michael Loewe, a specialist in the Han period and from whom a steady stream of scholarly articles and books was to flow during the last quarter of the twentieth century, and Jack Gray, a Scot, who had expertise in nineteenth- and twentieth-century China. Gray had just come back from a teaching stint at the University of Hong Kong, where two of my fellow PhD students, Yan-kit So and Sophie Wong, had been his prize students.

Actually, Yan-kit So and Sophie Wong were two of the students I was assigned to meet on their arrival in London as part of the Student Union mentorship program. Sophie Wong was quiet and reserved. The daughter of a banker, with a large house on Victoria Peak in Hong Kong, she eventually decided history was not for her and became an international lawyer. She and Margo became good friends.

Yan-kit So, or Nancy as she was called, was much more outgoing and from a poorer part of Hong Kong. She was engaged to Po Yat, a young surgeon in Hong Kong. She very much took to life in London, except for its lack of good Chinese food. At that time there were only two Chinese restaurants in Central London, each of them too expensive for students. Cheaper ones could be found down in Lime House in the East End, but they were far away and the food was not all that good. In desperation, Yan-kit would come to our cold-water flat in Onslow Gardens to cook barbeque pork (*char hsiu*), which we dubbed Charles Liu. Yan-kit and I became close friends and shared an interest in food. She did marry Po Yat in Hong Kong, but shortly thereafter divorced him. London and England were in her blood. She finished her PhD and married Briton Martin, an American scholar, a specialist in the history of India. She bore a son, Hugo, shortly before moving to Poona, India, with her husband where he was given a prestigious post. Sadly, he died shortly afterward while still only in his thirties, leaving Yan-kit to raise their son. She returned to the United States and oversaw the publication of her husband's thesis. Suffering from nervous exhaustion, she was advised to rethink her life and to do what she liked best. What she liked best was cooking, and what she was to become was a famous chef on British television under the name of Yan-kit Martin, credited with introducing the English to the finer points of Chinese cuisine. She authored beautiful cookbooks and a scholarly work on the history of Chinese food.[12] But all this was yet to happen. In 1955, we three—Sophie, Nancy, and I—were naive but eager beginning graduate students, searching for a topic and the archival sources to go with it and trying to figure out how to write a thesis.

Rescued by NATO

When I began my studies at SOAS, China was ending its first five years of Communist rule. Mao and his colleagues faced problems on all fronts: illiteracy, poverty, disease, and starvation at home; and trade embargoes and hostility abroad save for the USSR, but even that relationship was showing signs of stress as the two communist parties increasingly disagreed on dogma. In addition, the Chinese rulers had a problem with their intellectuals, many of whom rejected outright the regime's approach. When efforts to convince the dissenters through popular campaigns failed, the Chinese Government resorted to re-education and reform through labour, referred to in the West as brainwashing.

While the Chinese experimented with creating a new China, with a new type of citizen, I found myself undergoing some self-inflicted brainwashing. Chinese history was too vast a subject and one had to choose some part of it to study. But which part? Would the part I eventually select give me a greater understanding of the whole? How well would I be able to think myself into the context of the past? How far should my future employability govern my choice? Never mind the future, how were Margo and I to manage the present?

CANADIAN INTERLUDE

By the spring of 1957, with our resources running low, Margo and I decided to spend what we had on boat and rail tickets back to Edmonton. We sublet our flat to another graduate student on a flexible term. I was yet to settle on a PhD thesis topic so it was a good time to take a break between formal courses and independent research. In addition, Margo wanted to consult her family doctor on the question of why we had not been able to begin a family. (It was an era when the failure to conceive was blamed on women but I am rather certain that in our case the fault lay with me.) She also wanted to spend time with her aging parents. Margo was to seek employment as a teacher until at least the following spring, and I was to try to find some high-paying summer work. We stayed with Margo's parents in Edmonton, but I was soon aware that there were no high-paying short-term jobs. I was encouraged by my former professors at U of A to go back to finish my degree.

However, I did not return to England before making a disastrous attempt at selling *World Book* encyclopedias door to door during the chilly days of October 1957. Sometime, I think it was when I was in grade six, my parents were convinced by a travelling *World Book Encyclopedia* salesman that a set of *World Books* was worth the financial sacrifice in order to assure me of a good education. And indeed, growing up, the *World Book* became a fountain of knowledge for me. Whenever I had a question, I was enjoined to look it up in the encyclopedia. Ironically, I found myself being recruited and trained in *World Book* sales techniques, and I set out to make my fortune. I chose to spend a couple of weeks with my sister Mary in the small town of Holden, east of Edmonton, where she was then living, to test my skills. Margo, meanwhile, had begun work as a supply teacher in Edmonton's high schools, but finding maintaining discipline to be a major problem, she took a position in the Correspondence School Branch, teaching social studies worldwide through the mail, living with her parents until she was to return to London at Easter. At Holden I came away from farmhouse after farmhouse without a sale but with a full appreciation of the hardships facing farmers. By the end of that month, I had sold one set, to my sister, and only because I gave her a price without my commission.

Putting my days as a salesman behind me, I returned to Britain by ship in November. My cabin mate was a young Irishman who had worked a couple of years in Canada's North in a mine. He had saved a great deal of money, half of which he spent on dance lessons at Arthur Murray's in Edmonton. With the remainder he planned to buy a small farm in Ireland and live in luxury for the rest of his days. I admired his optimism.

Back in London, I faced two tasks: settle on a thesis topic; and find work that would enable me to carry on research and pay my rent. The question of a thesis topic was influenced by my experience while in Edmonton. Before I had left England to return home to Canada, I was attracted to the history of the Tang dynasty, which would mean working under Denis Twitchett. He wrote me in Edmonton to suggest a topic relating to Tang administrative history, which, to this day, I wish I had taken up. But in Edmonton I was advised that if I wanted to be marketable as a Chinese historian, I had better do something more modern. I searched for a subject that would reflect the languages I knew, eventually settling on a topic that involved the history of French, British, and Chinese diplomacy regarding China's southwest frontier in the last half of the nineteenth century. Jack Gray at SOAS was my immediate supervisor, but because he was only a lecturer, Professor Beasley was my official supervisor. At the same time, I continued taking classes in classical Chinese.

My search for gainful employment once back in London was more haphazard. I was shown some pity by a friend who offered me part-time work until Christmas. Findley McKenzie was the son of Chinese missionaries, a student of Chinese history and art, and a socialist. He attended the University of Alberta where he was dubbed "a Communist" because of his wedge fur hat, similar to those worn by Soviet Russian leaders. Findley married June Wiseman, a former student of Margo's, and moved to London. Earlier in 1957, Findley had persuaded Collett's Holdings, socialists who owned a number of bookstores in London, which despite their best efforts, made a profit, to open a Chinese bookstore. He became the manager of a beautiful new shop on Museum Street across from the front gate of the British Museum. The shop featured Chinese art, scrolls, prints, cards, and figurines on the ground floor. Upstairs were books about China in English and Chinese, as well as magazines and journals imported from the People's Republic. I was to assist in the shop to deal with an anticipated Christmas rush. I worked each day in the basement, unpacking cards and envelopes, preparing them for sale on the first floor. Some cards had Christmas or New Year's greetings printed inside, others were blank. Their outsides bore traditional Chinese scenes of nature, some with people, some with pagodas and temples, while others featured reproductions of Buddhist art. The job lasted less than six weeks, but I enjoyed my time in a socialist bookstore, selling Buddhist Christmas cards from Communist China. On my departure, I was given a four-volume English translation of the *Jin P'ing Mei*, *The Golden Lotus*, a famous work of Chinese erotica. The job also offered me a 10 per cent reduction on books, but I was not really in a position to take full advantage of it. Collett's was but one of a line of bookshops on Museum Street full of temptations. I purchased some books during my time in London, but they in no way reflected the opportunities I would have had if I had had the money.

I spent that Christmas with my cousin Reg Poole and his family. They lived near Pimp Hall, Chingford, just beyond the district called Edmonton, in North London, a long bus ride from 6 Onslow Gardens. Reg and his wife Betty had two sons, Geoffrey and Christopher, not yet in their teens. In addition, Betty invited her brother Phillip Podd, his wife Doreen, and their two young daughters for Christmas Day. Because Reg's mother and my mother were sisters, the day followed a pattern with which I was familiar. Unlike some English families, my cousin served turkey rather than goose. I was used to a houseful of people because during my childhood my parents invited the only other Welsh family in the district to share Christmas Day with us. Mr. and Mrs. Foulkes would arrive just before noon by horse-drawn wagon after a drive of over three hours. They were usually accompanied by one or two of their sons who specialized in teasing me. With this background I was happy to tease the children gathered at my cousin's house. There was one outstanding difference between Christmas in North London and in Taber and that was topography. One would search in vain in White Ash for a holly bush, never mind one laden with bright red berries. Nor did one leave our house in White Ash to enjoy an after-dinner walk on a grassy heath surrounded by tall oak and chestnut trees. In London, one felt much, much closer to Dickens.

Margo and I would spend subsequent Christmases with my cousin but in 1957 we were separated, relying on letters. I found the days between Christmas and New Year's Day particularly lonely as the gloomy and dank days dragged on. The cinema was reasonably cheap, but at Christmas Londoners gathered in theatres to watch pantomimes, something that I could not afford to do. Separated from Margo, I tended to neglect my diet. My mother had sent me a Christmas parcel with Christmas cakes and shortbread. I used a good slab of cake as a type of K-ration to keep me going. Along with the occasional parcel, my mother wrote us weekly the whole time we were in England, in her neat clear script, keeping us up to date on family news and local politics.

That Christmas, during conversations with Phil Podd, my cousin's brother-in-law who was a schoolmaster (principal), it came out that I was in need of money. He offered to help me get work as a substitute teacher. Late in February, I was offered a stint teaching a class of twenty six-year-olds at Hornsey primary school, a forty-minute walk from Onslow Gardens through lower Highgate Woods and beyond. It seems the school had trouble keeping teachers, and I soon knew why. The job was mine until Easter, but it did not take me long to find out that this was not for me. Discipline was a problem. To get them to be quiet, I struck a cricket bat on a wooden table with a resulting loud bang. This worked only once—after that, they made noise just to hear me hit the table again. A senior teacher suggested I tell them about Canada but they showed no interest. Another teacher told me that they loved to paint. I seized on this, but one could not have them paint all day.

The weather was cold that February. On my long walks to and from the school, I wore my wedge fur hat, but I was not hailed as a communist. Instead, little children followed me in the street singing, "Davy, Davy Crockett," from the film that was all the rage at the time. My spirits were very low. After a week of teaching, mainly painting classes, I suggested to the headmaster that he find someone else.

Meanwhile, having decided on a topic for my thesis, I began the research. Research materials were to be found in a number of places, not very far from SOAS. They included the Senate House Library and the Institute of History, housed in the same building; the British Museum Reading Room (BM) nearby; the Public Record Office (PRO) some distance away on Chancery Lane just above Fleet Street; and the India Office Library, a little further away, off White-hall, near Number 10 Downing Street. I gained entry to each of these places with an identity card, which I had to renew each year. None of the buildings were that comfortable to work in, each being cold in the winter and humid in the summer. I also had to make sure I arrived early in the day at the PRO and BM, since seats were at a premium and quickly taken up by other researchers. During the winter months it was doubly important to arrive early at the PRO to find a seat close to the fireplace. The BM held other hazards. A friend, who used a book one day, requested it the next day only to receive a slip that read: "Unavailable, eaten by worms during the war." At the India Office and PRO, one dealt with original documents, mainly handwritten, bound in leather. At the India Office Library in particular, the leather bindings shed, staining one's shirts and sweaters. Notes in each of these places had to be taken by hand, usu-ally in pencil. Xeroxing was at least a half-decade away, but, if one could afford them, one could order photocopies or microfilm. The process was lengthy and required special permissions. The one advantage of these research sites was their variety, that and the rare coffee or tea shop en route. Only the British Museum's newspaper collection at Colindale, north of London, lay outside this inner circle, reachable only by a long train ride.

Today, almost all of the original sources I spent hours and hours searching through are available on the Internet in searchable form. I daresay I would have been able to complete my research from Canada in eighteen months without ever going to London had the Internet existed sixty years ago, but it would not have been such fun and such a great adventure. There is something about being the first researcher to sort through documents on the site where most of them were created or received. Moreover, the Internet cannot provide the physical context in which the creators of the documents lived and worked. Given the choice between speedy convenience and historical atmosphere, I choose the latter. But today the choice is not so clear, because documents have been rehoused, relocated, and removed from their physical context. I feel I was lucky to do research when and where I did.

When I first arrived in London in 1954, the city was still suffering from the aftermath of war. The last of the rationings, sugar, ended in February 1954. Everywhere were bombed sites, houses and office buildings shored up with cables and wooden buttresses, or vacant lots where a historic church, or another fine edifice, once stood. Londoners went to bed early. Apart from the theatres in the West End around Covent Garden, Soho, and Shepherd's Market, there was very little light, or life, after dark. The famous Lyon's teahouses were mere shadows of their pre-war selves, serving poor-quality food and syrupy tea on well-stained trays and tables. There were pubs, of course, but there were no coffee shops, small cafés, or restaurants in which to spend an evening. Smoking was allowed everywhere. Things began to change with the introduction of cappuccino in the late 1950s and the Italian cafés that dispensed it, but it would be some years before London nightlife showed signs of a full revival. Like me, most Londoners had little ready cash. Their workdays were long and evenings were for family and the "telly," if they could afford one. The radio was an essential medium and it provided lots of comedy shows to cheer people up. This was the time of the *Goon Show* featuring Peter Sellers, Spike Milligan, and Harry Secombe, as popular then as *Monty Python* remains today and with a similar approach and content. In addition, comedians Tony Hancock, Jimmy Edwards, Kenneth Horne, and many, many others provided escape into a world of ridiculous situations and fantasy. On stage there was the birth of the angry young man made famous by playwright Harold Pinter, and plays mirroring working life, while on film the Carry On Gang were soon to keep movie audiences in stitches. The days of the Beatles, Mary Quant, and Carnaby Street, and the good economic times of Prime Minister Harold "you never had it so good" Macmillan were still to come.

THE FIRST TIME I SAW PARIS…

With Margo's return to London in the spring of 1958, our financial fortunes improved. She found a job with a travel agency located near Hyde Park Corner, which provided us with rent money and a little more to spare. Meanwhile, I looked at the help wanted ads. One day in early spring, in answer to an ad for a mimeograph operator, I presented myself at an office on the third floor of an old building at 15 Victoria Street, not far from Westminster Cathedral and Parliament Square. A pretty, dark-haired girl with blue eyes and a tailored suit to match invited me in and asked me what I wanted. I listed my qualifications. She told me to come back the next day: I was to start at five pounds a week. Later, I learned the young lady had been hired only the day before and in hiring me she had greatly exceeded her authority. A senior member of the organization had planned to give the job to a relative, but the offer to me was honoured. I was to be in charge of a room with four electrically operated mimeograph machines.

The organization, of which I was now a member, was completely unknown to me. The NATO Parliamentarians' Conference (NPC) was in its infancy.[1] It was not an "official" NATO organ, but an outgrowth of the Charter that contained a section, said to have been inspired by Lester B. Pearson, which encouraged contacts among parliamentarians from NATO's member countries. Elected representatives from national assemblies on both sides of the Atlantic saw this as an opportunity to influence NATO policy. The first conference of two hundred parliamentarians from fourteen NATO countries was held in Paris in July 1955, chaired by Senator Wishart Robertson, Speaker of the Senate of Canada; it resolved to hold similar meetings in the future. The formation of the NPC was spearheaded by a handful of representatives from the United States Congress, the Canadian Parliament, and the British Houses of Lords and Commons. A small secretariat was set up in London. The second meeting was held in Paris in November 1956 under Representative Wayne L. Hays of the United States. The organization was funded by grants from the fifteen member countries according to NATO's funding formula. The United States contributed about a quarter, the United Kingdom about a fifth, with France and Germany each contributing just a little less. Canada provided nearly 6 per cent of the funding. Many countries fell behind in their funding, so the key to financing annual meetings was a vote from the United States government. Hays was largely responsible for garnering a vote in favour of supporting the Secretariat and the annual meeting. He was a most unpleasant person, but he exercised great power through his influence on the budget. His womanizing was obvious, particularly to the secretaries in the NPC office. Affairs with secretaries were to lead to the end of his Washington career some years later.

A standing committee composed of one representative from each NATO country met regularly between conferences and guided the work of the organization. The president was selected each year by the Standing Committee. NPC members were organized into five committees: Political, Economic, Cultural, Military, and Scientific & Technical. The committees were co-ordinated and supported by the Secretariat. The Secretariat under an executive secretary was small, but in the run-up to the annual conferences extra temporary office staff was added, such as typists, translators, and a mimeograph operator: me. Most important of all, however, was Mrs. Dingley, the tea lady.

Each year the executive secretary, along with the committee chairmen, solicited discussion papers from parliamentarians and academics. The papers were translated into French, or English, and distributed to committee members prior to the annual assembly meeting in November, timed to coincide with a pause in the American legislative schedule. I was hired to speed the preparations for the fourth annual meeting to be held in Paris. The system was pretty simple and straightforward, the problem was the personalities involved. Many of the papers had to be reprinted and reprinted because of poor phrasing; faulty translation; people constantly changing their minds about what they had written; as well as further arguments and consultations.

Leading up to the meeting, I went through a great deal of paper and began to work long hours just to keep up. Most of the papers were lengthy and had to be printed on both sides of the sheets. The system for collating papers at that time was crude, but of the standard for the day. Piles of separate pages were spread in numerical order on the tops of tables. Then I, and anyone else (Mrs. Dingley was tireless) who wanted some exercise, walked around with rubber-tipped fingers, putting the pages into a complete document that we then stapled. Once a final revised version was deemed acceptable, it was mailed to the committee members. At the annual meeting, the committee members discussed the papers, along with any last-minute entries, and came up with a brief report and recommendations. These recommendations went to a plenary session of the elected representatives for adoption and forwarding to the Secretary-General of NATO. If possible, the assembly agreed on a general communiqué that would be released, along with the final resolutions, to the press.

The executive secretary, Douglas Robinson, who was in his mid-thirties at the time, was a person with minimal formal education, but with an engaging personality and great energy. He came to the Secretariat from the *Scotsman* newspaper, whose owner-publisher, Roy Thomson, a Canadian, and the future Lord Thomson of Fleet, was his mentor. Robinson had been active in the promotion of the Declaration of Atlantic Unity, signed by prominent people in the United States, Britain, Canada, France, Belgium, Norway, Denmark, and Netherlands urging NATO to extend itself beyond a military organization. The NPC was a result. The position of executive secretary gave Robinson a good salary, living allowances, and travel costs, plus an expense account. It also gave him an impressive identity card that was useful when stopped by the police from time to time when driving home at night in haste. Because he no longer held a valid driver's licence, he fumbled in his pockets, at last revealing his NATO security pass. That, plus an explanation about leaving his licence in his other suit, regularly saved him from a summons or reprimand. His job took him back and forth to the United States, a country with which he had completely fallen in love. As a child he knew the austerity of wartime, but once in the States he was like a kid in a candy store. He tended to live well beyond his means, using his expense account to dine in the most exclusive places. He acquired an expensive house near Hyde Park Corner, where he and his wife and young children lived, but he was often away. He had no skills in French, or any other foreign language, but he, for a number of years at least, knew how to handle members of the standing committee, particularly Mr. Hays, which was the most essential factor in maintaining his position. I liked Robinson very much and we got on well, although at heart I thought him a bit of a rogue. But he was very sympathetic to me and provided me with the ladder for what would become a Gilbert-and-Sullivan-style "rise to power," from lowly mimeograph operator to Documents Officer with major responsibilities for the annual conference.

Robinson was travelling when I was hired and I did not meet him until I had been working for a few weeks. Five days a week I produced documents, collecting my five-pounds-plus-overtime pay, twice a month, while getting to know a beautiful part of London during my lunch hours. The entire Secretariat was amused to find that they had a PhD student in Chinese history running the mimeograph machines. In a short time, I became an essential part of the operation. I was told in September that I had to go to Paris, where I would have the position of Documents Officer with a staff of secretaries, translators, and mimeograph operators under me to prepare for the November 17–21, 1958, conference. I would be paid ten pounds a week, plus travel expenses and a three-pound-a-day living allowance in keeping with the British Foreign Office's idea that Paris was a hardship post.

The flight to Paris Orly airport took all of twenty-five minutes and I was in Paris before I knew it. It was my first time in Paris and on the continent. The city lived up to its depiction in films; the air was filled with the scents of perfumes, Gauloises cigarettes, *steck frites*, and wine. Leaves were still changing, giving parts of the city a golden fringe or halo. Apart from a whirlwind walking tour on my first evening of the Île de la Cité and the Left Bank to see the lights and thriving restaurants, I saw little beyond the conference location. I counted on Margo joining me at the end of the conference for a week of combined holiday and research. The conference was held in temporary buildings overlooking the Seine, in the front gardens of the Palais de Chaillot, originally constructed to accommodate an early session of the United Nations. The buildings were drab, detracting from the beauty of the Palais, and infested with rats, but not the talented ones from the film *Ratatouille*. I was assigned a large room filled with mimeograph machines, paper, ink, and lots of tables for collating documents. My staff was a collection of typists recruited from Fleet Secretaries, a office temp agency run by Mrs. Fay Pannell, an energetic and very "with it" business woman. She supplied staff to the NPC in London and had supplemented those with others, all under her supervision, to form a pool for the conference. The translators and editors were recruited from a circle of young intellectuals acquainted with Miss Patricia Wood, the special assistant to the executive secretary. Some of them could be temperamental. One, a pale, wispy poet named Bill Anderson, refused to assist with unpacking a crate full of documents because he said handling a hammer would ruin his delicate hands.

In order to save as much as I could from the money I was being given for living allowances, I shared a room in a modest hotel across the river and near the Eiffel Tower with one of the translators, a veteran of trips to Paris and a little older than I whose name has left me. Next to the hotel called the Eiffel, which shook each time a train went by on the elevated Métro line, was a small neighbourhood restaurant where I was introduced to two standards of Parisian restaurant life: peas hard as bullets, and the habit of every newcomer shaking hands with those already there. Luckily, the hotel was handy to the conference site, only two stops on the Métro. For a fledgling organization, the conference went quite well, with no major disasters evident to the outside world.

Once Margo joined me in Paris immediately after the conference, it was time to enjoy the thrill of being in the city. Paris, the City of Light, was dimmer in those days, as well as much more French and less international, apart from a thin patina of American culture evident in places like the brilliantly lit Le Drugstore at the top of the Champs-Élysées near the Place de l'Étoile. Here one could get American-style sandwiches, salads, and desserts served with flair and style. The cityscape was not yet marred by golden arches, white-haired colonels, and red Coca-Cola billboards.

Paris had escaped the destruction of war, although one saw the placards marking where a brave soldier died when fighting for the liberation of the city. Usually the wall on which the placard was affixed had the pock marks left by bullets. But the beauty of the grand boulevards and the formal parks was undiminished. Even though slightly subdued, there was plenty of glitz and glamour. With a limited budget, Margo and I could not participate even a little bit in the glamour, but the glitz was free for the viewing in the beautifully dressed windows of the Rue du Faubourg Saint-Honoré and other homes of the fashion industry. Tourists were relatively few. Travel among European countries had yet to be fully revived and expanded. The boom in trans-Atlantic tourism awaited the appearance of long-haul jets. Few Britons strayed onto the continent. The average worker did not have the money for travel of this kind, or else the currency restrictions and the thought of a rough Channel crossing dissuaded them. The travel agency in London where Margo worked specialized in select and seasonal tours. It was a time when the famous headline in a London paper, "Fog in the Channel, Continent isolated," did not seem that strange or funny to British readers. Popular images of France were shaped by Brigitte Bardot in *And God Created Woman* and the good-humoured bumbling of Jacques Tati in *Monsieur Hulot's Holiday*. Considering ourselves fortunate to be in Paris, Margo and I walked to the Louvre, Notre Dame, Saint Chapelle, the Opera and the Grands Magasins, Place des Vosges, Bastille, and the Jardin des Plantes, and strolled through the outdoor food and flower markets. Like all visitors, we fell in love with the Luxembourg Gardens. Although Parisian streets are hard, the city is compact, making it a delight for walkers. We ate in inexpensive cafeterias and each evening tried a sidewalk café for coffee and hot chocolate.

I took the week to begin research work in French government records at the Quai d'Orsay. It confirmed what I had been told about French archives. There was no point asking for advice, one had to know in advance what one wanted. Of course, if you knew in advance, why were you there asking advice? The trick was to find a reference in an already published work to a series of documents that appeared to relate to what you were interested in. You then asked for one of that series. This convinced the keeper on duty that you knew what you wanted. If you struck a dry well, then after a few days you might enquire if there was a related series of documents of interest. Only then might one get some expert advice. Clearly, the French did not want anyone wandering in off the street seeking warmth and a place to while away the hours. Naturally, the number of volumes allowed at any one time, and on any one day, was strictly limited so as not to tax the keeper or to encourage the researcher to try to stay later than the proscribed hours. After ten days of this routine, I was ready to return to London, carrying with me the knowledge of what I was going to ask for next time.

Going back to London, we took the train to Calais to catch the ferry to Dover and from there the boat train to Victoria. On the train from Paris we were quizzed by a French Customs Officer as to what we were taking out of the country. With my French teacher beside me, I indicated that we had purchased a beautiful tray decorated with jolly French flowers. "*Un plafond*," I said, pointing above my head to the luggage rack. He looked at me hard. "*Un plafond?*" (A ceiling?) "*Oui.*" At this point Margo intervened: "*Un plateau*," (A tray,) she said. "*Ah, un plateau.*" And he departed smiling.

After a rough Channel crossing and a crowded train from Dover, we boarded the No. 134 bus at Victoria Station in the early dark of a December night. There was only room under the stairs leading to the upper deck for my battered Gladstone bag, a relic from my days at Hussey's furniture store. We carried Margo's to the front of the bus and sat dozing until the flashing orange Belisha Beacons that marked the pedestrian crossing from the end of Onslow Gardens to the entrance to Highgate Wood came into view. It was time to ring the bell to get off, the long day's journey over. I reached under the stairs for my bag, but it was not there. I called the conductor. "Someone must 'a nicked it mate," he said and signalled the driver to be on his way. I was stunned. First, I should have known better because the sign said: Keep an eye on your luggage. But my eyes were tired and the only seats available to us when we left Victoria were at the very front of the bus. My bag contained my clothes, the wedge fur hat, and loud shirts and ties that proclaimed I was from North America, my shaving gear, and—oh gawd—*my notes*. Not just the notes I had taken in Paris, but all of my thesis notes. With the usual graduate student's paranoia, I took all my notes with me for fear of what might happen to them if I left them behind. A year's work had vanished. The next morning I reported my loss to the police, who, while being sympathetic, gave me little hope. They did not spend time lecturing me on my stupidity. Instead, they assured me that what had happened to me was a common occurrence. A thief would board the bus at the station, or at the next stop, and when the conductor went upstairs to sell tickets, he would grab a bag and get off when the bus stopped at traffic lights. It happened all the time, they said. My chances of recovering anything were very close to nil.

Oddly enough, after my shock had passed, the theft gave me a sudden rush of freedom, a sense of intellectual weightlessness. I was free to choose another topic, another career, or to find a full-time job that paid a decent salary. The news spread like wildfire among my fellow SOAS students. Some were shocked as deeply as if it had happened to them. Others congratulated me and said they wished they could be that lucky. My euphoria lasted for about ten days, until one evening, a policeman came to call. He was holding a piece of paper and asked, "Are you Brian L. Evans?"

"Yes."

"A student at the Senate House of the University of London?"

"In a sense."

"Does this belong to you?" He handed me a call slip for a book from the Senate House Library.

"Yes."

"Yes."

"At last," he said with a relieved sigh. "Do you know that there are six Brian L. Evans registered at the University of London? We tried the other five first!"

My bag, he explained, was thrown over a wall of a garden at the Elephant and Castle on the south bank of the Thames. It was empty except for some notes. Suddenly, the world closed in on me. The next morning I made my way to the Elephant and Castle police station to claim my bag. My notes were intact. "He can't have been an intellectual," observed one officer about the thief. "Or else he has gas heating in his digs," said another. Years later, the police in that area raided a house. Inside they found rooms full of suitcases and stolen merchandise. I never enquired as to whether they found a fur hat or my shirt with bull fighters on it, the latter of which I wore to a tea party offered by Professor Cyril Philips, director of SOAS, shortly after I arrived. Although the purpose of the event was to greet new students, Professor Philips, when he saw me, said: "Ah, Mr. Evans, you will be leaving us soon, I understand." Maybe it had been the shirt, or perhaps his Welsh clairvoyance. If it was the latter, he was wrong: I remained at SOAS for seven years.[2] The real change brought by the theft was evident in my appearance. I began to look like all young male Londoners in their twenties who got their clothes at Marks and Spencer's. There would be no more chants of "The Ballad of Davy Crockett" when I passed children in the street.

The return of my notes was but a prelude to more good fortune in the New Year. In Paris, the NPC resolved to celebrate NATO's first decade and to discuss its future with a special meeting in London, June 5–10, 1959. Called the Atlantic Congress, it was a proto-parliament for the whole of NATO. The Queen, along with Prime Minister Harold Macmillan, agreed to open the congress at Church House, a large auditorium close to Westminster Abbey, and Sir Isaac Walton wrote a special fanfare for the Queen's arrival. The meetings would end with a final plenary session and a midnight gala performance of *My Fair Lady*, at Drury Lane. After Paris, some changes were made to the NPC Secretariat. A number of countries were unhappy that the Secretariat was exclusively British. As a result, a new assistant executive secretary was brought on, Otto Van H. Labberton, I believe the *H.* stood for Hinloopen. He was a retired military officer from the Netherlands, tall, slim, moustached, every inch the gentleman, but taut like a coiled spring. Douglas Robinson chose to ignore him and Labberton appeared to be content to fill his days with long lunches, gin, and watching belly dancing (London clubs provided all sorts of entertainments). He was harmless enough, so it seemed. Meanwhile, in December 1958, the Secretariat moved to 37 Great Peter Street, even closer to Westminster Abbey than before.

Between the Paris meeting and the Atlantic Congress, the NPC paid me a monthly retainer to ensure that I was available when needed. I was embarrassed because I saw it as a thinly disguised means of helping me through the lean months of winter, but I was assured that it was common practice and no Englishman would ever question it. I thought I should at least do some work for it, but no, I was told it was not necessary. Early in the New Year, I received additional good fortune in the form of an invitation to teach a course for the University of Maryland Overseas. There were two American doctoral students at SOAS. Jack Gerson, a Quaker, had served in China with a stretcher corps in 1948–1949 at the close of the Civil War. His face bore the marks of a rough, delinquent youth in New Jersey, but he was, nonetheless, a pacifist and married to an Englishwoman who was also a pacifist. His thesis was on a topic in nineteenth-century Chinese history so he and I took special courses in classical Chinese together from the famous Tang poetry specialist A.C. Graham. Graham was very shy and would not look at us, but sat at right angles looking at the classroom door while he puffed up a dense cloud of blue smoke from his pipe. Gerson smoked as well, but only cigarettes. At least I think he smoked. He always had a fag dangling from the corner of his lips. He "sipped" at it just often enough to keep it going, it was more like an incense stick than a cigarette.

Nearly a decade older than I, Jack saw all sides to a situation and was a stickler for detail and nuance. He was a deconstructionist before the term was invented: he split hairs already split. His wife Elisabeth had the same tendencies. A meal or evening with them was spent in defining the terms of an argument, without getting to the argument. A couple of years later, Jack accepted a position at Memorial University in Newfoundland, and later became a professor at the University of Toronto, where he mentored a number of brilliant students, while driving many of his colleagues wild.[3]

The other American, John McMaster, came from a protected environment in upstate New York. He was a very quiet man. He was estranged from his father, but he doted on his mother who paid him annual visits in Europe. His service with the US Army in Japan sparked an interest in Japanese history, so he became a student of Professor Beasley.[4] It was John who recommended me to the director of the University of Maryland Overseas Program. With so many troops stationed overseas, the American Military gave the University of Maryland a contract to provide university courses for credit, to be offered in the evenings on the various military bases. I was to teach a course called Far Eastern History.

I was sent to the West Drayton army base on the western outskirts of London. One spring evening in 1959, I appeared before a class of about thirty eager young men, anxious to learn about the Far East. The textbook was by Paul Hibbert Clyde, and my only advantage over the students was that I was a few pages ahead of them. Not until nearly the end of the course did I feel comfortable teaching. I agreed with an older student, who each evening before class checked for bugging devices in the room, who said at the final class: "I am sure that one day this will be a good course." Apart from the valuable experience, for me the importance of the course was that it paid US$350 a month. The American dollar was slightly below the Canadian at the time, but it converted into nearly a hundred pounds, i.e., over thirty weeks' rent money for every four weeks worked. It eased our financial situation considerably. The final two weeks of the course at West Drayton coincided with the run-up to the Atlantic Congress, so I had to suspend my research.

The congress was patterned on the NPC and the various committees and sub-committees were to meet in some of the most expensive hotels and restaurants in London's West End, while the plenary sessions were to be held in Church House. Nonetheless, in preparing for the assembly, extra space was rented, particularly to accommodate my side of the operation. New staff, some of it for me, was found, with the upper levels being recruited from the old boy network and the lower from student ranks. Medical students from St. Bartholomew's hired to distribute and collect documents, prepare meeting rooms, and run errands were a particularly lively find, but some of the old boys were duds. I liked the British way of letting the unsatisfactory old boys go. We were attending a splendid lunch in the United Services Club on Pall Mall, when the person, who had been brought in to be my assistant, was told he was no longer needed. He was a former military man, who had served in the army with our host who had recommended him for the job. Perhaps because they knew each other so well, the firing was done with finesse, no hard feelings, and with great appreciation for such a good lunch. I quite liked the man who was leaving, but his main contribution to the operation had been to demonstrate how best to keep one's suede shoes from losing their shape, accomplished by having them resoled before you wore them, thus retaining the original sole and the shape of the original shoe.

The weeks leading up to the assembly were extremely busy and as the opening day approached, I worked all night, heading home at around three or four in the morning. Night buses were infrequent, and it was much more refreshing to walk part of the way, particularly via the flower and fruit market of Covent Garden, which was just beginning its day. One morning, to make Margo appreciate how important it was that I stay out all night, I took her a water-bucketful of carnations in assorted colours. Although I was working hard, getting exercise, and burning nervous energy, I was no longer the slim fellow who arrived in London five and a half years earlier. I learned that I was now known as "Cuddles" to the female members of the staff.

Money flowed during the run-up to the Atlantic Congress. Hired cars, taxis, expensive lunches, overtime pay, all of it contributed to budget overruns that came to light in the weeks after the meeting. Mrs. Pannell was contributing staff and her boyfriend at the time, Eric Pink, was hired to run important documents between the hotels and the Secretariat. He rented a Rolls Royce from a dealership on Regent's Street as a delivery vehicle. Then he went missing—he took a run down to Brighton for the day. If anything, the congress was over-organized. On paper, it was a planner's dream, but making it work took a lot of crisis management. The major committees' sub-committees all had reporters, drawn where possible from the academic community. Among them were Max Beloff, Gladstone Professor of Government and Public Administration at Oxford, Dr. Henry Kissinger, then on the brink of receiving tenure as a professor of history at Harvard, and Maurice Faure, a former French Cabinet minister, out of office between governments.

Eventually, the committee meetings and preliminary plenary sessions were over and it was time for the release of the final communiqué, and for the midnight gala on June 9. I had an invitation to the gala, but I was unable to attend because I and a skeleton staff were standing by for the final communiqué. Some time after the gala began, we learned that the communiqué was at the gala in the pocket of Jean de Lafforest, the head of translation, an expat Frenchman who had set up a translation service in London. He was a man of great talent but erratic to the point of being certifiable. He told his staff of a dozen or so to "stand by" for the important task of translating the final words from the assembly. I waited with them at their address on Villiers Street. Like so many international meetings, the final communiqué was bland, harmless, and reasonably unexciting. It was also short. Sometime after 2 a.m., de Lafforest returned. He was in tie and tails, a thin wiry man of medium height in his early fifties. After climbing atop a table in the middle of the room, and doing a little tap dance, he announced he was going to dictate the final communiqué to his staff in English, and each of them was to translate it into French. He would grade their efforts to see who came closest to the perfect rendition. None of them met with his approval, and he repeated the process. Growing weary of this farce, I demanded he give me a final version. He prepared it himself and half an hour later, around 3:30 in the morning, my weary colleagues were able to reproduce it for distribution. At additional expense to the congress, they went home by taxi because the hour was so late (early.) I walked home, wondering whether this was typical of international meetings and diplomacy. Fortunately, as I was to discover fourteen years later in Beijing, it was not.

My research took another beating five months later in November 1959 when I was invited to the NPC meeting in Washington, DC, to mark the organization's fifth anniversary. I spent almost three weeks in the United States, leaving Margo hard at work in London. Although born and raised only fifty miles away from the American border, I had never visited the USA. We flew by KLM chartered super Constellation to Washington, and arrived on November 5, ten days before the conference. The charter was filled with members of Parliament who were taking advantage of the early flight to carry on business. After a stop for fuel at Shannon in Ireland, we settled in for the long flight.[5] The meal served by KLM that day remains the most sumptuous and lengthy I have ever had in the air. Course after course was trundled down the aisle, accompanied by expensive wines. Each course was served on fine China and the separate wines in beautiful glasses, although I did not drink in those days. I would like to have that meal over again, a hopeless dream given the steady downward spiral of today's in-flight meals and services.

We arrived at Washington National Airport very late at night to be met by Representative Wayne Hays, who waived off the customs officers, both as a welcome to us and a demonstration of his power. I was to stay in an apartment hotel on the Hill, within a stone's throw of the Old House Office Building where the conference met. Once again I was Documents Officer. This time, the NPC contracted with a bilingual group from the Library of the House of Commons in Ottawa. We worked in the rooms of major congressional committees, and I had a direct line to the White House from my office. The last year of the Eisenhower administration was approaching and security was extremely lax. I had unrestricted access to the entire building, made famous by the Army-McCarthy Hearings in 1954. I was challenged only once, by a cleaner, at two in the morning on my return from a late dinner with Douglas Robinson and other members of the Secretariat. The guards in charge of the building were university students from various parts of the US. The rotunda of the building held a circle of marble busts of former speakers of the House, set on plinths. In the evenings, the security guards put their caps on one or two of the speakers and sighted their handguns at them. There was nothing else to do of an evening.

The reason I had such easy access was because I was recognized as "Wayne Hays-approved," and Hays controlled the appointments of all those who served the building as guards, elevator operators, etc. He was chairman of the House Administration Committee. [6] It was said the no one dared cross him for fear that their air conditioning would be shut off. The day after my arrival in Washington, I was taken to meet another of Hays's boys, a self-styled dirty-neck printer from Ohio, who was in charge of the government printing operations and secretary to the Committee of the Library of Congress. When he learned that I was a student, he gave me a letter of introduction to the librarian of the Library of Congress, urging him to give me anything I wanted to assist with my research. His office was under the Capitol Dome and it was approached by a curved hall. He had a lookout window in his office through which he could see the parking spot reserved for Wayne Hays. He said to me, "When I see his car, then I make myself scarce." He had not had a face-to-face meeting with Hays for months. Our meeting over, I asked him why there were so many documents piled in the hallway, nearly blocking access to his office. "Look at the title page," he said, "and you will understand." The documents in the piles bore the title: Report of the Committee for the Elimination of Waste in Government Printing.

Within my first thirty-six hours in Washington, I learned that there were two ways of getting things done. One was by going through all the bureaucratic channels, filling out dozens of forms in multiple copies. The other was to invoke the name of Wayne Hays. I saw little of Washington, apart from Capitol Hill and some of the major monuments on the Mall. Otherwise, it was like Paris—all work and no play, but unlike Paris, I could not look forward to a post-conference break with Margo, except there was the prospect of a couple of days in New York before leaving the US. Each day of the conference was like the other, although I remember, curtly, telling George Brown, the ebullient British Labour MP, to call his own cab after he had issued me an order to do so, but generally I kept to my job. The 1959 Washington conference offered some impressive speeches, but its work was overshadowed by a major international conference on the Antarctic held in Washington at the same time.

The conference over, a car full of us headed for New York to catch an El Al charter to London. The night before, I saw the movie *Porgy and Bess*, which had just opened in Washington. I was shocked that the audience was segregated into white and black sections in the theatre. From my limited observations of Washington, I concluded that it was a very black city, and I expected better of the capital of the world's greatest democracy. My experience at the movie house revived my nascent anti-Americanism, which had mellowed during my time in England. My fellow British students were anti-American, but to me, they were anti-American for the wrong reasons. I began to re-examine my own views, which I realized were just as parochial as those of my British friends. But the movie house gave me some concrete evidence for my earlier feelings. The longer I worked with the NPC, the more Americans I met. I developed a tremendous admiration for many of them who attended the annual meetings and had been present at the Atlantic Congress, like Senators Jacob Javits, and William Fulbright, but others provided an unfortunate counter-balance. The car trip to New York was memorable for its speed. The Englishman driving thought 120 mph was about right. Back in London at Heathrow, there was no Wayne Hays to waive customs, and even the most important of British MPs looked nervous at the approach of the inspectors.

Fortune continued to smile on me. On my return from Washington, I was asked to teach a second session for the University of Maryland. It was the same course, this time on the base at Brize Norton, outside Oxford. Once a week in the late afternoon, I took a train to Oxford where I had supper in the Randolph hotel before being picked up by a military car. A professor of language and speech from Norman, Oklahoma, was involved in the same routine, so we began travelling up to Oxford together. He was very pleasant and we talked of many things, which kept my nerves calm for the evening lecture. Then, one or two weeks before the end of my course, on the train to Oxford, I raised the question of the treatment of blacks in America. Suddenly, he changed into a virulent white supremacist, a transformation that I found breathtaking.

I suppose I should have been prepared for this, because his views were coming to the surface in what was widely regarded as tolerant, fair play Britain Beginning in the late 1940s, Britain became host to a growing number of immigrants from the Caribbean, particularly Jamaica. Londoners who were used to receiving white refugees from Europe were now faced with black immigrants from the Empire and Commonwealth coming home to "mother." The new arrivals were educated in English to English standards, and they began to take jobs British workers were reluctant to do. One morning in late February 1957, after a light dusting of snow, which never fails to snarl London traffic, I took the No. 134 bus down to the British Museum. It was a normal trip, punctuated as always each morning by the Druid, swathed in white, who got on at Kentish Town about halfway along my journey. At Camden Town a black man got on. The bus was crowded and under union rules only five people were allowed to stand in the aisle, in order to give the conductor room to sell tickets. The black man was one of those standing. The driver, in order to avoid a collision as he approached Euston Road, touched his brakes suddenly, enough to bring the standing passengers into collision with each other. The black man lost his balance and as he straightened up, he smiled and said, "Driver, you better sharpen your brakes." His humour was lost on the passengers around him who snarled back variations on, "Go home to Jamaica, you're not wanted here." I was amazed that such a good-humoured, innocent remark could provoke such a reaction. I was upset enough to write a letter to the *Times*, but it was returned to me as irrelevant. Yet what I witnessed was among the beginnings of racial tension that would grow into riots at Notting Hill at the end of August 1958 and elsewhere in the late 1970s and 80s. It was an object lesson to me, because I had begun to accept the mantra of "tolerant, fair play" Britain.

In August 1959, between the Atlantic Congress and the Washington meeting, I began to write my thesis, carefully feeding a sandwich of six thin sheets of paper, interleaved with carbons, into my portable Remington. I was under pressure from Jack Gray, my immediate supervisor, to produce a chapter. I did, and then he misplaced it for several months. Meanwhile, I had not yet finished my research in Paris, so Margo, having taken leave plus holidays owed from work, and I set out the next March for six weeks in the City of Light. I had received a research grant from the University of London: nine pounds fifty shillings for travel, and twenty-five pounds for living expenses. At SOAS I consulted an Australian student, Les Marchant, who had spent some time in Paris living on a shoestring. He gave me a short list of places to stay and the names of some inexpensive restaurants.

Once in Paris, we checked into the absolute cheapest of the hotels. All I can say is that it was fortunate that Margo was a good sport and that she had spent part of her teaching career living in primitive circumstances in small rural towns. The Hotel Senlis was cold and austere, but the lady concierge was very pleasant. And the price was right: ten francs, roughly C$1.50, for the two of us each night, with breakfast. Moreover, the location was ideal, halfway between the Pantheon and the Jardin de Luxembourg. From the Senlis, I could walk to the Quai d'Orsay and the Foreign Ministry's archives. Professor Patrick Honey, the Vietnam historian at SOAS, had given me a letter of introduction to Professor Georges Taboulet who had recently published an extensive collection of documents from the French archives relating in great part to my thesis topic. Then recently retired, Professor Taboulet invited Margo and me to his apartment to discuss my research. He had spent years in Vietnam as a French civil servant and he was clearly unhappy that the French were no longer a major factor in that country's future. He was happy to discuss with me the days of France's former glory in the nineteenth century. After an afternoon of stimulating discussion and tea, we left him in his book-lined study where his wife had made runners to cover the tops of his uniformly leather-bound books to keep them free of dust.

During the day, I went to the archives, while Margo had Paris to herself, exploring galleries, museums, bookstores, libraries, and the side streets of the Left Bank. Paris was beginning to feel the impact of the New Wave film directors like Jean-Luc Goddard and François Truffaut, as Jean Moreau replaced Bardot on cinema placards. We found the best place to eat, a cafeteria-style restaurant on the second floor of a building opposite the entrance to the Luxemburg Gardens. The food was fresh and excellent, particularly the pastries, and modestly priced. Because the weather was cold, in the late weekday evenings and on weekend afternoons we would stop in a café for a coffee and hot chocolate, as we had done on our earlier trip. We did not seek out the restaurant near the University of Paris School of Medicine recommended by Marchant, where he said, "You can get a good sheep's head and chips for under a dollar." It was not just my allergy to mutton and lamb that kept us from that experience.

On our return from Paris, I learned of a bloodletting at the NPC Secretariat. Douglas Robinson, whose free-spending ways had brought him into conflict with Wayne Hays and others, was forced out and Otto Van Labberton emerged as the new executive secretary. He had been working behind the scenes, lobbying for a further internationalization of the Secretariat. Indeed, one of his first moves was to give the position of his assistant to a chic, highly competent, and beautiful French woman, his mistress. The Secretariat was to be moved from London to Paris, to be near the splendid new A-shaped building at Porte Dauphine on the edge of Bois de Boulogne that was to be NATO's headquarters. I did not know Labberton well, but in July he asked me and Mike Jenkinson to assist in the move and with setting up the new office in a building on the rue La Perouse, just off the Arc de Triomphe. Mike, an actor and artist, was also an accountant and was employed from time to time to do the NPC books. We were flown to Paris aboard an Olympic Airways Comet in July 1960, the first passenger jet in service. Our time in Paris was short, just over a week, and our working hours coincided with the hours that the archives were open, so I could not do any research. I gave in to fate and enjoyed the long lunch hours and Paris summer evenings. I was paid generously, twenty pounds for a week's work plus a daily living allowance of five pounds, eight shillings, and six pence per day. Foreign exchange restrictions were still in place in Britain and I was allowed to take out of the country thirty-eight pounds for my trip expenses.

Before the NPC moved to Paris, Mike and I were contacted by Douglas Robinson, now secretary to the Liberal Party of Britain, to work in his office. His departure from the NPC had been made with fine words. His role in the establishment of the NPC could "not be overestimated." In the beginning his "youthful imagination, initiative and drive...were far more important than the political and administrative experience and the languages which he lacked." But in the end it was decided that the NPC "needed as Executive Secretary someone with experience of working on an international staff and with a good knowledge of European languages." Douglas had taken his removal hard. In debt, he flew to the United States one last time, resolved to jump off the Golden Gate Bridge. Once in California, however, the weather was so nice he changed his mind, hired a car, and toured the wine country. Having financed all of this on his credit card, he returned to London, and his family, even further in debt. One of his friends from the NPC, Stanley Clement Davies, whose father had been leader of the Liberal Party when it was still of some importance, invited him to become the party's secretary. The party was a mere shadow of its past, and lacked resources. My work with them was very part-time and petered out quickly when they moved from central London to the City, into further reduced circumstances.

It seemed I was fated to remain with the NPC as Labberton invited both Margo and me to work at the 1960 meeting to be held in Paris at the new NATO headquarters in the Bois de Boulogne, on November 21–26. We crossed on the Channel ferry, arriving in Paris on November 15, where we were put in a good hotel and given living allowances on top of wages. I was Documents Officer and Margo helped with translating the reports. We remained for a few days after the meetings so that I could check some references in the archives before we took the train and ferry back to London. Well along in writing my thesis, I was anxious to finish in time for my defence, which was projected for late May. By Christmas 1960, I had been a student at SOAS for just over six years. I was unique in having to work my way through. Kathleen Wooding, the registrar, showed great sympathy for my circumstances and interpreted residence requirements and time limits generously in my case. (She was one of the first to congratulate me on completion of my PhD.) I fear that without the NATO parliamentarians and the University of Maryland I probably would have given up my studies to take a different path. Through the NPC, I made many good contacts, some of which made me interesting offers.

Even the NPC itself would have been happy to give me some permanent status. I had grown fond of the people who worked for the annual conferences, and although my links with the NPC were to be maintained until 1965, I was never seriously tempted. The NPC gave me a good view of another way of life, but it could not lure me away from China. In retrospect, it was probably because I did not think the NPC a substantial organization, or perhaps it was bedrock parochialism that made me fear major change, or perhaps, like Groucho Marx, I did not want to involve myself permanently with an organization that would have me as a member.

Nonetheless, I met many exciting and talented politicians. At the NPC meetings in Paris there was always a major reception at locations such as the Assemblée Nationale and Le Senat. At one of these events, I was invited to meet American Senator Estes Kefauver, who had a tremendous reputation as a fighter of corruption and who had run unsuccessfully as Adlai Stevenson's candidate for vice-president against Eisenhower and Nixon. A Democrat from Tennessee, he was liberal in his views, including those on race. On shaking my hand, he immediately offered me a job. It was an offer I felt I could refuse. Later, I learned that an offer was an automatic reflex among American Congressmen. I did not get as close to Lyndon Baines Johnson, but he attended meetings and it was fascinating to watch him in action. On one occasion at the Paris meetings he asked his staff to get the sheriff of Dorchester County on the telephone. The request was relayed to a conference worker and very soon Johnson was told his party was on the line. He stood up, and the American delegation drained out of the room, as though a plug had been pulled from a basin. They were back almost immediately when Johnson found himself speaking to the sheriff of Dorchester, England, not Texas. Congressman John Lindsay, later Mayor of New York, was also very impressive, and kind enough to grin from ear to ear when, not knowing who he was, I told him bluntly at a meeting in Paris that I was too busy and he should look for it himself, when he asked me for some information. I very much liked Peter Rodino from Rhode Island, who later became a type of folk hero during the Watergate hearings. But then I came across parliamentarians from Portugal and from Italy who wanted my opinion as to whether or not black people had white souls. And there was always Congressman Wayne Hays, who was nearly impossible to like.

I had the same negative reaction to many of the representatives from NATO countries, including Canada, whose behaviour left much to be desired. Every member country, with the exception of Canada it seemed, sent the leaders of their elected assemblies to the meetings, the choice being that of the various parliamentary speakers. For some reason, under Prime Ministers Diefenbaker and Pearson, the NPC meetings became junkets for backbench MPs. Perhaps it was looked upon (likely correctly) as a low-level international experience and a good training ground for the uninitiated. This practice backfired in November 1962, when the Canadian delegation to the annual NPC meeting in Paris was accused by Montreal's *La Presse* of spending more time in *Pigalle* than at the meetings and of behaving in a way that brought discredit to Canadians.[7] Their behaviour was highlighted in the *Globe and Mail* and in other dailies. The delegation, individually, denied the charges in interviews, but the damage was done. I was in no position to observe the behaviour of the delegation, but on the evening before the conference began, the delegation leader, William Skoreyko, who happened to be a backbencher from Edmonton, not knowing who I was, approached me with a question: "I am the leader of the Canadian delegation. Do you know what I should be doing?"

SPIES 'R' US

After the 1960 NPC meeting, my academic fortunes changed. In January 1961, with five months to go before I defended my thesis, I received a notice from the Canada Council that I had been awarded one thousand dollars to enable me to finish my studies. Every year for three years, I had applied for support and each year I had been refused. My first reaction now was to refuse the money—I had gone this far with no encouragement from them, so why not remain pure? My initial anger dissipated when I considered how much easier that money would make our lives in our last months in London. In retrospect, after serving on scholarship committees for the Canada Council and many other granting organizations, I realize that committee members do their best with the information and money they have. The last thing they are concerned about is the emotional state of the recipient. But I still find it ironic that a fellow student from the University of Alberta, studying at the University of London in another field, who received two or three years of full support from the Canada Council, never finished his PhD, while I did.

And January 1961 held other surprises. On January 7, a man by the name of Gordon Arnold Lonsdale was arrested outside Waterloo Station.[8] He was carrying a shopping bag containing microfilmed plans of the British nuclear submarine being developed at Portland Down. The bag was handed to him by a man named Houghton and a woman named Gee. In addition, a Mr. and Mrs. Kroeger were arrested in west London.

It was the Gordon Arnold Lonsdale I knew as a fellow language student six years earlier. I met him first in the SOAS student common room. He arrived the year after I did, and he was introduced as a fellow Canadian student studying Chinese. Even more interestingly, he was Ukrainian and formerly a used car salesman in Edmonton, the latter of which helped to explain why he looked older than the other students. He had weak eyes and frequently missed classes, but his spoken Chinese was good. After our first meeting, when we talked about Edmonton, he was rather cool and standoffish. I had no money to socialize and he appeared to bond closely with a young Canadian diplomat named Pope, who threw lavish parties fuelled by duty-free liquor. At one of these parties, Lonsdale was present along with Charles Elwell, who later became his MI5 tracker. Neither knew it at the time, but Lonsdale later incorrectly believed that MI5 had been on to him earlier than they were.[9] Lonsdale lived in an apartment in a building called the White House on the edge of Regent's Park, a very good address. It was rumoured to be full of deep-pile Chinese carpets, beautiful scrolls, and other bits of Chinoiserie.

Lonsdale operated a small business while at SOAS. He had a number of coin-operated jukeboxes, and candy, gum, and drink machines scattered around the London area, and a small van that he used to service them. One of his regular stops was the American Air Base at West Drayton where I taught my first course for the University of Maryland. (It turns out the older student who looked for electronic bugs each evening before my class was not far off the mark.) I remember Lonsdale had asked around SOAS to see if anyone wanted to go into business him, but the only known taker was a fellow from the Colonial Office. When MI5 raided Lonsdale's flat, they found Chinese scrolls with hollowed-out ends used to keep American dollars, microfilm, and micro-dots. A radio and more US dollars were found in a floor cavity. MI5 touted Lonsdale as the greatest Soviet spy yet caught in the Cold War. His trial, and that of his accomplices, was set for May.

A few days after his arrest, I called at SOAS to collect my mail. The students' common room was reasonably large with a huge round table in the centre, a tea wicket in one corner, and open pigeonholes for mail just inside the main door. The mail was sorted each day by the school porters and put in the pigeonholes. In the hole marked D-F, I found a letter, marked "Confidential," addressed to me. Inside the envelope was another one addressed to me and marked "Strictly Personal and Confidential." The letter inside was brief: "We have reason to believe that you may have information of interest to us. If you are willing to assist us, please phone..." And there followed a Whitehall number. I went out to a red call box on the corner of Russell Square, dialled the number, pressed Button A, and talked to a voice at MI5. I was invited down immediately for a chat.

The chat turned out to be an interrogation of sorts, with me sitting staring across a desk at a sunlit window, with my questioner pacing up and down behind the desk between me and the window. He quickly found that I knew very little. All I could contribute was that Lonsdale seemed to know very little about Edmonton. He was unable to remember the name of the used car dealership where he had worked and he did not know anything about a very colourful car salesman who regularly advertised on the radio in Edmonton. From my questioner, and later, I learned that Lonsdale, at a very young age, was sent from Russia to live with an aunt in California, but as a teenager he asked to go back to Russia where he went to university and learned Chinese. Later, probably around 1953, he entered Canada from a ship that docked in Vancouver. He applied for a passport in the name of a dead infant whose tombstone was in a rural cemetery in Ontario. Eventually, he sailed for England and SOAS. He had never been near Edmonton. The interview over, I was sent on my way with a promise that if I remembered or learned anything else, I would call again.

Lonsdale was tried, found guilty, and sentenced to twenty-five years in jail, the longest sentence in the Cold War up to then. His accomplices were sentenced to ten years. Just a few years later, Lonsdale was swapped in Berlin at the Brandenburg Gate for Greville Wynne, an "innocent English businessman" whom the Soviet authorities were holding on a charge of spying. Not long thereafter, in 1965, Lonsdale's memoirs were published in Britain. One of his anecdotes from his time at SOAS is worth repeating: "In our class, we had an American named Bredt [*sic*]....One day...he nudged me and whispered: 'Listen Gordon. Except for you and me, they are all spies here.' (Of course, he was wrong about one of us)."[10] Gordon's memoir is misleading and mischievous, designed to discredit MI5 and to undermine the reputation of Scotland Yard. He insists that his name was Lonsdale and that he was a Canadian businessman, but at the trial he was found to be Konon Molodi, a Russian. He died in October 1970 at the age of forty-eight, while picking mushrooms. Later reports said that his name was Lonov and that he had been born and raised in Moscow.

Much later, Lonsdale's son wrote that his father's activities were completely unknown to him and his mother, and that they believed he was doing business in the West.[11] His son also relates that although Lonsdale received a hero's welcome on his return to Moscow, the KGB did not trust him and treated him as a suspected turncoat. Lonsdale died frustrated and angry. The fact remains, however, that he had a Canadian passport in the name of Gordon Arnold Lonsdale and that he entered England in March 1955 on a ship from Canada. In his book, *Spycatcher*, Peter Wright, the man who brought him in, accuses his boss at MI5, Roger Hollis, of being a Soviet agent. It was Hollis who had interviewed me.

My PhD thesis defence, on the subject of French, Chinese, and British diplomacy regarding China's southern frontier in the last quarter of the nineteenth century, in late May 1961 took place at the same time Gordon Lonsdale was sentenced. My result was pleasanter, and as luck would have it, I too was being invited to spend some time in an institution. My initial term would be for three years, extendable to thirty-five for good behaviour.

FOUR ★ ★ ★ ★

The Far East in the Far West

By 1960, China studies in Canada were not very advanced. Efforts were made at McGill University and at the University of Toronto between the wars, but the Depression was not kind to them. McGill could not maintain its book collection of seventy-five thousand volumes; the Gest Collection was moved to Princeton in 1937.[1] The University of Toronto was the one place with the semblance of a program. Southern Ontario was the focus of Canadian intellectual interest in China. It was the home of many missionaries working in China, or returned from China, and of the University of Toronto Museum (since 1968, the Royal Ontario Museum), with its major collection of Chinese art and artifacts, some of them courtesy of Dr. William C. White, the Anglican Bishop of Henan, China.

With such a collection close at hand, and with prominent citizens with Chinese experience, the University of Toronto hired White in 1934 to head a school of Chinese Studies, which concentrated on classical China. Returned missionaries were important to the growth of Chinese studies internationally, but their interests were not in modern studies, they concentrated on Chinese classical texts as they sought to understand Confucian China. White retired in 1948 and in 1953, W.A.C.H. Dobson became chair of the department and served to 1964. By 1960, the University of Toronto had the only firmly established China Studies program in Canada. The University of British Columbia, a younger institution, was a late beginner. The first course in modern Chinese history was offered in 1948, with other courses in Asian Studies in other disciplines following. A fledgling language program was launched in 1957. UBC and Canada benefitted from McCarthyism in the United States when the Institute of Pacific Relations (IPR) in New York City was forced into bankruptcy in 1959.[2] Its journal, *Pacific Affairs*, and its director, William L. Holland, were invited to UBC where, in 1961, Holland was named the first head of Asian Studies. In 1960, at the University of Alberta, the Department of History was thinking about China, no longer believing that there was no future in it, as more and more students wanted to have courses related to Asia, particularly China and Japan. But the supply of Asian history specialists was limited, particularly Canadians.

BACK TO THE FUTURE

In April 1961, I received a letter from Dr. Walter Johns, president of the University of Alberta, formally offering me a position as assistant professor in the Department of History. Close to gaining my PhD in Chinese history, I was a rare commodity and because I was already known to the University of Alberta History Department and because my letters of support were strong, I was selected as a candidate for appointment. This news spurred me on in my last weeks of thesis preparation. My oral defence was scheduled for the third week of May at SOAS. The examining committee was chaired by Professor Beasley and included Professor Victor Purcell, a distinguished civil servant, poet, and scholar of Southeast Asian history from Cambridge and another from London. The examiners expressed some surprise at my conclusions and at my syntax. I had concluded that the Anglo-French rivalry over the southwestern border of China was not as intense as they (and was popularly) assumed. They felt I was sometimes remiss when I bent sentence structure when aiming for a pun. They did have a point, however, on my spelling of the word, "withdrawal." My omission of the second *a* they kindly assumed to be a Canadianism and after about an hour invited me to wait in the Senior Common Room. There I found Jack Gray, my real supervisor, who looked at my copy of my thesis and said: "Ah, so this is what it looks like." Shortly afterwards, I was called back in and congratulated on a good thesis, well defended. Professor Purcell returned his copy to me as he left. I noticed later that he used the fee schedule for examiners as a bookmark, with the fee for PhD theses circled. He must have liked my thesis because almost immediately he set one of his students on a topic arising from it.

The 1960s were a time of further hardship and turmoil in China. The disaster of the Great Leap Forward coincided with years of poor harvests to usher in the decade. Then came the Cultural Revolution and internal chaos. Chinese universities were particularly disrupted. In contrast, in Canada, the decade of the sixties saw an unprecedented growth of universities. Established institutions expanded and were joined by brand new ones, in an effort to meet the burgeoning "Baby Boomer" enrolments. In Alberta, two new universities were added before the end of the decade: Calgary and Lethbridge. Because they lacked the capacity to produce enough graduates to fill the growing number of academic positions, Canadian universities experienced a growth in American influence, which continued into the early seventies as American academics left the United States in protest over the Vietnam War. At the same time there was an influx of British-educated academics. Prior to 1960, Canadian institutions very much reflected the influence of the British Empire and Commonwealth, in some disciplines more than others. In the case of history departments, British and European histories were a priority, with American and Canadian history following behind. There was a snobbishness shown toward Canadian history— it was considered neither complex nor difficult enough to be worthy of the respect shown the histories of the British Isles and the countries of Western Europe. Canadian history did not begin to come fully into its own until after the centennial year, 1967. With university growth, history departments in larger universities were able to expand their offerings to include Africa, Latin America, Russia, and East, South, and Southeast Asia, depending upon the availability of staff.

With my appointment, and that of Don Weidner, an Africanist, the History Department at the University of Alberta was a pioneer in the trend toward expansion of the range of histories to be offered to their students. Unaware of the context, Margo and I were more concerned with the fact that I was getting a job at all, which not only offered a reasonable salary but also paid the cost of moving us back to Edmonton. We suddenly had money and prospects and celebrated by purchasing an eight-by-ten handwoven Chinese carpet (the first of many more to follow) at Heal's, the famous furniture emporium on Tottenham Court Road in London. The carpet became by far the most substantial item in our meagre household goods to travel home with us.

We arrived in Edmonton in late July 1961 and settled in with Margo's parents, taking over the upstairs two front rooms. I took a week to visit my parents and found that my father was keen on putting in a septic tank, the hole for which he set me to dig. Because the term did not begin until the third week of September, on my return to Edmonton I turned my hand to carpentry, remodelling our two rooms into one large one. The Burwash house is located just off the south end of the university campus and about ten blocks from the office I was assigned in the old power plant at the north end of the campus. It was convenient for me, but Margo, who resumed her position at the Alberta Correspondence School, faced long bus rides north across the river. A year later, we moved into an apartment in Whitehall Place, an easy walk to Margo's work and an easy bicycle ride for me to the university. For the first time, we had space in a well-built and well-heated building and could entertain old friends.

Our apartment building was inhabited by other university types. The chairman of the university Board of Governors, Mr. C.M. Macleod, lived directly above us. Macleod and his wife were model tenants and we had no reason for any contact beyond nodding to each other in the elevator. Most of the tenants were conservative politically, a fact that was brought home to me when I began campaigning in our building for Tom Pocklington, a colleague in political science who was running for the New Democratic Party. I called on one lady who demanded to know how I got into the building. When I replied that I lived there, she said, "Really, they used to be more careful." Pocklington lost and garnered few votes from our building. He did get the votes of Fred and Barbara de Luna, two colleagues from the university, who lived down the hall from us. Fred, a specialist in nineteenth-century France, and Barbara, a specialist in Elizabethan English literature, were left-leaning Americans, graduates of the University of Iowa. They were late risers, but some days of the week our schedules coincided and I was invited to ride in their '57 Chevy to the university. We became good friends, but I sometimes found the free trip to the campus trying. Barbara smoked nonstop while she and Fred argued loudly some point that had seized their attentions earlier in the day, or was left over from the night before.

Edmonton in 1961 was different from the small provincial capital inhabited by government officials and university professors and students that Margo and I had left seven years earlier. It was in the early stages of a building boom spurred on by oil revenues. Its commercial centre was enlivened by entrepreneurial immigrants from Europe. Countries set up consulates, marking the growing international awareness of the province. Edmonton had grown, but was still a small city. Public transport was adequate, but infrequent in the evening, a hardship during cold winter nights. The commercial heart of Edmonton was still Jasper Avenue, with all the major department stores located either on it, or close by. The Chinese community remained small despite an influx of immigrants reuniting with families following the slight easing of Canadian immigration restrictions after 1947. Dining and entertainment was also centred downtown, except for concerts and other shows that were accommodated in the Jubilee Auditorium on the university campus. The university was growing along with the city. The university enrolment of around three thousand students in 1954 was now about five thousand. U of A was on the brink of major expansion for which the government provided generous funding. For a few years, because it remained the only university in the province, along with a branch in Calgary, there was no competition for government funding. In 1960, the academic staff received a major salary increase. The starting salary for an assistant professor was six thousand dollars, twice that of a full professor just the year before.

The university professoriate in the 1960s was well integrated into Edmonton society and there was no feeling of "town versus gown." There was, however, tension between the university and the provincial government. They faced each other across the North Saskatchewan River. Nonetheless, the university did well by the Social Credit government of Earnest C. Manning, as money generated by the oil industry was invested in geology, chemical engineering, chemistry, the library, general staff recruitment, and in the physical plant. Professors in the humanities found it difficult to associate Manning's evangelical religious beliefs with his government's actions. A number were bent on demonstrating his hypocrisy, as they saw it. Nevertheless, the arts were not neglected. The construction of a new library, the Cameron, signalled the beginnings of major book purchases that would lay the foundation for the university's collection, eventually becoming the second largest in Canada. New academic staff were being recruited in all fields, but often they moved on just as quickly as they arrived. The demand for staff was Canada-wide and Edmonton was physically remote, bitterly cold in winter, and isolating for families with young children. Many stayed, however, and later the university was to benefit from a number of fine American scholars who, as I mentioned earlier, could not tolerate the Vietnam conflict and the actions of their country.

Along with the city and the university in general, I found that my department, the History Department, had also changed. First and foremost, it was larger: two of the older professors, Morden Long and Ross Collins, had retired and six more had been added.[3] The History Department owed its growth, not only to the increased enrolment but to the fact that an introductory course in European history was considered basic to an arts degree. As more students entered the introductory course, the department generated more money for appointments. On the initiative of Professor L.G. Thomas, head of the department, steps were taken to recruit female historians to leaven the male-dominated ratio of staff. Within the following decade, seven women historians were appointed.

I approached my first term rather naively, counting on my University of Maryland experience to carry me through. I soon found I was fooling myself, partly because I thought I would be teaching more courses on Asia. Instead, I faced two sections of a survey of European history as the bulk of my load and as a result I spent most of my first year preparing lectures and marking from dawn to dusk. Moreover, I felt very junior, particularly in my relations with the older professors, two of whom, Lewis G. Thomas and Donald Blackley, had been my teachers in the early 1950s. I found it difficult at first to view myself as their colleague and peer, to get used to calling Professor Blackley, Don, and Professor Thomas, Lewis. Of course, they in no way expected deference on my part and did everything possible to make me and other new staff members feel included. Moreover, they opened their homes to Margo and I, inviting us to meet other members of the university over dinner. Only Professor W.J. Eccles, a historian of New France, felt that the newer appointees should take note of the hard work that went in to establishing oneself as a full professor and show the proper respect. As the department expanded rapidly in the 1960s, the younger staff outnumbered the full professors and with the introduction of greater democracy in the running of the department any feelings of rank dissipated.

Although I found the preparation of lectures in European history a burden, I was more than delighted to be introducing the first regular course in Asian history to be offered at the University of Alberta. It was called the History of the Far East and concentrated on the history of China and Japan. I also began teaching one honours student some classical Chinese before introducing a course called Chinese for Historians the next year. It was the first Asian language course to be offered at the U of A. The university term began the third week in September and ended late in April. Classes were offered six days a week and lasted the full length of the university year. In addition to three courses, I was also expected to teach honours and graduate students. Class enrolments were around twenty students, so marking, though time-consuming, was not an overwhelming chore. Library resources for the history of China and of Japan were limited. As well as attempting to build the university's collection, I developed my own to supplement it.

From the first year, Far Eastern history received good student support, which grew after 1966 during the time of the Cultural Revolution. Students were captivated by Mao and the history of student protest movements and their impact on the course of modern Chinese history. One of the major movements was called the May 4th Movement after the protests that erupted in Beijing and Tianjin against the treatment of China in the Treaty of Versailles of 1919. In 1964, the final examination in my course fell on May 4. My students who wrote in a large gymnasium, along with students from other courses, marched in carrying placards and slogans from the original protest of 1919. The tension from examination jitters vanished from the gym.

After the Cultural Revolution began in 1966, some of my students were caught up in Mao Zedong's criticism of university teaching. They did not realize just how formal and rigid classes in Chinese universities were, with students expected to stand when the professor entered the room and not to ask any questions. Mao encouraged students to challenge their professors and copy off other students during examinations if they saw a better answer. I found it ironic when a few of my students stood up and demanded a more democratic atmosphere in the classroom. When I asked them for suggestions on how to improve matters, they had none. Like many of the student Maoists of the time, they had little knowledge of what Mao was actually about.

I took steps to enrich the Far Eastern history program, for example by linking with the University of Toronto and UBC to bring in major China scholars such as Charles Patrick Fitzgerald, professor at Canberra, Australia.[4] But the department, as well as the university in general, was still very much Anglo-European oriented in its outlook. I too reflected this by carrying the title of "Far East" on my early Asian history courses. Within a couple of years, however, I adopted the more accurate and neutral description of "East Asia." My long-term hope was that the university would accept the study of Asia as a natural part of its curriculum.

Beginning in my first year, I also took steps to meet my peers in the field of Chinese studies. I joined three academic associations, all of them American: The American Historical Association (AHA), the Association for Asian Studies (AAS), and the American Oriental Society (AOS), and subscribed to their journals. The AHA met every year between Christmas and New Year, while the AAS and the AOS met in the spring around Easter, usually in the city where the AHA had met a few months before. The AHA was very inconvenient because it took me away from Margo during Christmas and involved travelling in the harshest and most unpredictable weather. It was also the least helpful. Nonetheless, during the first decade and a half, I visited many American cities in the course of these association meetings and visited many fine collections of Asian art, whose publications and coloured slides enabled me to add depth to my lectures on Chinese culture. Except for those of the American Oriental Society, the meetings were crowded with huge programs and an overwhelming amount of information. The AOS was more like a group I belonged to as a student in London.[5]

Unlike the AHA, The AAS meetings provided an opportunity for me to meet my Asianist colleagues from across Canada. In their search for new staff, Canadian universities found themselves with staff of a broad range of interests, many of them Asian with expertise in their own country's history and culture, but there were few full-time appointments dedicated to the study of Asian history per se. Two of these were held by friends of mine from SOAS, both Americans: Jack Gerson, who was now at the University of Toronto, and John Spellman, the Bostonian who objected to our program of meeting new students in London, who held an appointment at the University of Windsor. Eventually, there were enough Asian appointments to represent a critical mass and in meetings held in Vancouver in April 1965, on our way to an AAS meeting in San Francisco, the Canadian Association for Asian Studies (CAAS) took shape.

GROWING PAINS

With the rapid growth of the university in the early sixties, the established administrative structures were severely tested and came under attack from students and staff for the "father knows best" paternalistic attitude that seemed to be endemic to them. During May 1968, caught up by the story of the Red Guards in China and the student demonstrations in France over physical conditions in the universities and their rigid hierarchical structure, the latter of which soon becoming political with unions joining in and producing a full-blown crisis, students challenged professors in class, staged sit-ins, and agitated for representation on all levels of university committees and government. The university was having further growing pains over the concept of an all-powerful head of department with life-long tenure.[6] It did not sit well with young appointees who wanted a greater say in departmental and university affairs.

One of the early serious challenges came from within the History Department. In 1963, Professor Lewis G. Thomas stepped down as head of the department, and after consulting the senior members of the department, decided to promote the African historian, Donald Wiedner, to the position. Wiedner was an exciting lecturer and could draw freehand on the blackboard detailed maps of Africa with all the current and past frontiers accurately placed. He had accomplished a great deal since his appointment. He published a history of Africa south of the Sahara and was key in establishing a national African History Association and its journal, but he was untried as an administrator. His appointment, announced as a *fait accompli*, left his peers, the younger members of the department, feeling uneasy.

Physically, the department was split, some members' offices being located in the Arts Building, while the rest of us had office space provided in the original university Power Plant building, which was also then used as an engineering lab. Wiedner was one of us, with an office in the Power Plant, but his appointment was seen as an arbitrary act on the part of those in the Arts Building who had a higher opinion of his abilities than we did. But what was done, was done, and to his credit, Wiedner was able to get from the central administration, as a condition of his acceptance, a grant of $50,000 for book purchases in history, a major breakthrough in library acquisitions, which I was placed in charge of. Nevertheless, he ran into difficulties over personnel issues within months of his appointment. This added to a growing mood for change within the department toward a more open system for selection of a chair, not a head, to serve for a set term.

But there was more going on than the internal struggles of the department. The University of Alberta, under President Walter Johns, toyed with the idea of establishing a centre for the study of international relations. To this end, a number of professors with international experience were appointed to the Political Science Department and they, along with internationally minded appointees in other departments and faculties, represented a growing critical mass out of which a centre could be formed. Among them were ambassadors, former high officials with the United Nations, international lawyers, and academic specialists in the international system and in international affairs.[7] The failure of the University of Alberta to capitalize on these riches is both a mystery and a tragedy. By the close of the decade, most members of the group went elsewhere. A major opportunity was lost largely because the practitioners and the theoreticians could not agree on the goals for a centre. The failure was a blow to the study of contemporary Asia, which certainly would have been one of the research areas of the institute and would have provided a firm foundation for my course on China and Japan and for my graduate students.

The failure pointed up a divide that continued to grow between scholars from the humanities and those from the social sciences with historians caught in the middle. The social scientists tended to discount the need to learn languages, while the humanists regarded them as basic. Loyalty to individual disciplines overrode the desire to co-operate in a centre. Despite this, the university benefitted in general ways, such as through participation in annual August conferences on international affairs held in Banff, and public-on-campus debates, in all of which I participated, often as a speaker. My courses on

Far Eastern history were enriched by lectures given by Ambassador Chester Ronning, living in retirement in the city of Camrose, who spoke of his childhood in China at the time of the Boxer Rebellion, of his experience as a teacher there in the 1920s, and his time as a diplomat in China in the years following the defeat of Japan in 1945. His anecdotes from the Geneva talks on Korea and Indochina in 1954, as well as his special missions to Hanoi in 1966, kept the students (and me) spellbound.

AWAY TO FAR CATHAY ·

In the summer of 1962, Professor John King Fairbank,[8] doyen of modern China scholars in North America, invited me to Harvard. I lived in the maid's quarters of a large house on Brattle Street owned by a minor biographer of F. Scott Fitzgerald whose name I cannot remember at the moment and who later committed suicide. I remained there for nearly two months before joining Margo and her mother for a tour of the Maritimes in late August and early September.

In the summer of 1963, I returned to England and France for further research in the archives that I knew well. In 1964, however, I did not go back to London—I went to China instead. Soon after I began teaching in Edmonton, it was thrown up to me by colleagues that I had never been to China, a serious omission for a China scholar. As it happened, Don Wiedner, the African historian, had not been to Africa, either. The joke was that the only person in the department who had visited either place was Don Blackley, who had visited them both during his service in the air force during the war. I studied in Britain, partly to have better access to post-1949 China and a more open political atmosphere than existed in the United States. A number of my instructors at SOAS travelled to and from China, when on leave. One of them, John Chinnery, was widely viewed as a Beijing fellow-traveller. In contrast was Arthur Waley, the famous translator of Chinese literature, who had never been east of Switzerland.

In the spring of 1964, a small travel agency in Edmonton advertised tours of China. This was extraordinary since travel to China, unless one was specifically invited, was near impossible at the time. Fred de Luna, a colleague of mine and a historian of modern France, suggested that I look into the offer. The only people I knew to have gone to China a year or so before were a group of extremely rich farmers from around Edmonton and central Alberta. Socialists, they were greeted on their arrival at the train station in Beijing with a banner that read: "Welcome delegation of peasants from Canada." Margo was enthusiastic about my going and for the opportunity for me to see Sophie Wong, whom she had befriended in London and in Hong Kong.

My trip to China took up the month of June 1964. Travelling on my own, I would be following what was called the "milk run," including Guangzhou (Canton,) Beijing, Changchun, Nanjing, Suzhou, Shanghai, and Hangzhou. Because there were no official diplomatic relations between China and Canada, I had to arrange for my visa after I got to Hong Kong. In late May I flew to Hong Kong, the delights of which included my introduction to dim sum, shown to me by Sophie Wong. Hong Kong was between war booms: Korea was in remission and Vietnam was just gathering speed. Not surprisingly, Hong Kong was very British, but its capacity was challenged by the flood of refugees from China seeking escape from the famines and disruptions caused by Mao's Great Leap Forward and People's Commune Movement, and years of bad harvests. Refugee shacks scarred the hillsides in Kowloon and on Hong Kong island. China International Travel Service (CITS) had an office in Hong Kong and I gave them my passport to be forwarded to Guangzhou for approval. It was returned to me the next day with the visa, on a loose sheet, inside. My passport was never stamped.

To enter China, I took a train from the old Kowloon station (now gone) to Lou Wu on the border of the New Territories[9] with China where I crossed a bridge on foot to change to the Chinese train for the onward journey to Guangzhou. Indeed, tourists were as scarce as hen's teeth, the main source of the Soviet Union and Eastern Europe having dried up because of the heated ideological dispute between Moscow and Beijing that broke out into the open in 1960. Even so, because my name translated into Chinese has the same sound as "Ivan," I was taken for a Russian by many ordinary people. After crossing Lou Wu bridge, I made my way to the Customs and Immigration hall to declare my foreign money, because on exit from China one was required to show receipts for purchases and any record of the exchange of money. No Chinese money was allowed out of China and had to be exchanged. The People's Liberation Army (PLA) officer on customs duty unpacked my bag and showed an interest in my newly purchased camera and a Chinese phrase book. He then repacked my case and pointed me upstairs where I could have lunch before boarding the train. Lunch was of a clear leafy soup, chicken with peanuts, rice, and a stir-fried plate of vegetables. My nervousness at entering China went with eating as attendants rated my skill with chopsticks. My rusty phrases remembered from first-year Mandarin classes appeared to work well, apart from occasional giggles and repetitions by my hosts. When left alone, I wrote postcards and letters home to Margo, to my parents, and to colleagues, some of whom thought I would return to Canada a hopeless brainwashed wreck.

On the train from the border to Guangzhou (Canton) I travelled with a group of British engineers on their way to Beijing for an industrial machinery show, and with a small number of French diplomats on their way to Beijing to set up the new French Embassy following Charles de Gaulle's decision earlier in the year to recognize the People's Republic. The engineers were sceptical about Chinese being able to master the intricacies of their machines, but later when I met them in Beijing, they boasted about all the free time they had because the Chinese demonstrators mastered the machines in half an hour. I stayed on in Guangzhou for a day to watch the celebrations of International Children's Day; to visit the sites of earlier rebellions; to visit Shameen Island, with its rows of European-style buildings where foreign traders lived in the late nineteenth and early twentieth centuries; and to visit public parks. It was hot and humid but it did not seem to curtail the energy of the children as they played around the huge white marble statue of a goat, the symbol of Guangzhou. Outside the city were rice fields being worked by men and women standing in the water or driving a water buffalo pulling a plough through the mud. Along the narrow roadways were white ducks, guided by duck herds. The paintings I had seen of China were suddenly coming to life.

I was the only non-Chinese foreigner the next day on the train to Beijing, a person of interest. But I was not as interesting as one of my compartment companions. She was a famous Cantonese opera star heading for Beijing to learn about the new style of opera being introduced by Jiang Qing, Mao Zedong's wife—a forerunner to the Cultural Revolution. At each station people crowded around her when she stepped onto the platform. My other fellow traveller was a geologist returning to Beijing from work on Hainan Island and carrying a large number of small bananas. We travelled north through Wuhan, passing over the Yangzi on the Great Bridge of which the Chinese were proud but which was built with Russian help.[10] The multi-decked bridge made it possible for speedy north-south travel of people and goods without resorting to the ferries of old.

Having gained some confidence at knowing what to order off the dining car menu, at breakfast the next morning I asked for congee, pickles, boiled peanuts, and cold steamed buns stuffed with vegetables. I ate carefully, attempting to look as though I belonged, but my solitude was broken by the words: "I don't

Beijing schoolchildren, June 1964.

know how they eat that stuff. I need bacon and eggs in the morning." Sitting across the aisle from me were three Chinese gentlemen from Singapore on a private tour. After I introduced myself, one asked if I could assist his son in gaining entrance to the U of A.

Although I travelled on my own on the trains, I was met and accompanied on tours of the cities by guides from CITS. They were young men and women, recent graduates from universities and competent in foreign languages. Their hard factual information on China in general was limited to what they read in Edgar Snow's newly published book, *The Other Side of the River* (1963), which was based upon information given to Snow in interviews with Mao Zedong and Zhou Enlai. Wherever I went, the country and the people looked very poor and economically depressed, but their revolutionary spirit and optimism was high. I was surprised to hear how much they sang in public. It reminded me of southern Alberta during the Depression and the war, when everyone was relatively poor but full of hope and promise for the future. In 1964, China was isolated internationally. It quarrelled with the Soviet Union, which withdrew its economic and technical assistance, and the United States had imposed a trade embargo against it. Moreover, the situation in Vietnam was worsening. There were no more than a dozen or so Western tourists travelling in China that June. In Beijing I encountered the crew from the famous CBC program,

Busy Beijing street, June 1964.

This Hour Has Seven Days and Charles Taylor, the correspondent for the *Globe and Mail*. *This Hour* was making a film to be called *700 Million*—the estimated size of China's population at the time.

Compared to today, Beijing's streets were virtually empty, there being no street vendors, few cars, and only some bicycles and buses. Most Chinese lived in housing supplied by their work unit and did not have to travel far. Chang'an, the main avenue passing in front of the Gate of Heavenly Peace (the gate is separated by Chang'an Avenue from the square that bears its name), was lined with pink-blossomed oleander bushes. One could get around quickly in the Polish-built Warsawa automobile provided by CITS. I visited Buddhist temples in the Western Hills that were later placed out of bounds during the Cultural Revolution, and went boating on the lake in front of the Summer Palace. It was a very hot day and many people were swimming, some using large lotus leaves to protect their heads from the sun. I was driven by CITS to the Great Wall on a day that threatened rain. I was the only tourist at that time of day. I was so excited that I took all my pictures with the lens cap still on my camera.

In Beijing, I stayed in the Xinqiao Hotel in a room down the hall from Charles Taylor's office and close to the rooms occupied by Patrick Watson and the CBC television crew. It was the Chinese practice of keeping guests separate according to who their sponsor was. Thus, I dined in solitary splendour, eating sea cucumber for the first time. It was a chewy gelatinous mass in an

The Great Wall of China.

interesting sauce, and was served only to special guests in these hard times. Behind the hotel was a stretch of the old Beijing city wall, which was slowly, stone by stone, being dismantled.

Mr. Hu Erh-chien, my guide for my one-week stay in Beijing, was a young recruit to CITS and fond of painting. He was delighted when we went to Liulichang, the street of antiques, books, and paintings, to buy scrolls and woodblock prints, because the shops next door sold paper, ink, and brushes. Nine years later, this street would be much subdued. Traditional paintings and block prints would be kept under the counter and would have to be asked for, replaced by those of revolutionary themes now on display. Antiques would also be hidden away and would be inexpensive, having fallen out of revolutionary favour. I would walk from the end of the street along the *hutongs* (lanes) to Qianmen at the south end of Tiananmen where there was a wholesale dry goods shop with a trapdoor that provided entrance to a whole network of underground rooms and facilities dug as shelters against an atomic attack from Russia in the early years of the Cultural Revolution.

In June 1964, the Cultural Revolution was two years in the future and Beijing was quiet and relaxed, unaware of the frenzy to come. My days were filled with sightseeing visits and eating. My guide Hu had a charming phrase to urge me to rest after lunch. "You better take a snap," he would say. One day, when I sneezed, he began to laugh. At first he would not tell me why, but I urged him to be frank. "We have a saying," he said, "that when a dog sneezes it is going to rain." And it did! We visited Beijing Normal University one morning. It was covered with banners and slogans left over from the Hundred Flowers campaign that had urged open debate and criticism of the government but that in the end led to the persecution of intellectuals. We were taken to some experimental agricultural plots where they were digging deep trenches for sowing grain. It was an idea from the Great Leap Forward that illustrated the triumph of ideology over common sense.

One day, Hu and I visited Tiananmen Square and I stood on the steps of the Monument to the People's Heroes to photograph youths and children with coloured flags welcome the motorcade of a visiting African dignitary. We passed under the gate, which at that time bore no large portrait of Mao, and proceeded to view the always impressive Forbidden City (Gu Gong), which was sorely in need of paint and repair. We inspected the royal apartments and the many clocks given to Chinese emperors by Western emissaries, before entering the Empress Dowager's garden just inside the north gate. Some exotic flowers were in bloom, a number of them gifts from abroad. After exiting the Forbidden City, we climbed Coal Hill to stand atop it, a little above the tree where the last Emperor of the Ming Dynasty was found hanging in May 1644. From this vantage point we could see all of Beijing with its low, grey-walled compounds and grey-tiled roofs interlaced with *hutongs*, contrasting with the imperial yellow tiles of the Forbidden City, and with the Temple of Heaven, its blue-tiled roof shining in the sun. To the north lay the broad thoroughfares cut by Soviet engineers beyond Beihai Lake to the Bell and Drum towers. Soviet plans to destroy many of the prime mansions that line the shores of the three small lakes to the north of Beihai to make more broad roadways were halted by Zhou Enlai, who had been lobbied by a famous Chinese architect and city planner Liang Sicheng, the son of the even more famous reformer Liang Qichao (1873–1929). Soviet advice,[11] however, was taken about enlarging Tiananmen Square, which stood out as a vast expanse flanked by the Great Hall of the People and the Museum of Chinese History. The view of Qianmen at its southernmost end was unimpeded, not yet blocked by Mao's tomb. I began to appreciate why old Beijing used to be considered one of the world's most beautiful cities.

When I departed Beijing, Hu and I promised to keep in touch, but without success. In later years I attempted to find him. Only after many inquiries did I find someone from CITS who knew of him. It seems he had been singled out during the Cultural Revolution and sent to the countryside, later becoming a tour representative in a small provincial town. It was Hu who introduced me to Beijing Cao Ya, popularly known around the world—even in Beijing—as Peking duck, and to Mao Tai, the over-proof clear liquor that tastes like sack cloth, at the "Sick Duck" restaurant off Wangfujing. As I wrote in a letter home to Margo: "I have just tasted Peking duck and I will never be the same again. What wonderfully delicious food." The fact that it was ingested at the same time as my first ever taste of alcohol may have affected my opinion, but it has really never changed: I am still addicted to a Peking duck meal with all of its ritual.

Before I left Beijing, Hu arranged for me to cancel my trip to Changchun and made it possible for me to visit the city of Tianjin (Tientsin). It is on the coast about sixty-nine miles from Beijing and functions as the port for Beijing. Tianjin was very rough indeed. I was barked at as a foreign dog, and heckled as a Russian. I was closely accompanied by two guides, one in military uniform, a stoic figure, who proudly wore my leather camera case on his shoulder.[12] I wanted to visit the city because of its role in Sino-Western relations during the late nineteenth century. It was the site of the Anglo-French invasion during the Second Opium War also known as the Arrow War.[13] I wanted to see the Dagu forts, which the Chinese had built to guard against the invaders. Unfortunately, I did not see the sites I wanted, but I did see the dock where Canadian wheat arrived and visited the Sailors Club where Polish sailors played pool in a room where slogans on the walls exhorted: "Workers of the World Unite against Common Enemies"; "The Test Ban Is for Fools"; "China Wants the Complete Scrapping of All Nuclear Weapons"; "China Is Confident that the American Negro Will Win the Struggle." My guides and I went to a new revolutionary play, the plot of which centred on union struggles. It was very poorly attended whereas the traditional opera the next night was packed.

From Tianjin I went by train to Nanjing, passing through areas of great flooding while the train's intercom carried the news of how all flooding in China had stopped thanks to Chairman Mao. In Nanjing, the air was filled with the scent of jasmine. I toured the sites of the Taiping Rebellion of the mid-nineteenth century and the office of Sun Yat-sen, first president of the republic, along with his imperial-style tomb on the side of the Purple Mountain outside the city.[14] At Nanjing University the dean of arts explained to me why his students were pulling up the grass in the forecourt. It was part of the New Socialist Education Movement that called for work to be combined with study. Personally he

Nanjing street scene, June 1964.

thought it ridiculous and he had the long fingernails to prove it. In Nanjing I also visited a doctor because I was suffering from stomach problems. She gave me pills for constipation, which was definitely not the problem.

On the train to Suzhou from Nanjing, my carriage had a uniformed officer with binoculars who surveyed all the hills as we passed along. He may have been a bird-watcher, but I think he was probably looking for signs of illegal activities by locals. The beautiful classic gardens of Suzhou were poorly attended and I had them all to myself. The other visit arranged for me was to the Silk Research Institute, which was the name for an embroidery factory where women embroidered intricate patterns with minute stitches, while the shop sold silk portraits of the Communist Party leaders.

After Suzhou, I travelled on to Shanghai, which was drab, minus neon signs and street life. Ma, my CITS guide, was a music major hooked on Beethoven and we often made detours to buy sheet music. I had agreed to a proposal from my old friend Jack Gerson that I purchase books in Chinese for the University of Toronto Library. (The U of A library at this time was not able to handle such materials because it had neither a Chinese librarian nor a collection.) Ironically, two years earlier Claude Bissell,[15] then president of the University of Toronto, had visited China, meeting, briefly, Zhou Enlai and even Mao Zedong at May Day ceremonies, but did not stop to buy books. I was daunted at the thought, but Ma took me to all the bookshops and slowly checked off my

A street corner in Shanghai, June 1964.

list of items, made up exclusively of history books, documents, and academic journals. Having filled the trunk of the car, Ma and I took the books back to the Peace Hotel on the Bund where I was staying and where the staff wrapped them up, sent them off, and presented me with a ridiculously low bill. After having done my duty by U of T, we visited communes outside Shanghai and at one, in the commune's school, children were singing a song called "Chairman Mao Is a Member of Our Commune." I remembered the title of the song for a talk I would be making to the University of Alberta Philosophical Society on my return. The school worked in two half-day shifts, with the morning students working in the fields in the afternoon and the morning workers going to school in the afternoon.

Before leaving Shanghai, I was given a dinner in a small private dining room atop the Peace Hotel by the deputy director of CITS, who quizzed me about Canada's likely policy toward China and about what I thought the US would do. It was an election year in America, but he had little hope for a change in US policy no matter who won. Looking to my own future, I asked his opinion on whether I could return to China in 1967 to do research in Yunnan province on the Panthay (Muslim) revolt (1856–1873), a topic arising from my thesis. He saw no reason why not.

At the end of June, after a stop in Hangchow to visit the famous dragon well (*long jing*) and to drink fresh tea, I left China, exiting the way I came. In Hong

Kong I was debriefed by Peter Roberts of the Canadian High Commission, who was originally from Lethbridge and a U of A graduate in history, and by the BBC correspondent David Willey for whom Sophie Wong was working. I was buoyed by my experience inside China. I found the spirit of the people inspiring and I was encouraged to see that traditional culture had survived the first fifteen years of the Communist revolution. It was clear people had gone through very difficult times, the full extent of which no outsider knew at the time. As someone who had worked his way through school and university, I was not shocked by the work/study ideas of the Socialist Education Movement, particularly in the face of the traditional distain of Chinese intellectuals for manual labour.

My views were quite different from those expressed in a *Time* magazine story printed the next month, stating how dreadful life was in China with power cuts, shortages, and no sex. Those were the days when *Time*, under the direction of the Luce family, dedicated itself to denouncing every aspect of life in China. The *Time* story painted a picture of life in a China that was regimented and fanatically clean, with no obvious differences between the sexes at first glance, where flies and birds had been eliminated and where relations between the sexes were strictly regulated to a highly puritanical standard.[16] I wrote *Time*, saying their story did not coincide with my observations during my trip, and pointed out that the large population surely indicated that some Chinese at least were having sex. They did not print my remarks, but replied saying their story was based on the observations of experts. Then in early August came the contrived Gulf of Tonkin incident,[17] used by the Lyndon Johnson administration to widen America's involvement in the war in Vietnam.

After my return home, as someone who had been to China, I was suddenly in demand. I was invited to give an illustrated lecture at the University of Toronto in late August, followed by another one two days later at Harvard at the invitation of Professor Fairbank. I had been greatly impressed by my experiences in China and my reputation for being left of centre perhaps got a little redder as though the very act of going to China was akin to being a Maoist. My comments were received with scepticism by some members of the Harvard audience, bombarded as they were almost daily by stories of China the enemy and Mao the ogre. I remember showing a slide of a particularly beautiful temple, which was well preserved. I was asked its age, something I did not know. Fairbank came to my rescue with the words, "Built by a Yale man in 1929."[18]

As I wrote earlier, when in Shanghai, I had asked the deputy director of CITS whether I could expect to carry out research in China in 1967–1968 when my sabbatical leave was due. Neither of us was aware of the Cultural Revolution Mao was planning. When the time for my leave came, travel from Canada to China was no longer possible, but since I was also going to spend some of my leave in London, I was sure it would be easier to travel to China from there.

In July 1967, shortly after Margo and I arrived in London, I went to a travel agent called Progressive Tours with good contacts with China to make a reservation for a tour. I was advised to prepare for the trip. In the meantime, Margo and I resumed the routine we had established during our earlier time in London: plays, concerts, and galleries, with weekend trips to historic places. We found a beautiful flat in a house at Golders Green, a rich suburb centre of a Jewish community. Golders Green was well served by London transport and it had a large theatre called the Hippodrome that featured a different play each week. It was often the last stop of theatre companies on their way to open in the West End, and the first stop of companies after they finished their London runs. We resumed direct contact with our London friends, often sharing a play and a meal in a local restaurant. During the week, I resumed my research, travelling to the British Museum and various archives during the day while Margo, either with friends or on her own, explored more of London. Later, she enrolled in short courses on London history. For the first time since we married, we were able to enjoy London without pinching pennies.

By mid-August, the news of the increasing disorder in China as the Cultural Revolution spread made me suspect that our trip to China was not to be, particularly when the revolution spilled into the streets of London. Late in August in Beijing, Red Guards began an uncontrolled rampage against foreign embassies and the Chinese Foreign Ministry. The British Embassy was sacked, burned, and diplomats were injured and one was killed in the attack. In response, the alley outside the Chinese Embassy in Portland Place, a fashionable section of London, became the scene of a battle between Chinese Embassy staff and London Police. Goaded by some Brits and under pressure to show their mettle in the heart of British Imperialism, Chinese diplomats attacked the bobbies with baseball bats and one axe. Injuries suffered in such fights in London and other foreign capitals brought the Chinese combatants great status in Beijing. Some were invalided home to a hero's welcome. Chinese ambassadors from around the world were called back to Beijing and issued new dress codes and rules of behaviour,[19] leaving China a diplomatic cripple in the meantime. By late September, Mao intervened to discipline the Red Guards, blamed extremists for the incidents, and placed the Foreign Ministry and international diplomacy off limits to Red Guard activity.

Shortly after the Portland Street brawl, I was told that our trip was off. China was closed—to us at least. I was determined, however, to return to East Asia at any rate. Hong Kong, which had become the main listening post for Western observers of China, was well worth a visit, particularly because the American Consulate there was collecting and translating materials on the current situation in China. This was of interest to me, but the fact remained that I considered myself a historian of Qing China, so the materials in the Hong Kong university library were the real draw. Margo proposed that we travel to Hong Kong by freighter, an idea that I resisted because having crossed the Atlantic twice in rough seas, I was not anxious to repeat the experience. I was wrong. The six weeks we spent on a Dutch freighter was one of the travel highlights of our lives.

Our trip to Hong Kong was made possible by the situation at that time in the Middle East. The Suez Canal was closed and as a result bookings were easy to get on Dutch express freighters heading for Hong Kong. There were many cancellations because the trip around Africa took much longer, and because of the continued international uncertainty. We became two of six passengers on the twelve-passenger *Mersey Lloyd* that left Rotterdam on January 26, 1968. The officers were Dutch, the crew Chinese, and the chef came from a famous Hong Kong Hotel. The captain was an engaging character who liked food and to talk, although one subject went unmentioned. On an earlier voyage, he had piloted his ship into Boston carrying an American scholar and his Chinese mistress among his passengers. When they entered Boston Harbor, the woman had disappeared only to be found floating in the water some time later. The captain had a rough passage over the incident and we were warned by the second in command not to mention it.

Our voyage turned out to be idyllic: calm seas, star-filled nights, excellent food, and good companions, including a Dutch couple on their way back to Kenya where he was a bank manager (they got off at Cape Town) and an elderly Scots brother and sister in their eighties named Thompson who were both intrepid travellers. I was drafting a couple of articles and I was able to sit in the saloon and watch the seascape as I worked. Because the freighter was part of an express service, it only paused in South Africa's Table Bay to deliver mail and drop off the Dutch couple who were to travel to Nairobi by train, before rounding the Cape and heading for Singapore, where we arrived on February 28, thirty-three days after our departure.

After one day in Singapore and one day in Manila, where the ship's crew noted with disgust that the cargo from their previous trip was still on the dock, we arrived at Hong Kong six days after leaving Singapore. Arriving by ship in Hong Kong is a special treat, particularly at night. Victoria on the island and Kowloon on the mainland, outlined in twinkling lights and flashing neon, were an open welcome invitation to the traveller. We were met by Jack Gerson, then on leave, who made arrangements for us to stay at Robert Black College at Hong Kong University, where William Saywell, also from U of T, was in residence. Hong Kong was not the ship's final destination. It was scheduled to go on to Shanghai, but try as I might, the captain was under strict orders not to carry passengers beyond Hong Kong, and having had one bad experience with a professor, he was not about to chance another. In any case, I was told by him that once they arrived in Shanghai they would be boarded by Red Guards waving Mao's "Little Red Book," demanding that they memorize the sayings to prove their redness. Neither the officers nor the crew were looking forward to Shanghai. Hong Kong, however, they loved, but they could not stay for long.

Hong Kong was still very tense after the bloody riots the previous year—an offshoot of the Cultural Revolution. The aftermath of these riots, during which the riot leaders were jailed, had provoked the Red Guard attack on the British Embassy in Beijing. The governor of the colony introduced strict censorship against any information that might promote anti-British feeling. Thus, the University of Hong Kong, a very conservative and British-dominated institution, was not allowed to show a documentary film on the growing war in Vietnam because of a scene that showed American warships refuelling in Hong Kong. Hong Kong was promoting an image of strict neutrality. We stayed in Hong Kong for nearly two weeks while I did research in the university library and Margo shopped and explored Hong Kong island. Then, after a day in Macau, which at that time was still a sleepy and slightly seedy Portuguese colony, we decided to continue our trip by going around China by crossing Russia on the Trans-Siberian railway, a journey we had often spoke of taking. Margo and I flew to Japan for six days in Tokyo and Kyoto before taking the Russian ship, the MS *Khabarovsk*, from Yokohama to Nahodka in the Soviet Union, south of Vladivostok, the latter of which was a military base and closed to foreigners.

The Russia, Trans-Siberian railway, April 1968.

The *Khabarovsk* sailed regularly between Hong Kong and Nahodka via Yokohama, so we loaded most of our luggage aboard in Hong Kong. At Yokohama we were reunited with our luggage, all fourteen pieces of it leaving very little room in our cabin. The ship was full of Japanese tourists and assorted Europeans and very lively they were too. The food was good but plain. The cabin attendants were beautiful, blond, and female. In the evenings they danced the twist with the passengers. After fifty-two hours, we reached Nahodka, but it was another five hours before we disembarked due to general Intourist[20] inefficiency. We had hoped to have time to walk around the city, but in the end we only just made our scheduled train to the city of Khabarovsk.

The train from Nahodka to Khabarovsk was marvellous. It was all blue plush upholstery with polished mahogany and cut glass trimmed in brass. We were looking forward to crossing Siberia in this splendid accommodation when we were taken off the train and told to wait for another train called the Russia that was coming from Vladivostok in a couple of hours. We were bottled up in a VIP lounge where we were on exhibit for the natives of Khabarovsk. It was snowing and looking very much like Edmonton.

The Russia was a mix of old passenger cars and shiny new ones. Its carriages were divided into hard and soft class with four berths in each compartment. We paid for soft class and were put in a new carriage with hot and cold running water, which as it turned out was actually hard class. The soft-class carriages were the old ones full of soft cushions filled with soot and only cold water. Each carriage had a pot-bellied stove at the end of the corridor for general heating and to boil water for the samovar from which the attendant dispensed tea at four kopeks a glass with sugar. Nearly all the staff on the train were female, charming, and friendly, highly amused at our sense of propriety. They would enter our compartment when the door was closed without knocking and thought privacy, limited as it was, was theirs to invade. I could not help but think of my days as a sleeping car porter and how hopelessly bourgeois and capitalist it would have appeared to them. One thing was the same—I had to make my own bed. They handed us towels, pillow cases, and sheets at the beginning of the journey and collected them at the end. It was up to you to make your bed when and if you felt like it. The train was comparable to the ones I had travelled on in China four years before, except the Chinese provided Thermos bottles of hot water instead of relying on a samovar.

The passengers on the Russia were not segregated according to gender, so we shared our compartment with a German lady, while a charming Dutch Canadian girl was put in with a male American student and an Australian lady in with three Russian men. The Australian later managed to move to a compartment with a nursing mother. We had already seen the German lady earlier aboard the *Khabarovsk*, but we did not make her acquaintance. When we first boarded the train, we found her already in the compartment and as our luggage was lugged in she kept saying, "Zo much lugagges, Zo much LUGGAGES. Never I have seen zo much luggages." She helped us bury various things and then sat down to tell us the story of her travels. As a traveller, she was nearly broke. Until she was able to return home, she was planning to keep alive on pills, bread, and canned chicken. She had a huge plastic container of pills of various colours. She also had a little tube of heart pills over which she panicked one afternoon when she thought they had been thrown out. She had left her home, husband, and son in Germany early in January to visit some friends in India. While in India, she got the idea that she might like to visit Angkor Wat and Bangkok, Hong Kong, and Japan. In Japan, without telling her husband or son, she decided to travel home via Russia. Once in Russia, she began to have second thoughts. As the trip lengthened, she kept saying, "Yugoslavia is beauty, Dubrovnik is very beauty, Zwitzerland is beauty, but ach Ziberia. Mine husband was right, why travel?" During the train trip she began to think she was being spied upon and woke us up at night with her nightmares in which she dreamed that someone was trying to kill her. This was because her mother was alive and came from East Germany, her father and brother were killed in Russia in the war, and she had spoken German to a Russian in the next compartment. When he answered in German, she asked him where he had learned it. "In a German prisoner of war camp," he replied. "My father died in Russia," she snapped back. She was a remarkable woman and had travelled all over the world. When we got off at Irkutsk, she stayed on the train for Moscow. She was determined to get to "Zwitzerland," where it was "beauty" for Easter.

Most of the Russia's passengers were Russian, but there were about a dozen or so of us non-Russians. Three were Frenchmen who remained French throughout. There were three German student types who migrated to Australia some years earlier and who were returning to West Berlin for kicks. There was the tall Dutch Canadian girl, already mentioned. She lent me a copy of *Bachelor's Japan* wherein I discovered what I had missed by never having been to a Japanese bathhouse. There was also the American student from her compartment. He was on a round-the-world tour when he jumped ship out of Saigon. He was reluctant to give his name, so he was called "the American" by everyone onboard the train and he sat around reading Galbraith. He turned out to be a very interesting dropout from San Francisco State. There was a man from Yorkshire with a huge silver steamer trunk, on his way back there to give his sister away at her wedding and who was to spend one day in Moscow en route to London. There was a German ship's architect from Yokohama. He was charming, handsome, and joined our compartment when we left Irkutsk after our stopover there. He had two very good friends, carpenters, in Edmonton. Also onboard was an Englishman from Hong Kong, who turned out to be a fellow graduate from SOAS who knew most of the people I knew. Among the others there was an Australian woman going to Moscow to join her husband who was a student there. Her husband was a student of the husband of Rosalind, the eldest daughter of our old landlord at 6 Onslow Gardens in London. It is amazing how your world has a way of travelling with you.

Although our fellow passengers were varied and interesting, there was plenty of time to look out the window as we crossed Siberia. Never had we seen so many silver birch trees, and because spring had not yet sprung, we were able to see for miles through the forests. Most of the snow was gone, but there were patches of it several hours long, and the odd snowstorm. The country around the city of Chita looked like Taber and the trip from Khabarovsk to Moscow was like travelling from Sudbury, Ontario, to Edmonton, via Medicine Hat, four times over, plus silver birches. There was one major difference—the towns, or lack thereof. What towns there were, were depressing to see. They were built of wood, unpainted, with outdoor plumbing, and mud for streets. They reminded Margo of northern Alberta before the war. The Soviet Union spent money on their space program, but little on infrastructure in Siberia.

The previous year, the Soviets had celebrated the fiftieth anniversary of the Bolshevik Revolution. At one of the stations where the train stopped there was a sign announcing fifty years of the revolution, along with a statue or bust of Lenin and perhaps of a buxom Olympic athlete or two. Standing by the tracks were bulky women dressed in black dresses with white aprons. They sold foods such as boiled eggs, cabbage, potatoes, and garlic. These were scenes quite different from the train stations I had seen in China where a range of foodstuffs were dispensed off carts. The further west we travelled, the wider the selection of food for sale and the better constructed the wayside stalls became, but there was never anything too exciting. We saw fresh fruit on sale once east of Irkutsk: apples at $1.50 a pound. East of Irkutsk, at stops, local people would come along the tracks to the dining car of the train to buy wines, sweets, or tobacco. They very rarely got any because the supplies of the dining car were limited. At times, the most persistent luxury-goods seekers received a boot in the face from dining car staff.

The dining car on the train seated fifty but there were only two ladies to serve. The front of the car was for foreigners and the rear for Russians. The Russians drank immense amounts of beer and from time to time accused the staff of serving the foreigners better bread. In the midst of it all was a little enclave of French culture where its three valiant representatives broke bread in the French manner and drank the abominable wine with elegance and grace. But one morning we came upon one of them who was sitting at his table in despair. He was sure he had ordered an omelette. He stirred it with a spoon, tasted it, and said, "I don't know what it is, but it is not an omelette."

Somewhere east of Irkutsk, the train stopped and picked up the latest newspaper from Moscow. In this manner we learned of the death of Soviet cosmonaut Yuri Gagarin, who had been buried the day before in Moscow. As it happened, we had heard the funeral service on the train radio the night before, there being a seven-hour time difference, but we did not have a clue what it meant. As it was, we learned of Gagarin's death in a silly way. We were eating lunch with the Frenchmen when the papers arrived. The lady in charge of the dining car came up to us and said, "Gagarin in heaven," and she pointed to the ceiling. We smiled at this because we thought he was circling the earth in some

Irkutsk, Soviet Union, April 1968.

new spacecraft. She saw from the look on our faces that we had missed the point, so she held up the black-bordered picture that took up most of the front page. Then we understood, but we thought it interesting that she would say he was in heaven. We wondered if she thought he might see Lenin and Stalin there.

News from the outside world did not get through to us while we were on the ten-day trip to Moscow and when it did, we did not believe it. After we left Irkutsk, a German-speaking Russian, who was reading a copy of *Pravda*, turned to the German-speaking American and said, "Johnson has quit." It turned out that the Russian had used up his entire German vocabulary on this sentence, leaving a mystified American with an unreadable article in *Pravda*. He ran through the train looking for someone to read the article to him, but found no one, and none of the staff had a sufficient grasp of English or any other Western European language to be of help. He happened on us and we discounted the story, saying that such things sounded ridiculous. When we got to Moscow, we heard the details about Johnson and learned of the assassination of Martin Luther King, but it was not until we arrived back in England on April 16 that we learned of Pierre Trudeau becoming prime minister.

The Russia became a world within a world for us as we proceeded, day after day, through aspen and white birch forests, over grassy plains, while winter gave way to spring. Despite the lack of outside news, however, I made an effort to sound out our fellow Russian passengers, and those we met later in the cities, regarding their opinions of the Chinese and the Cultural Revolution. They were all aware of the antics of the Red Guards and of the battles over the islands in the Ussuri River, which marks the border between Siberia and Northeast China. The Chinese, I learned from the Russians, "had gone crazy,"[21] and the Cultural Revolution was "the result of Mao's madness." The Chinese represented "a threat to the Soviet Union"—"they wanted to flood it with their excess population."

The nearly four days from Irkutsk to Moscow took us through more settled areas and through the science city of Novo Sibirsk.[22] We were transferred now into a soft-class sleeping car. Our compartment companions were Russian, one of whom was a sort of Russian version of Jack Armstrong, the all-American boy. He constantly smiled, was kind to little old ladies, and friendly to us. One thing about the Russians, they believe if they speak Russian to you long enough, eventually you will understand.

When we arrived in Moscow early on the morning of April 7, we were met by a huge station wagon. Obviously, the news of our copious luggage had gotten around. Our Intourist welcomer was drunk and greeted us with, "Goodbye, I hope you enjoyed your visit." Fortunately, he was only with us until we got to the Metropole Hotel, which, though old, was well situated for the sights of Moscow. A hotel desk dispensed ballet, theatre, and circus tickets to tourists. The first night we went to the Boshoi Theatre to see the ballet *Giselle*, and the next night we went to the Moscow Circus to see the famous clown Popov and the fabulous Russian bears.

There was also an Intourist desk at the hotel, where I got into an argument I could not win. I failed to understand why I could not get the full amount for the twenty-two-rouble-and-fifty-kopek voucher given to us in Irkutsk because we had been put in hard class for the first part of the trip to Irkutsk although we had paid for soft class. The Intourist agent insisted that 10 per cent had to be deducted for a service charge, and even after I went along to argue at their head office that it was their mistake in the first place, they still gave me only twenty roubles and twenty-five kopeks. When I got back to the hotel, there was a call to tell me that I owed them twenty roubles, twenty-five kopeks, because I had changed our train bookings from Moscow to Leningrad. I decided that I was in Moscow to see the city and not to engage in endless fights with Intourist, so I gave up. My experience with Intourist was in sharp contrast to CITS, who, after I left China in June 1964, calculated it owed me money and

Red Square, Moscow, April 1968. Lines of people await a chance to see Lenin.

sent the cash in American funds to me in Canada. CITS was patterned after Intourist in name only.

Moscow was magical, particularly the Kremlin, its colours contrasting with the freshly fallen snow. The scenes of public drunkenness were hard to ignore as were the young men, black marketers, outside the hotel offering five times the official exchange rate. We took the underground and marvelled at the fabulous stations, architectural wonders beneath Moscow's streets. But the most exciting thing to happen to us in Moscow took place during our last few hours there. We were booked on the midnight train to Leningrad on April 10 and having been to the ballet and the circus, we thought that our chances of finding another entertainment in time were slim to none. The ticket lady in the hotel told us that there would be no tickets for anything until after 6:30. Besides, it was the opening night of a new production of Aram Khachaturian's ballet, *Spartacus*, choreographed by Yuri Grigorovich, so another trip to the Bolshoi was out of the question. We spent the afternoon viewing French Impressionist paintings in the Pushkin Museum. On our return to the Metropole, we were held up by a conversation with the Englishman from Yorkshire we had met on the train. He had run out of money and called on the British Embassy for a loan. It was now just after seven and because most things began at 7:30, we resigned ourselves to grabbing some supper and packing. But before we reached the stairs, the ticket lady ran up to us with two tickets for *Spartacus*. There being no time for food, we dashed to the Bolshoi Theatre.

The evening was spectacular, and we settled on a glass of champenski for supper. We just made the train, much to the amusement of the luggage porter. The Intourist guide seeing us off was as drunk as the one who had welcomed us and bade us farewell with, "Welcome to Moscow. I hope you will enjoy your visit." We were installed in a compartment for two on the Red Arrow, the most comfortable and luxurious train compartment for two I have ever travelled in. It was large and brightly lit with soft velvet curtains, no upper berths, wide comfortable beds, and a window table with flowers and water in cut glass containers. After a cup of tea served by the blonde lady attendant, we were off to Leningrad.

Nothing can compare with a first visit to Leningrad (except perhaps for the first visit to Saint Petersburg). The city was already greatly restored from wartime damage and all of the delights of its eighteenth-century architecture were there to see, along with the fabulous art collections of the Hermitage. Both Moscow and Leningrad were enchanting, emerging from winter with occasional light dustings of snow in the early morning. But the scene was blighted by drunks. To be sure it was not always the Russians in this state. Our hotel in Leningrad had more than a dozen Finns sprawled around the lounge, besotted with vodka at nine in the morning. In the evening, the bar was crowded with British school groups, underage, but intoxicated nonetheless because the barman never refused any hotel guest a drink.[23] Although we had paid to be greeted and seen off in Leningrad, Intourist did not bother. We were compensated by a tour in a black ZIM, conducted by a very knowledgeable young woman. On our tour, we encountered little bands of children of kindergarten age, led by a teacher and tied together with string. The children were looking every which way, except in the direction the teacher was guiding them. I took this to be symbolic of the relationship between the Soviet government and the people, but I did not say so. As our guide told us of the storming of the Winter Palace in 1917, the string broke on a line of children, forcing the teacher to run about gathering up her scattered brood. I think now it foretold the end of the Soviet Union in the final decade of the century.

In Leningrad we went to the Kirov ballet, but it was clear the Bolshoi had picked the best resources. We sat in the royal box, Leningrad being fresh out of royalty, and we learned the true purpose of the ballet: the intermissions; there were four of them. During each one you could buy huge oranges, or go into an old-fashioned ice cream parlour where ice cream, cream cakes, tea, coffee, and lemonade overflowed. It was another world. When we came out of the theatre, it was snowing and we went for a walk. The facades of the yellow, cream-coloured building were spotlighted and the statue of Peter the Great, astride his horse, was galloping through the snowflakes. It nearly made one forget the twenty million Russians who had died in World War II, millions of them in Leningrad during the siege, and who are buried outside the city.

Leaving Leningrad after three days was interesting. At the train station, a porter lit several matches in order to read our luggage tags before discerning we were headed for Poland. He guided us among small sloughs to the platform, which looked like a refugee camp. Margo and I caught the train at midnight only to learn Intourist had been up to its old tricks. We had paid for soft class, but we, and everyone else, were on a new train that was all hard class with four to a compartment—everyone's reservation had been fouled up. We were in a carriage filled with the graduating class from an engineering school in Poitiers, France, along with the Dutch Canadian girl we had met on an earlier train, and an American exchange student from Cornell, who was very much impressed with the Soviet Union.

We reached the Polish frontier in the late afternoon and it was snowing. While we were still on the Soviet side of the frontier, passport and customs officers came through the train. They made the American student empty his pockets and give them his film and notebooks. He later got them back. They did this to every American as a matter of routine. Unfortunately for us, they were short of Americans that day and an officious Intourist official advised the officers that we should be investigated thoroughly. The Dutch girl knew German, as did the customs officer, so she acted as our interpreter. After a few questions, the officer wanted to see everything in our fourteen pieces of luggage. I began with my book box and handed him a stack of Japanese postcards. These were of little interest to him, so I handed him a pile of my research notes. These interested him even less. Obviously tired of the game, and with more people to see, he wished us a happy trip. The train moved forward a few hundred yards and then stopped. Three soldiers came through the train checking compartments and counting the number of passengers. One of them was tall and specialized in looking in the luggage racks. Other soldiers walked on top of the train while their colleagues looked under it. Only then were we allowed to cross the frontier, passing through lines of armed guards. Such scenes in which agents of the Soviet Union acted rudely, roughly, and completely without sensitivity made me even more sympathetic to the Chinese side of the dispute with Moscow.

We arrived in Warsaw in the evening, about thirty hours after leaving Leningrad. It was snowing and we waited half an hour for a taxi, which we shared with the Dutch girl to the Grand Hotel. We had no Polish money, so I gave the driver an American dollar, which, at the official exchange rate, equalled the fare. He gave me back the equivalent of two dollars American in Zloty in change. I had just made my first black market deal. We went upstairs in our hotel to the Olymp Bar where a quite magnificent band played "Puppet on a String." We felt we were once again in Europe. Wherever we went in Warsaw, we were sung at by moneychangers: "Do you want to change money?" It was never clear just who they were because it was usually done when we were in a crowd waiting to cross the street. The next afternoon I decided to buy a little more money and I went to look for a changer. After many cloak and dagger manoeuvres, I was finally asked seriously if I wanted to change money. I replied yes, but my request for two dollars worth was greeted with heavy scorn. Because the two dollars I offered were American, I feel I did the USA a disservice. The restored portion of Warsaw looked wonderful, but progress had not been as great as in Leningrad. Nonetheless, the city reminded me of drawings from children's fairy tales with stone buildings and irregular-tiled roofs, turrets, and cobblestone streets. With little Polish money, we set out on a quest to find an inexpensive eating place. We did: a milk bar. Never was a language barrier so great. Margo wanted bread and cheese. I got her hot milk and tea. I had an omelette with syrup, tea, and bread.

Once we left Poland by train on our way back to London, we stopped a couple of nights in West Berlin, which was still very much war-ravaged, with little to see. It was very expensive. Margo and I both found East and West Berlin depressing. I spent some time going from one to the other trying to retrieve a wristwatch. I had left it on the sleeping car we arrived on at East Berlin. Of course, there was no trace of it, but it was interesting to go through the process of applying to get it back. I checked our luggage through from Berlin to London. It was costly, but I had grown tired of lifting 350 pounds of Chinese rugs we had bought in Hong Kong, as well as gongs and books. On our arrival at Harwich, we had to pass through customs. The officer looked askance at our huge pile of luggage but let us through without a curious peek. Starved for news I could understand, I bought a copy of the *New Statesman*. There, to our amazement, was the story of Pierre Elliot Trudeau's elevation to prime minister. After being away for three months, it was great to be back in England. Then it began to rain...

My experience of the Soviet Union and Eastern Europe did not compare at all favourably with my previous experience in China. CITS treated its travellers like guests, while Intourist appeared to find them an inconvenience. Soviet society, unlike Chinese, was abusive of alcohol and less polite. Food and basic household goods appeared to be better distributed in China and more readily available. Judging by opera and ballet crowds, there was evidence in Russia of Djilas's "new class,"[24] while part of the purpose of Mao's Cultural Revolution was to nip in the bud such a tendency he saw growing among the Chinese Communist Party elites. The Soviet Union had denounced Stalin, but the Communist Party remained rigidly in power, supported by the military, its leaders emulating Stalin's style. By the spring of 1969, when a halt, but not an end, to the Cultural Revolution was called, the shattered Chinese Communist Party, still maintaining the efficacy of Comrade Stalin, was once again dominated by Mao Zedong, relying heavily upon the People's Liberation Army. In 1968, the state apparatus of the Soviet Union remained intact, but in China the organs of the state were severely damaged and the economy was in a slump, problems that the redoubtable Zhou Enlai set about to repair by attempting to be a pragmatic modernizer in the face of inflexible Mao Zedong thought.

My effort to return to China had been a failure, but my compromise gave me an opportunity to gain some perspective on the Cultural Revolution as seen by China's immediate neighbours. I looked forward to comparing notes with other China specialists in Prague in late August at the meeting of the Junior Sinologists. It was the time of the Prague Spring, the May upheavals in Paris, and the assassination in June of Robert Kennedy. The very morning of the day Margo and I were to leave London for the conference, Russian tanks moved into Prague[25]—our trip was cancelled. In early September 1968, Margo and I returned by ship to Canada, Margo to resume her position at the Correspondence School and I to assume the position of chair of the History Department, a position I held for five years.

CHAIRMAN ME

In June 1968, after Margo and I had returned to London, I began to receive phone calls from my colleague Fred de Luna. It seemed that Lewis H. Thomas, who had succeeded Don Wiedner as chair of the department, had had enough and wanted to resign. Fred was keen for me to let my name stand for the chairmanship. I was less keen but with each succeeding call Fred announced that support for me had increased. I looked on the selection process as one similar to penguins on an ice floe, pressing forward until one of them falls into the water. I finally agreed, saying that I would take the position as an acting chair for one year. Margo and I returned to Edmonton in early September, taking up residence in a larger apartment in a new building near our old one. As before, the de Lunas were in the same building. The History Department was also in a new location in the Henry Marshall Tory building where it had moved in the summer of 1965. Professor Lewis H. Thomas had managed the move and under his chairmanship the department had developed a new cohesion.

Assuming the chairmanship of an expanding department was a daunting task. Most of the members were young with less than a handful of the department being full professors. It was made clear to me from the start that I had everyone's support, but I had been around academic life long enough to know how quickly support can dissolve. With so many members of the department being new, a dozen or so having been hired within the first three years of my time as chair, I thought it was important for me to get to know everyone, paying them regular visits in their offices, and through an annual Chinese dinner to which all members of the department and their partners, along with chairs and their spouses from friendly departments, were invited. I felt it to be a good investment of my chair's honorarium. The dinners were held in the Bamboo Palace and catered by its owner, Ned Lee, an excellent chef, who once fed John Diefenbaker dim sum. Lee was a regular on local television cooking shows and a leader in the Chinese community.[26] The atmosphere was relaxed, particularly after the consumption of large quantities of pre-dinner sherry. The dinners were at least one way of bringing department members into direct contact with an important aspect of Chinese culture.

During my tenure as chair, the department underwent further expansion, offering women's history, black history, and history of Ukraine. By the end of my five-year term (1972–1973), the department numbered thirty full-time appointments, plus eight sessional instructors. The department's geographical reach was wide, offering courses in African, American, East and Southeast Asian, British, British Commonwealth, Canadian, European, Latin American, Russian, Ukraine, and diplomatic history. The department was intellectually lively and young, with a mix of personalities, some grating on others, but in a civil and generally good-humoured way. The university was suffering growing pains with space shortages, an ambitious construction program, and outside attacks over the number of Americans on its staff. Student radicals, some fashioning themselves as Maoists, sought to embarrass the upper administration and did so through marches and sit-ins. One radical student leader, John Bordo, borrowed the history departmental hammer in order to nail some demands to the office door of sociology.

While chair of the department, I continued to teach two courses (equivalent of four today), along with supervising honours and graduate students. In my last two years, I gained some relief from teaching through the work of a visiting professor. Leon Jankelevitch was French-born of Russian Jewish parents, a scholar of classical Chinese language, and a brilliant teacher. He had served in the French Foreign Service in China on Hainan Island before the revolution. He gave the impression of being anti-Chinese yet he and his wife had an adopted Chinese daughter on whom he doted and who was married to a French restaurateur in France. But Jankelevitch avoided returning to France because his brother Vladimir, who held the chair of moral philosophy at the Sorbonne, was a very controversial figure, often the centre of protests, and from time to time, thrown in jail. Jankelevitch taught in California, but was asked to leave because of his age, even though he had won teaching awards. He and I held different views on modern China, he being much more critical, but we were certainly compatible as colleagues. In fact, I took advantage of his presence and superb knowledge of written Chinese to deepen my knowledge of classical Chinese and Tang poetry, through private sessions spent reading classical texts. He was very deaf and his lectures could be heard well beyond the classroom door. Unfortunately, my term as chair ended during a budget crisis and it was impossible to extend his time in the department. His wife, who did all the negotiating for him, said sadly that they had no alternative but to return to France.

Jankelevitch was not the only addition to the department's East Asian section. The former Burmese ambassador to Canada and the USA, James Barrington, began his time at the university in the Political Science Department, but later he became a full-time member of history, offering courses on the history of Southeast Asia. His first-hand experience in diplomatic negotiations with Zhou Enlai, Mao Zedong, Lyndon Johnson, Lester Pearson, among others, made him a tremendous resource on the modern history of Asia. His self-deprecating manner and quiet style also made him a very popular teacher.

Apart from history, the department developed a program in Chinese and Japanese languages during my time as chair. The leader of this program was

Professor Hazel Jones, a specialist in the history of modern Japan, who, with the assistance of her friend Mrs. Miyakawa, set up a complete introductory program in Japanese. Because of her own experience, Hazel was able to attract funding from the Japan Foundation to assist with library-building and to fund instructors. Her role was matched by the work of Stanley R. Munro, a first-rate teacher of the Chinese language. In general, members of the department were very tolerant of these developments, particularly once the new East Asian Language program was housed elsewhere. Overall, development of the program was monitored by a committee on East Asian Studies, made up of scholars who were teaching in departments in the Faculty of Arts.[27]

I managed to survive five years as the chair of the department relatively unscathed (I think), but I remember being roasted twice by colleagues, both Canadianists. In the first case, in 1969, I extended a leave of absence taken by our Commonwealth historian in anticipation of her eventual return. She did not and we lost the position in the first round of university cutbacks in 1972–1973. My Canadianist colleague and good friend Robert Hett let me know that he had clearly predicted this would happen and I had to eat crow. The second incident did not involve a loss but a gain. In the spring of 1971, the department had a visitor from Harvard in Ukrainian history. He was excellent. That August, as the Social Credit government was dying, the department received an offer from the provincial Department of Education to make his appointment full-time and in the base budget. It was late in the summer and few of my colleagues were around. I tried it out on one or two of them and they said yes. Not long afterward, a different Canadianist and friend David Hall visited me to express, in the strongest terms, his disapproval of how things had been done. I agreed one should not allow the government, or others outside the department, to dictate its staffing, and that one must look fully and carefully into the mouth of every gift horse. In this case, I thought I had, and it turned out to be a very a good one.

My time as chair did not go unmarked by personal sadness. In 1968, after thirty-seven years in Taber, Alberta, my parents were given a big send-off when they moved to be near my sister Mary in the resort town of Sylvan Lake. They moved when I was travelling in Europe, so I did not have a chance for one last visit to the old house or to retain souvenirs of my youth which they, probably wisely, threw out, or gave to the new town library. My parents moved into a small house not far from the lakeshore and not far from my sister's home. There they entertained their growing number of grandchildren, gardened, and got to know their neighbours. Margo and I tried to visit at least once a month, and we managed a ten-day family trip to Vancouver and Victoria in the late spring of 1969. However, three years after moving to the greener pastures of Sylvan Lake, my mother died at the age of seventy-six. She fell in the garden late in August 1971 and broke her hip, but the doctor diagnosed her condition as one of a bad back and gave her some painkillers. She died at home on September 8, a couple of days before her birthday. I took her death badly. I was due to pay my parents a visit the weekend before she died, but I had to take care of a professor from Australia on a short visit to Edmonton and could not make the trip. Margo and I went to Sylvan Lake for the funeral and made the trip back with the casket to Edmonton where she is buried. It was a cold day with snow flurries. My mother was a gentle, kind lady, who after a hard life on the dried-out prairie deserved more time by the lake.

ALBERTA AND THE FURTHER WEST

Politically, it was an opportune time for the promotion of East Asian Studies. The Conservative government of Premier Peter Lougheed had launched an effort to expand the markets for Alberta beef, canola, and oil field technology, looking westward to East Asia as a prime target. Agreements for mutual benefit were reached with Kangwon province in South Korea, Hokkaido in Japan, and by 1980, an agreement in principal was reached with Heilongjiang province in China. Lougheed considered linguistic and cultural understanding as basic to the growth of these relationships. To facilitate Alberta's outreach to Asia, the Alberta government established offices in Tokyo and Hong Kong. Initially, the Tokyo office handled Korean affairs until an Alberta representative was appointed to Seoul within the Canadian Embassy.

Moreover, Lougheed was anxious for the University of Alberta to have the resources to support his initiatives. By the spring of 1978, the new Department of East Asian Languages and Literatures cleared most of the lower-level university hurdles, but it still faced top-level committees and the Board of Governors. There was little opposition save for one very British member of a planning committee who voiced a concern that it was all a waste of time because every Chinese would soon be speaking English. The proposal for setting up the department passed to the Board of Governors where I sat as an elected academic representative. I had the pleasure to speak to it and to the work of all my colleagues. Approved by the Board, the proposal went to the provincial Department of Higher Education for funding and in the spring of

1979 the department was formally established within the Faculty of Arts. It was given temporary space in a house on Saskatchewan Drive and an acting chair, which turned out to be me, was appointed while a search for a full-term chair was carried out. In the summer of 1981, Stanley Munro was named the new chair. The following April, Hazel Jones left Edmonton to take up residence in Japan, never to return to the university or to the department that she had worked so long and hard to establish.

Meanwhile, the university was recruiting more and more Asian students, particularly from Hong Kong, Malaysia, Taiwan, and Singapore. They were joined in the early 1980s by increasing numbers of students from China. On the students' own initiative, they laid long-term plans to establish a library of Chinese language books and periodicals primarily for student use, but open to the broader community. Students Lawrence Lau and Kim Hung began the library in 1970, taking two shelves in my office for a once-a-week distribution of reading materials. They soon outgrew my office and were given a small office within the department, but this too proved too small. Eventually, the Chinese Library Association was allowed to take over the old law library reading room in Rutherford South, before moving to a lounge in HUB Mall on campus. In the spring of 2010, the library moved downtown to the Chinese multicultural centre where it continues to function as a valuable supplementary source for students at the university learning Chinese.

It took eighteen years, from my first appointment in Chinese history to the establishment of the Department of East Asian Languages and Literatures, and a great deal of volunteer effort on the part of professors in the humanities and social sciences to achieve success in establishing East Asian Studies at the university. The East Asian Studies Committee constructed a BA program in East Asian Studies to which the teaching of languages was key. In the beginning, before languages were offered, our best students were sent to other places to learn Chinese and Japanese. To many in the university and the province, this was a satisfactory situation. They did not take seriously Canada's growing involvement with Asia and Alberta's role in it.

Underlying this view was a 1964 report of the Canadian Universities Foundation's Commission on International Studies in Canada, chaired by Professor Norman MacKenzie, a former president of UBC.[28] The report concluded that during the next decades, three universities should be encouraged to develop Asian Studies: UBC, U of T, and one francophone institution yet to be identified. Unfortunately, this three-centres-only view became fixed in the long-range plans of the federal government well beyond 1974. The U of A committee was of a different view. It was building a strong language program that quickly outstripped the enrolments at UBC and Toronto. Moreover, the Japan Foundation recognized its importance and had regularly included Alberta in its annual book donation and staff support programs. The university enjoyed the personal support of a series of Japanese Consuls-General who served in Edmonton. Between the university and the government, a critical mass had developed in Edmonton that was favourably received internationally, but which was not accepted nationally. Matters came to a head in 1986 when the Japan Foundation gave the federal government six million dollars for Japanese studies in Canada and it promptly divided it among UBC, McGill (with Université de Montréal), and University of Toronto (with York University). My loud protest on behalf of the University of Alberta, backed by the Government of Alberta, brought about a reconsideration, but not a victory. The money was divided two-thirds to the three major (so-called) centres, with the remainder shared among six institutions, of which Alberta was one. Thus, the largest Asian Studies program in the country received one of the smallest shares. It was difficult to overcome another prejudice in Ottawa, which held that Alberta was rich and could fund itself. Meanwhile, the Alberta government provided funds for educational and cultural exchanges with its three sister provinces in Asia: Heilongjiang (China), Hokkaido (Japan), and Kangwon (South Korea). On alternative years, the History Department sent its students to Heilongjiang and Hokkaido to further their language training.

The University of Alberta Asian Studies program grew and consolidated during its first decade. It passed internal and external reviews with flying colours, but under Dean of Arts Patricia Clements it was transformed into the Department of Asian Studies in 1994. This action flew in the face of the concept of the original committee, which was to integrate the study of Asia among departments in a multidisciplinary way. Instead, some departments are content to leave the task to the East Asian Studies Department. From the late 1980s to the mid-1990s, the university developed closer ties with Chinese, Korean, and Japanese universities, particularly in the fields of education, science, engineering, agriculture, and pharmacy and medicine, following the interests demonstrated and encouraged by the Province of Alberta. The Department of East Asian Studies introduced courses in the Korean language and the Economics, Political Science and History departments held a series of conferences with Yonsei University in Seoul. In the twenty-first century, the

Alberta government has been less aggressive in its approach to East Asia, and the university's Korean interests have been muted to a degree. With the rise of China, however, more and more departments throughout the university have developed a China dimension, but with less attention paid to Japan.

Although it took many years to establish East Asian Studies as part of the Faculty of Arts and the program has won national and international recognition, it remains vulnerable to the old thinking that Asia need not be a focus of study in all Canadian universities. The department has weathered the threat of extinction at the outset of the new century at the hands of a dean of arts appointed from outside who had to be educated on just why Asia is so important to Alberta. New-style university administrators who concentrate on the bottom line easily lose sight of the academic goals of universities in the search for a budget cut.

My experience as a university administrator, and in developing the program in East Asian Studies, as well as my brief experience in China, enabled me to adjust quickly to life in the Canadian Embassy in Beijing, to which I would be appointed as cultural officer for a year in July 1973. The Cultural Revolution as I witnessed it influenced my study of China. I was now less of a nineteenth-century diplomatic historian and more of a budding student of the history of contemporary China. Moreover, I became greatly interested in Canada–China relations to the point of offering a course in Canadian–East Asian relations after my return to the university in 1974.

FIVE

Old Dog, New Tricks

During my time as a PhD student and the first decade of teaching at the University of Alberta, I had come to think of myself as a specialist in late Qing Dynasty (1644–1912) history. Like the proverbial chicken that will not deviate from a line drawn in the sand, I did not stray far from my specialty. To be sure, the courses I taught dealt with China up to the founding of the People's Republic of China and a little beyond, but I was not what was called "a China-watcher." Even on my first trip to China in June 1964, I was most interested in Qing Dynasty sites, to the extent that when I was asked in October 1964 to give a talk to the U of A Geographical Society, I dedicated most of the evening to Yunnan province in the nineteenth century. Even my illustrated lectures at the University of Toronto and Harvard were along the lines of "what I saw in China last June." Moreover, in November 1964, the lecture I gave to the local Philosophical Society entitled "Chairman Mao Is a Member of Our Commune," made me nervous because it was a "little out of my field."

To be sure, I had opinions about Mao's China based on what I had seen and heard while there, but I was not familiar, except in a broad sense, with the policies and personalities of contemporary China. Trying to make sense to my students of the Cultural Revolution that began in May 1966, however, drew me into a more serious study of Maoism and Communist China. By the time of my first sabbatical leave beginning in July 1967, I found that I could not ignore events in China, if only for the fact that they were fouling up my research plans. On my return to Edmonton in September 1968, I was much more engaged with the study of current events in China. As fate would have it, five years later I was given the opportunity of a lifetime to observe China first-hand for a year at a time when it remained closed to Western academic researchers. Not only was I able to become an inside China-watcher, but I was, at the same time, able to play a small role in Canada–China relations, the history of which I was soon to learn.

Direct relations between Canada and China were limited in the first decades of the twentieth century. From the end of the nineteenth century, Canada had trade commissioners overseas with offices established in Shanghai and briefly in Tianjin. The Chinese had a representative in Ottawa and consuls in Vancouver and Winnipeg. Immigration was handled separately by Ottawa, but Canada remained content to have its diplomatic relations with China handled by the British and to enjoy the special privileges that the British had garnered during its wars with China. In fact, Canada was very slow to establish diplomatic posts abroad. The Department of External Affairs was formed in 1909: Canada's first missions were established in Britain (1880), France (1882), and the United States (1926). After considerable debate, and in the face of strong opposition from the Conservative Party, who regarded it as an unnecessary break from Britain, the Liberal government of Mackenzie King formalized relations with Japan in 1928. Pressure mounted to do the same with the new Republic of China established in Nanjing in 1927, but Ottawa relied on the embassy in Tokyo to cover China. This proved problematic when Japan extended its empire on mainland Asia at the expense of China.

The Canadian government also received information about China from Canadian missionaries and, as could be expected, the views of those engaged in work in China were different from those working in Japan and within its expanding empire. Between July 1923 and the Japanese attack on Pearl Harbor in Hawaii on December 7, 1941, the size of the Chinese community in Canada shrank as a number of people returned to China and Hong Kong. Some rejoined their families, from whom they had been separated without hope of reunion in Canada because of the Exclusion Act, while others had given-up hope of succeeding in a country that had no use for them in its state of economic depression. Still others went back home to die as they had reached an age beyond employment in Canada.

After Pearl Harbor, Canada joined in the war against Japan as an ally of China. Moreover, in the months prior, Canadian troops were sent to Hong Kong to defend the colony against the Japanese. Hong Kong fell to the Japanese on Christmas Day 1941; Canadian troops were killed, or taken captive by the Japanese to experience horrendous conditions in Japanese prisoner of war camps. Within Canada, sympathy for China, growing since the Japanese invasion of Manchuria in September 1931, grew stronger by the time the Japanese launched their invasion south of the Great Wall in July 1937. Pearl Harbor not follow—no Canadian embassy was ever established there. The Chinese ambassador in Ottawa remained as the accredited representative of the Republic of China whose capital was now Taipei. This arrangement remained in place until October 1970. Chester Ronning, the Canadian representative in Nanjing, stayed on, expecting Canada to recognize the new Communist government in Beijing, but early in 1951, following the outbreak of the Korean War and the subsequent branding of China by the United Nations as an aggressor, he was ordered to close Canada's embassy in China and to return to Canada.

Although there were times when Canada seemed prepared to recognize the new government in Beijing, it was not until the prime ministership of Pierre Trudeau that it happened. In 1961, Prime Minister John Diefenbaker initiated the signing of the first of a series of annual wheat agreements with China, a major fillip to the farmers of western Canada. Grain ships left British Columbia for China, in spite of American criticism, and US government efforts to prevent Canadian shippers from obtaining the pumps needed to load them. Opinion polls taken throughout the 1960s showed Canadians were split on the issue of the recognition of China. Generally, the west was of the view: "If they are good enough to trade with, they are good enough to recognize." But central Canada, particularly Quebec, was not enthused. At a meeting on international affairs, sponsored by the University of Alberta and the University of Calgary, held in Banff in August 1965, Paul Martin Sr., Secretary of State for External Affairs in the Lester Pearson Liberal government, was bombarded with questions on why Canada had not recognized the People's Republic of China; was it due to American pressure? Martin parried the questions skilfully, alluding to a number of factors among which American pressure was but one. Those of us in attendance remained unconvinced. In the lounge after Mr. Martin's performance, someone asked his executive assistant: "If the United States recognized China tomorrow, how long would it take Canada?" "About sixty seconds," came the reply. Nearly thirty years later, at a conference on Canada and China held in Montebello, Quebec, Mr. Martin, long out of office, confided to us China specialists in attendance that one of the key factors delaying Canada's recognition of China was the anti-Beijing attitude of the Catholic Church in Quebec and its influence.

Western Canada was increasingly unhappy with Ottawa's failure to recognize the People's Republic of China. Ever since the wheat sales to China of 1961, the farmers on the Prairies had come to rely upon the China market. Advocates of a policy of recognition had a ready audience in western Canada. At a meeting

united Canadian opinion in favour of China against Japan, as Canada an[
became allies. Meanwhile, anti-Japanese sentiments, always latent, l
overt and gathered strength. In 1942, the King government, respon
unproven charges that the Japanese Canadian community on the we:
harboured spies and fifth columnists, ordered the evacuation of all Ja
from the Pacific coast to a depth of 350 miles inland. Their propertie
confiscated and they were herded like cattle onto trains bound for ca
the interior of British Columbia.

Under these circumstances, the Canadian government established re
with the Chinese government of Chiang Kai-shek headquartered in the
Chongqing (Chungking), high up along the Yangzi River, where it had re
in the face of the Japanese assault. Ignoring advice that Canada's amba
should be someone familiar with China, a civilian, and not from Brit
lumbia, King chose Major General Victor Wentworth Odlum, a Libei
former newspaper publisher from British Columbia. In June 1943, M:
Chiang Kai-shek, the striking Soong Meiling, visited Canada as part of he
of North America to bring China's struggle to the attention of its alli
June 16 she addressed a joint session of the House and Senate, the first fo
dignitary to do so. Her speech was impressive, delivered in flawless Engli
she was a graduate of Wellesley College in the United States. From his
iour during the visit, and from the entries in his diaries, it is abundantl
that Prime Minister King was completely charmed. In November, Cai
representation in Chongqing was raised to the level of ambassador. D
the next three years, Odlum discussed plans for Canada–China relation
the war, including matters of immigration and postwar assistance. Durii
war, Western powers gave up their special privileges in China given und
Unequal Treaties and pressure began to build for Canada to end its excl
of Chinese immigrants, but the Exclusion Act was not amended until 19

Canada's first embassy in China, opened in Chongqing in 1942 under O
was small. The compound where the embassy and its staff was housec
noisy and rat-infested. It was not a desirable posting. In 1946, the eml
moved to Nanjing, following the Nationalist (KMT Guomindang) Repub
government as it re-established itself in its original capital. Conditions
better but still difficult. Civil conflict between the Nationalist and Comm
parties broke out soon after the war's end, leading to the proclamation o
People's Republic of China, on October 1, 1949. The Republican governi
under Chiang Kai-shek withdrew to Taiwan, but the Canadian Embass)

in Banff in August 1966, bringing together academics and foreign and Canadian diplomats, China and the Vietnam War were the prime topics. Among those in attendance were Paul T.K. Lin, a Chinese Canadian back in Canada after fifteen years in China working in Beijing, sometimes with Zhou Enlai; Chester Ronning, a retired diplomat fresh from debriefings in Ottawa and Washington after his peace mission to Hanoi; Ivan Head, a professor of international law at the University of Alberta who was soon thereafter to become foreign affairs advisor to Trudeau; and myself. The conference strongly reiterated to the government the importance of recognizing Beijing. Two years later, Pierre Trudeau, Canada's new prime minister, pledged during the general election campaign to recognize China. It took some time to accomplish. The sticking point was the status of Taiwan.

TRUDEAU'S FAR WEST

During his first year in office, Trudeau ordered a review of Canada's foreign policy and consulted widely on the issue of foreign relations. On March 12, 1969, along with about a dozen other academics representing a range of foreign policy interests, I, on Ivan Head's recommendation, was invited to 24 Sussex Drive for a dinner and an evening seminar on foreign policy conducted by our host, Pierre Elliot Trudeau. An aspiring sinologist and a historian of nineteenth-century China, I half-suspected they had invited the wrong person, so I nervously pressed the doorbell at the Prime Minister's residence after being delivered to 24 Sussex by Margo's sister and brother-in-law who happened to live in Ottawa. Expecting to meet a valet or butler, I was completely nonplussed to be welcomed by Trudeau himself, who took my hat and coat and said with a warm smile, "So pleased you could make it Brian Evans. Ivan has told me of your China prowess." Ivan, he explained, was absent due to a bout of the flu.

When we were all seated at dinner, Trudeau broke into the general hubbub and began to ask questions. One political scientist suggested our role in NATO was ineffective and another said we would have more influence out of NATO than in. "No one knew we were in NATO until we said we might get out," Trudeau quipped. He was due to meet US President Richard Nixon that same month before the Department of External Affairs finished the foreign policy review he had requested. "If you say we are to withdraw after you have seen Nixon, then you embarrass him. If you say on your return we are staying in, everyone will say—we know why," were the comments offered. To this Trudeau responded, "Perhaps I should not tell tales out of school, but I am a bit of a politician in this. When I announced the foreign policy review should be complete by March 15, I already knew I would be seeing Nixon on the 23rd, although it was not yet announced. The opposition said the 15th was too early and more time was needed. I offered the 30th. Now the opposition is on record asking me to delay my review until after I see Nixon."

The discussion continued on these broader lines and on the meal's completion everyone withdrew to the drawing room for coffee. I asked for tea and found myself drinking Chinese tea with Trudeau. I asked him if he had had any protests over his China policy. "A few grumbles, but nothing in the form of a formal protest from the US," he replied. "And the Russians?" I asked, unaware he had been briefed by the Soviet ambassador for forty minutes earlier in the day. "I cannot really say anything about that," he responded, before asking me how I thought "our China policy" would work out. I thought he was joking, but he assured me he was not. "But surely," I said, "we are recognizing Beijing—De Gaulle showed the way. Taiwan will withdraw recognition." "Ah," he rejoined, "but we do not know all about the French recognition. De Gaulle made the grand gesture, but we do not know exactly what went on between France and Taiwan. We may find out when those fellows have to move out of their embassy here. But what do we do if Chiang Kai-shek says he will give up claims to China, if we will accept separate status for Taiwan?" I looked at him in disbelief. "It will never happen." He said, "I don't think so, but what if it does?" I responded, "It will be a diplomatic breakthrough." He countered, "But for whom?" I told him back in Edmonton we were working on a plan to swap Vancouver Island for Taiwan. He laughed at this, but one of the other guests from Victoria objected. Trudeau then asked me about the border troubles between the Soviet Union and China. I replied I was so pro-China I was willing to believe the Russians provoked them. "What's in it for the Russians?" he then asked, but we were interrupted, and the discussion went unfinished.

Later that evening, a more general conversation ensued about anti-ballistic missiles and other matters until someone among the guests attacked the Department of External Affairs as rigid and using out-of-date methods. Trudeau agreed, saying he had been trying to shake them up, but with no success. Another guest, a former diplomat turned academic, defended the department, its traditions, and the system that required the lower appointees to report only to those immediately above them. Everything he said confirmed Trudeau's view that nothing new came out of the system, just the same old policies, nothing creative, albeit of high quality. As the evening broke up, I noticed, to my great embarrassment, I was still wearing toe rubbers on my shoes. It was not a fashion statement I had wanted to make, but it was a fair indication of how awed I could be by power, particularly when wielded by a gracious and intelligent host, who just happened to be the prime minister of Canada.

Eight months later, I saw Trudeau again, but this time I was properly shod. Further foreign policy consultations took place at the Liberal Party policy conference at Harrison Hot Springs in November 1969, to which I was invited. On this occasion, there was a foreign policy panel organized and chaired by Mel Hurtig. At the time, Hurtig was a Trudeau enthusiast.[1] He was also the dynamic owner of Hurtig's Books, an intellectual oasis in downtown Edmonton. Hurtig did much to bring town and gown together; he was a generous host at book signings and promotions. He had travelled to Japan and succeeded in becoming the Canadian distributor for Tuttle of Vermont, a publisher who specialized in works on Asia, particularly Japan. He began to publish reprints of early works on Canadian exploration, eventually leading him to the production of the *Canadian Encyclopedia*. Among the panel he put together at Harrison were advocates of withdrawal from NATO, and for a change in Canada-Asia policy. My contribution was a rather blunt call for Canada to look at Asia as it was, not as we wanted it to be. My paper was found useful for the review of Canadian foreign policy, which became the box of four booklets published in 1970 called *Foreign Policy for Canadians*. At the conference, one young Liberal from British Columbia, David Anderson, strongly objected to my reference to Hong Kong and other European outposts in Asia as the flotsam and jetsam of imperialism.[2]

At the time of the Harrison conference, Trudeau's campaign promise to recognize the People's Republic of China remained unrealized, stalled over the question of Taiwan. Fitful talks were taking place in Stockholm, where both countries had embassies. Moreover, John Diefenbaker was badgering Trudeau about it in the House of Commons. Diefenbaker, whose government had scored a breakthrough on wheat sales, was unhappy with Trudeau's approach. He had learned from the *Canadian Intelligence Report*, a Right-wing publication, that Professor Paul Lin of McGill had just visited China.

Paul Lin was a controversial figure, at least as far as the Right-wing and pro-Taiwan (Nationalist/Guomindang/KMT) forces were concerned. Born in Kamloops, B.C., Lin took a degree in business at Harvard shortly before the Communist victory in China. He had organized pro-revolution Chinese students in the United States, and like many overseas Chinese at that time, Lin went to Beijing to help build a new China. In China he was involved in communications, radio, and film. His voice was a familiar one on China English-language broadcasts and on film soundtracks. Through marriage, he was related to the Soong family and to Sun Yat-sen's widow, Soong Chingling, who was a non-Communist honorary president of the People's Republic of China. In 1965, on the eve of the Cultural Revolution, Lin and his family returned to Canada, to Vancouver where he took up a temporary position at UBC. Not long after, he moved to McGill to head the Asian Studies Department there. He was a popular lecturer and much sought after for his first-hand knowledge of China and its leaders. On his return to Canada, he was met by a series of hostile editorials and reports, inspired by Taiwan. He was said to be Zhou Enlai's agent and the future choice for ambassador to China from Canada. Based upon this speculation, Diefenbaker attempted to establish a link between Lin and Trudeau. Trudeau's response was unequivocal:

> The right hon. member said that I was a friend of Professor Lin, a person I have never met and whom I do not know. Second, the right hon. member stated that he had reported to me. That is another falsehood. I have never met him nor read any of his papers.[3]

This was no doubt true, but Paul Lin was well known to Ivan Head, Trudeau's friend and foreign affairs adviser who, along with Lin, had participated in the 1966 Banff conference on international affairs. At an evening reception at the Harrison policy conference, I saw Trudeau surrounded by a group of eager Liberals.

"Prime Minister," I called, "I know Paul Lin!"

"You know Paul Lin?"

"Yes!"

"Well, why hasn't he reported to me?"

Trudeau's eyes were dancing and he grinned broadly as he spoke.

The recognition talks languished in Stockholm, entering a period that the Chinese call "duck diplomacy": on the surface, matters appear calm, but there is a lot of activity going on underneath. This lasted until September 1970, when Canada came up with an acceptable formula on Taiwan. It was simplicity itself, but effective. It is generally credited to Mitchell Sharp,[4] then Secretary of State for External Affairs (1968–1974). The document announcing agreement on mutual recognition, dated October 13, 1970, barely fills one page, but the key clause reads: "The Chinese Government reaffirms that Taiwan is an inalienable part of the territory of the People's Republic of China. The Canadian Government takes note of this position of the Chinese Government." It was a formula that thirty or more other countries would adopt as the log jam on recognizing China was broken. The step was taken sixteen months before Richard Nixon's famous journey to the Great Wall in February 1972, and over eight years before Washington and Beijing agreed to exchange ambassadors in January 1979.[5] Canadian diplomats and the Prime Minister's Office (PMO) were particularly proud, the pride Canadians feel when they manage to do something before the Americans. It is often stated, incorrectly, that Canada was the first Western country to recognize the People's Republic of China. This is patently false given that Britain had recognized it in 1950 and France in 1964, to name just two. Canada was, however, to succeed in the midst of the heated anti-Western rhetoric of the Cultural Revolution, which Mao Zedong launched in August 1966 and two years later spun out of control.[6]

Ironically, when official recognition was announced on October 13, 1970, Canada was pre-occupied with the October Crisis and it did not gain the attention of most Canadians. Arthur Andrew, director-general of the Asia Pacific Bureau and former Canadian ambassador to Sweden, took the ambassador of the Republic of China out to dinner the evening of the day the new Canadian policy on China was announced. It was a fine meal at Madame Burger's in Hull, Quebec, widely considered to be the best restaurant in the Ottawa area. The street in front of the restaurant was patrolled by Canadian troops. It was the ambassador's second meal at Madame Burger's in as many days; Mitchell Sharp gave him lunch there on the October 12, also under the watchful eyes of Canadian troops. Before lunch, the ambassador handed Sharp a letter stating that the instant Canada recognized Beijing, the Republic of China would cease to recognize Canada. Trudeau's fear of a separate status for Taiwan vanished. The Republic of China closed its embassy in Ottawa on October 13, 1970, the day Canada recognized the People's Republic of China, just as the ambassador had told Sharp they would.

OPENING DOORS IN CHINA

Late in 1970, a team under the direction of John Fraser, who was in charge of the China desk in the Department of External Affairs, and a former high commissioner to Hong Kong, went to Beijing to prepare for the opening of a Canadian embassy in 1971. Canada was offered a small vacant embassy at 571 San Li tun. It was an unfortunate number given the political events in China that spring. A military uprising called Project 571 was planned for May and its code name was Wu Chi I (571), the sound of which can mean "May 1971" or "a military uprising." Consequently, shipments destined for the Canadian Embassy came under suspicion and were subject to delays. Nevertheless, the embassy was in order for the first ambassador, Ralph Edgar Collins, a senior member of External Affairs, the son of Chinese missionaries, and a graduate of the University of Alberta, to assume his tenure beginning April 8, 1971.[7] After Collins retired a little more than a year later in June 1972, John Small, another "mish kid," succeeded him.[8]

In July 1973, almost a year to the month that Small was appointed as ambassador, I was appointed to the embassy for a year as part of an experiment. Because the Department of External Affairs did not have enough officers with China expertise, it opted to supplement the staff of the new embassy with a Canadian academic, trained in Chinese studies, to serve as the cultural officer. Ideally, the academic would spend half of their time dealing with embassy affairs and the other half on academic research and study. A diplomatic appointment was a boon to a Canadian academic because it provided unprecedented access to China at a time when academic exchanges did not exist and visas to study in China were very difficult to obtain. This experiment lasted for thirty years until the Department of Foreign Affairs and International Trade felt that it had an ample number of diplomats with China experience, and academics were increasingly reluctant to take up the position because direct access to China for full-time research was easy. The title of the academic portion of the job was sinologist-in-residence. The holder was assigned a diplomatic rank in keeping with their experience. The first to serve was Professor William Saywell of the University of Toronto. He was a specialist in modern China and a catalyst in the development of East Asian Studies at the University of Toronto and across Canada. He took up the position of Sinologist-in-residence and First Secretary in Charge of Cultural Affairs in July 1972. His appointment was for one year. In the early winter of 1972–1973, the Department of External Affairs began looking for recruits to replace him. I was asked to apply, and to my surprise and delight I was selected. It was said among colleagues in Toronto that it was because I was from the West. This may be partly true. Within the embassy I found an unconscious bias in favour of central Canada and British

Columbia, with little real knowledge of the Prairies, and a tendency to ignore its universities in favour of Toronto, McGill, Queen's, and UBC.

Although I had to report to the embassy in July, Margo followed later, after the debilitating heat of a Beijing summer, and when our apartment was ready for occupancy. She arrived in Hong Kong in September where I went to meet her. We each had diplomatic passports, which made border crossing a mere formality. Margo fell in love with China immediately and became a fascinated observer of Chinese life wherever we went.

Prior to my departure from Canada, like other embassy staff I spent a number of days in Ottawa for briefings from relevant agencies and government departments. In addition, there was a security briefing on how to conduct myself in a communist country. Lacking any information on China, those doing the briefing used materials and film related to the Soviet Union. They were sure that all communist states were alike, but not everything translated. It would be very bad indeed to be found in bed with a blonde Chinese who was not your wife! After my Ottawa briefings, I returned to the University of Alberta to wrap up my lectures on modern China. On the final day of class, a young man came up to the front of the class to the lectern and told me he was with the RCMP, but that his purpose was "to learn about China." Later, just before I left for China, another RCMP officer visited me in my office to invite me to keep my eyes open for anything untoward I could report to the force.[9]

I arrived in Beijing on a scorching hot mid-July day by plane from Guangzhou to be greeted by Saywell,[10] who during the next few days introduced me to the job. I concluded it required a whirling dervish not an academic. He told me the ambassador was away, the First Secretary Consular John Paynter was on the brink of leaving,[11] the embassy was being painted on the inside, and the apartment he occupied would be mine, but only after he left and things were done to it. And, by the way, was I interested in buying some steaks he had left over?

It would soon become obvious to me that the academic side of my appointment was impossible to carry out. Libraries were closed and academics of repute under suspicion. I became, in fact, a full-time embassy officer. There were a couple of academic activities attached to it. There were regular meetings with members of other embassies who were China-watchers. The dean of the group was Steve Fitzgerald, an Australian professor, who was his country's ambassador. At times, we pooled our ignorance, but often there was reliable inside information to be gleaned. The other academic aspect of the job occurred weekly, when possible, when language sessions were held with Professor Wang Benxu. The Cultural Revolution had put Wang's career on hold. A graduate of Beijing University (Beida) in the early 1950s, and a champion speed skater who had trained in Norway, Wang was the son of a factory owner and thus relegated in the Cultural Revolution to the lower rungs of the class ladder. His wife was a career diplomat, posted abroad, where he could not go, so the Chinese Diplomatic Service Bureau (DSB) assigned him to the task of giving language lessons to diplomats.[12]

An academic entering an embassy to work faced a number of potential pitfalls, ranging from how to work inside a security-conscious environment to the possible animosity of professional diplomats toward a well-meaning amateur. As mentioned earlier, the ambassador I served under, John Small, was a mish kid, born of parents connected to a Canadian Methodist mission in Sichuan. Prior to Beijing, he was Canada's representative in Pakistan. Small was pragmatic, tolerant, humane, and virtually unflappable, a down-to-earth gentleman. I have warm memories of my year at the embassy under Small. He tolerated my eccentric behaviour, which included not wearing a tie very often, and my sense of humour. One evening, thanks to him, I was present at his official residence when Qiao Guanhua, China's Deputy Foreign Minister (later Foreign Minister), was a guest. Small managed to keep him late, drinking his favourite Maotai as he spoke to us of China's foreign policy and of his days as a student in Germany.

Because China was now a priority in Canadian foreign policy, a bright and able group of Foreign Service officers were assigned to Beijing. The next senior member of the embassy was the Minister-Counsellor Maurice Copithorne, a graduate in law from UBC, a scholarly figure with a boyish grin. He had a good sense of humour, but not when it came to poor prose. Political Officer Don Waterfall,[13] a PhD in philosophy from Yale, had excellent linguistic skills to assist ultimately Ottawa, but not Copithorne, in China-watching. The senior commercial officer, Bob Godson, had a permanent private residence in Hong Kong, and a deep knowledge of business on the China coast. He was joined by Armand Blum, another senior commercial officer who was originally French but with a career in the Canadian Foreign Service. Blum was a great cook; his idea of basic supplies included multiple cases of cognac. Blum and Godson also worked with a junior member, John Higginbotham, who was trained in economics at McGill. He brought a quick and restless mind full of innovative ideas and offbeat humour to the job. Still another member of the economic group was Margaret Cornish from Toronto, who was actually a Chinese hero.[14] In charge of consular matters was Gilliane Lapointe, whose linguistic prowess would later be on display during Trudeau's visit to China. She possessed a robust sense of humour and an infinite capacity for difficult work. Bruce Jutzi, quiet and efficient, was the officer in charge of embassy administration. The military attaché was another "mish kid," Colonel David Struthers, a senior member of the Armed Services, with a calm exterior under which lay great wisdom and a gentle sense of humour. Like the ambassador, he was born in China in Shandong where his father was a medical missionary. His secretary, an officer named Victor Lee, spent his youth in Shanghai during the Japanese occupation of the International Settlement in 1941–1945, much of the time in a small room in his family's apartment. The 1984 novel, *Empire of the Sun*, by J.G. Ballard tells of a young boy's similar experience in Shanghai at this time.[15]

Beyond the confines of the embassy were two members of the press from Canada stationed in Beijing: John R. Walker for The Canadian Press, and John Burns of the *Globe and Mail*.[16] Embassies tended to be wary of reporters from their own countries. Burns, in particular, filed a number of stories raising issues that had repercussions on the work of the embassy. Although I had good relations with Burns and Walker, I formed a close friendship with the correspondent for the *London Times*. David Bonavia was one, if not the only one, of the English-language newspaper correspondents in Beijing who was a trained sinologist. A student of Chinese under E.G. Pulleyblank at Cambridge,[17] he graduated with a double first in French and German and Chinese. He had previously learned Russian as a hobby while at school. In 1967, he joined the *London Times*, reporting from Hong Kong and Saigon. He married Judy, an Australian journalist and author from Perth, and in 1969 they moved to the *Times* bureau in Moscow. Three years later, he and Judy were expelled from Moscow because of contacts they had with dissidents. Reassigned to Beijing as the first *Times* correspondent since the revolution, David was welcomed by the Chinese who were engaged in a bitter ideological dispute with the Soviets. Judy and David worked as a team throughout David's career, which ended sadly due to complications from the abuse of alcohol. The Bonavias left Beijing in 1975 for Hong Kong where they had an apartment on Pokfulam Road.

Throughout the remainder of his China career, David lived sometimes in Hong Kong and sometimes in Beijing hotels. He filed stories for the *Far Eastern Economic Review* and for the *Times*. While Margo and I were in Beijing, we lived in the same apartment block on Jianguomenwai, overlooking the willow-lined moat and the tower atop of which were Jesuit-designed astronomical instruments. As products of British-style sinology, we became good friends, often having meals together in the nearby International Club, or drinks on the big red Chinese drum he and Judy used as a coffee table.

While my role in Beijing had changed greatly since last visiting China as a tourist, the city of Beijing in the early 1970s appeared little changed from when I saw it in June 1964, just two years before the Cultural Revolution. The Stalinist wedding-cake-spired buildings that housed the major government ministries remained the dominant features of the skyline. They now sported the only neon signs in the city, proclaiming, "*Mao Zhuxi Wansui*" ("Long Live Chairman Mao"), which were turned off after 9:00 in the evening when most folks were expected to be at home in bed. There were a few more low-rise apartment buildings, but the core of the city remained the same. Much had been going on underground with the building of a metro, and the creation of underground shelters, including hotels, hospitals, and stores in case of an attack by the Soviet Union. This was all done in keeping with Mao's dictum: "Dig tunnels deep, store grain everywhere." When driving about the city, one could see the Temple of Heaven and Coal Hill, icons of the imperial past, silhouetted against the sky. In 1964, the city of Beijing began to knock down the old Beijing city wall; it was now a road.

There were more people in Beijing in the 1970s, of course, and more cars. The taxis and diplomatic cars were now in the main Toyotas or some Western European models instead of Polish Warsawas and Chinese Shanghais built from Mercedes Benz dies. The leadership relied on home-built Red Flags, large luxurious cars, usually in black. The Public Security Bureau had a fleet of British Jaguars. Traffic was still a mix of bicycles, two-wheeled tractor carts with high handle bars called "Peking Easy Riders," donkey carts, horse-drawn wagons, with the occasional camel thrown in. There were blue and cream trolley busses and some diesel ones as well. There were some traffic lights at major intersections that were operated manually by policemen in raised booths on the street corners. The paucity of traffic and street lights made driving at night hazardous. It was never clear to me whether any one needed a licence to drive. Night life, and street life, was even less in evidence than in 1964. The Cultural Revolution had cast a puritanical pall over life.

With an increasing number of countries recognizing China, there was a rising demand for new embassy buildings and housing for diplomats. At the turn of the twentieth century, in the days of the Boxers and the Siege of Beijing, the so-called Legation Quarter, where most embassies were located, was on the same street as the Xinqiao hotel.[18] This was true into the 1950s, until the People's Government provided more space for embassies in the west and north of Beijing. The first wave of embassies to China were located near the Altar of the Sun Park. The British Embassy, attacked and breached by the Red Guards in the rabid period of the Cultural Revolution, was here. The Canadian Embassy, as I mentioned earlier, was in San Li tun, an even newer section further north where the Chinese had built a number of nearly identical small embassy compounds separated by high walls amid streets lined with willow trees.

The small embassy offered the Canadian government was actually the former Pakistani Embassy. It was usually the case that countries began in these smaller accommodations, eventually building larger premises. Canada was a long time realizing this process; other countries like France, Mexico, Australia, and the USA built more distinctive buildings sooner. If you went to the French Embassy, you had the feeling of entering France, to the British, Britain, to the Mexican, Mexico, but when you went to the Canadian Embassy, you knew you were in Pakistan. I exaggerate, of course. The embassy was built to house both offices and residences and it had a swimming pool. The staff of the Canadian Embassy, though small, was still too large to allow for anyone to live in the building: the rooms of the residence became offices. The embassy had officers to handle diplomatic, consular, cultural, commercial, military, and security matters. It had a small but efficient and dedicated support staff. The receptionist, as well as the translators, interpreters, drivers, gardeners, and caterers, were provided by the DSB and generally, perhaps because of the memory of Dr. Norman Bethune,[19] Canada was provided with good people, some of whom in later years became ambassadors themselves.

EMBASSY LIFE, BEIJING-STYLE

In the early 1970s, Beijing was in the midst of a diplomatic boom as more and more countries reached recognition agreements with the People's Republic. With the opening of the Canadian Embassy, more staff had to be brought in and housing found for them. The Chinese were building accommodations as swiftly as they could, but they lacked equipment and materials. Furniture and appliances were imported from Canada. For someone accepting a posting to Beijing, there were at least two general reactions. One was a sense of adventure, working in a country that was virtually unknown to the majority of Canadians. The other was a sense of dread at being far from home in a country of uncertain and unstable politics, with difficult transportation and communications links, in a completely foreign environment where few of the items, taken for granted at home, were available. At first, the sense of adventure was paramount, but it did not take long before the dread asserted itself. However, in Margo's and my case, the sense of adventure was never lost.

Life in Beijing in the first decade of the embassy's existence was hard on staff. Secretaries, or guards and communicators on shift work, had a particularly difficult time. Their housing was adequate but in no way luxurious. Unlike embassy officers who had allowances for entertainment, a cook, and a maid, they had to look after themselves. Western restaurants were very few in number, and only two in easy reach for embassy staff. Chinese restaurants that were open to Westerners were greatly in need of repair and redecoration. Those patrons with nervous stomachs had only to hear the cook clearing his throat of Beijing dust to hesitate about consuming the food. The most reliable restaurants were in hotels like the Beijing, Xinqiao, and Minzu, and the three other establishments that served Peking duck. Of the latter, the large restaurant, south of Tiananmen Square on Qianmen, was called the Big Duck. It also housed a smaller restaurant on its ground floor called the Little Duck. The third restaurant was located off Wangfujing, on a side street leading to the Capital City Hospital. It was called the Sick Duck. Peking duck (*Beijing Kaoya*) might have been the gastronomic highlight to a short-term visitor, but to people posted to the city for a long term it could take on the spectre of a visit to McDonald's. Fortunately, that spectre never visited Margo and me.

In Beijing, shopping was a daytime-only occupation, and the range of stores was limited. Stores along Wangfujing, the formerly famous shopping street, lacked style and glamour. Qianmen, running south of Tiananmen, had shops specializing in household items that were more interesting. One street haunted almost entirely by foreigners was Liulichang, the place to buy antiques, scrolls, reproductions, and books and art supplies. In one bookshop located here, you might find pre-revolution books in classical Chinese. The Foreign Language Bookstore on Wangfujing carried the currently approved range of titles in various translations, and you might find old Western language books in a corner of a nearby market. There were also the occasional dusty antique markets. Margo and I visited these shops and markets on weekends, often in the company of other members of the embassy or the Bonavias. When it was allowed, we would go by train to Tianjin where the antique market was said to be superior. Foreigners could only visit stores where FEC (Foreign Exchange

Certificates) were honoured, but you were up against the limited range and shortage of large sizes. The special Friendship Store, an oasis for foreigners, which was close to where we lived and became a favourite haunt of Margo's for its Chinese handicrafts, had a narrow range of Western-style clothing, but was equipped with a tailor's shop willing to copy anything. The store also sold some Western foodstuffs, but most members of the embassy depended on shipments from Hong Kong or Europe. Fresh fruit and vegetables were available only in season and were available in piles dumped on the earthen floor of the local shop. During the winter, cabbage was the staple.

Entertainment for foreigners ranged downward from extremely little to nil and mostly involved passive involvement. Television, mainly a propaganda outlet, was in effect nonexistent and this was well before VHS, DVDs, and the Internet. There were some public showings of Cultural Revolution films or live performances of revolutionary ballets and operas, which did not bear much repetition. More popular were the circus and acrobatic shows. Twice a year, on May 1 and October 1, there were usually colourful celebrations, mainly involving children. At the Spring Festival, when most Chinese attempted to go home to be with their families, there were flower shows and exhibitions in public parks. Sometimes tickets were available to see visiting sports teams, but once the long nights of winter came, life was very dull. Some embassies, like the French and Mexican, held film festivals in January and February. The round of dinner parties exchanged among friends helped to pass the long nights of winter. In addition, for embassy officers, there was a perpetual round of receptions.

Except for the occasional appearance of the moon and a cloudless sky, Beijing at night during the winter was black and cold. Heating for the residences of foreigners was provided from mid-November to mid-April. Beijingers relied on padded clothing and sitting outside in the sun when the opportunity afforded itself. They cooked with soft coal briquettes, with the heat and smoke from the kitchen stove being diverted through pipes under the raised family bed, the *kang*. During winter, embassy employees looked forward to their leaves when they could escape to a resort in Southeast Asia or elsewhere. Very few employees had cars—most people depended on embassy cars, taxis, or bicycles. Should a foreigner be involved in an accident in which a Chinese citizen was injured, their embassy sent them out of China as soon as possible to avoid their having to face draconian Chinese courts.

In general, most foreigners felt they were being watched and embassies thought they were being bugged, whether they were or not. The fact was that

The Summer Palace in winter, February 1974.

foreigners stood out against the background of Chinese life and even their most casual activity was observed and could be recounted by ordinary citizens if they happened to be asked. Any rides I took around the city on my bicycle were noticed by many people and no doubt the subject of speculation as to where I was going and why. Most people would offer directions if I asked, but conversations went no further. There was almost no fraternization with the Chinese, except at official dinners and lunches. Casual meetings were impossible and one had to watch what one said, not so much for oneself as for the sake of one's Chinese listeners.

Beijing is a large city rich in history, but you could grow weary of the historic monuments, at least the few that were open to foreigners in the early days of the embassy. Travel outside Beijing was very difficult. Permission was rarely granted. Because you had to enter China by train from Hong Kong via Guangzhou (Canton), or by air via Pakistan, entry and exit was time-consuming. The only guaranteed trip requiring no permission was the one to the Great Wall and the Ming Tombs. This took the better part of a day, usually with a picnic lunch, because there were no tourist facilities at that time. You could also make trips to the Summer Palace on the edge of the Western Hills, where there was a good restaurant that normally had to be booked in advance. You were free to explore Beijing by bicycle, dodging donkey carts and fellow cyclists on the streets and in the *hutongs*. Foreigners had to get used to being the object of stares, gazes, speculation, or the occasional "*Waiguoren!*" (Foreigner!) shouted by an excited youngster.

Worst off among the foreigners in China were the Soviets. Once the closest friends of the Chinese, they were now pariahs and shunned, as the ideological war between Beijing and Moscow raged on in the 1970s. They had limited social interaction with the rest of the foreign community, except for the weekly Sunday hockey game during January and February. The games were played at the Soviet compound, once the Jesuit mission,[20] on a small lake on its grounds. Here the Soviet Embassy team took on a pickup team called the Rest of the World, defeating them each week. The Rest of the World only got together on the day, while it was rumoured that the Soviets practised. Each Sunday, Canadian Embassy drivers, Chinese, were pressed into service to drive embassy members to the game. Having no hockey skills, I made certain there was plenty of hot buttered rum to ease the feelings of defeat. The people who felt the weekly losses the keenest were the drivers, who slunk as low as they could when driving in and out of the Soviet compound. On one of these Sundays, I was approached by a member of the Soviet Embassy and invited to his flat for coffee and a brandy. His apartment was big, obviously built during the 1950s when Sino-Soviet relations were good. I asked him how many times he had been to China. His reply showed the depth of his disaffection: "Twice, this is my first and my last!"

Matters picked up for the Rest of the World one Sunday morning in early 1974, the day after a Soviet Embassy official, who happened to be their best player, was expelled for accepting some microfilm under a bridge. The Soviet team was in disarray and the Rest of the World enjoyed a rare victory, one reported in the *Globe and Mail*. Everyone was happy, but the happiest were the embassy drivers who sat tall and smiled broadly as they exited the compound. The embassy had a supply of Canadian films to loan to eager Chinese. Unfortunately, because of the Cultural Revolution, no Chinese was eager to borrow them, except for the film of the 1972 Canada-Russia hockey series. That one could not be kept on the shelf.

TULUDOU LAI[21]

One or two days after my arrival, I was invited to my first diplomatic lunch in a dusty tree-shaded street in old Beijing. The lunch was given by the Chinese Foreign Ministry (Waijiaobu) to say goodbye to John Paynter, and to welcome me. It was a jovial affair because Paynter's joie de vivre was infectious. Or so was the case until one of the Chinese officials asked, "Where will Prime Minister Trudeau like to go on his visit to China?" This was the first time the embassy had heard that such a visit was in the offing. With the reply, "We would value your advice as to which places he might visit," the Canadians at the table tried to hide their surprise about the upcoming trip by their own prime minister. Through gentle probing, we learned Trudeau would be coming early in October in time to celebrate the third anniversary of the announcement of mutual recognition on October 13. We also learned it was very likely that Mrs. Trudeau, though pregnant, would be coming with the prime minister.[22] It seemed the invitation for a state visit to China had been issued to Trudeau over lunch in Ottawa, but Trudeau's acceptance had not yet been communicated to the embassy in Beijing. Meanwhile, John Burns learned directly from the Chinese Foreign Ministry that Trudeau was coming. He reported it in the *Globe and Mail*, whereupon the PMO chastised the embassy for leaking the information to the press. It did not bode well for the visit.

July was normally a slow time diplomatically, for Westerners at least, who were tied to the rhythms of the routines of their home government when many people took holidays. This was true of the Canadian Embassy once hosting the Canada Day celebration was over. From the outside, the Canadian Embassy looked calm. The soldiers from the People's Liberation Army, dressed in their olive green uniforms and canvas shoes, stood straight, seeing all by not appearing to see anyone. Donkeys pulling night-soil carts toiled by amidst the din of cicadas. The occasional embassy car entered or exited, and members of the local staff came and went on their bicycles, dismounting to show their passes to the guards. From time to time, a taxi could be seen waiting outside the embassy gates. It was business as usual. Yet, inside the phones, telex machines, and diplomatic mail pouches were generating mountains of work involving visits to various government ministries to deliver or receive messages of importance to an aspect of Canada–China relations. Official relations between Canada and China were not yet three years old, and the embassy had only been in full operation for under thirty months, but already routines of long hours and hard work were well established.

Recognizing China had raised great expectations among Canadian commercial, scientific, educational, cultural, and athletic circles. In the afterglow of recognition and in a continuing effort to take advantage before the Americans could exploit the Nixon initiative, a steady stream of Liberal Cabinet ministers journeyed to China to explore linkages with Canada. Each was anxious for opportunities. The commercial sector, in particular, was determined to sink its roots in before America entered the race. In August 1972, Mitchell Sharp led to Beijing the largest trade show and delegation Canada had ever sent abroad. On top of high-level government visits, there were also Canadian tour groups and individuals who looked forward to a visit to the embassy, and perhaps a reception at the ambassador's residence. China was a closed society and internal travel was difficult, so tourists, no matter how unobservant, had something to offer in fleshing out the embassy's view on what was happening outside Beijing. In addition, there were sports teams and numerous commercial groups, each coming at the invitation of their Chinese counterparts.

The last ministerial visit organized by embassy staff, which included myself, prior to Trudeau's state visit was headed by Jeanne Sauvé, then Secretary of State for Science and Technology. Sauvé, a newly appointed minister in a newly created portfolio, was anxious to make her mark internationally. She arrived in Beijing with a large entourage on September 29, 1973, in time to be a guest of honour at the state banquet on September 30, the eve of China's national day. The Chinese host for the visit was Guo Moro, the eighty-one-year-old head of the Chinese Academy of Sciences, a prolific writer of poems, plays, and essays with a huge national and international reputation. He was deaf in one ear, the result of a teenage illness. He was particularly well known in Japan, where he had lived off and on for a number of years before 1950. He was one of the most highly regarded members of the Chinese government.

Making arrangements for the Sauvé visit was a slow process; the Academy of Sciences did not reply to my requests in a timely way. The embassy was inclined to regard the delay as deliberate, but two decades later, the person who dealt with our requests confided to me that the reason for the delays was because the academy was very short of staff. "Most of my colleagues had been sent to the countryside," he told me. Sorting out details once the minister arrived was more difficult; Sauvé would deal only with the ambassador. Other members of the embassy were deemed to be of too low a rank, even though they were better informed on the different issues. Consequently, I spent a great deal of time with the minister's support staff, one of whom was an American and an old Cold War warrior. He was very nervous, frequently commenting in a hushed voice: "This country is full of communists." His preparations for the trip included cards, the size and shape of name cards, only they were not name cards: they were thank you cards, tri-lingual thank you cards. At the top were the Chinese characters for *Xiexie*, the common term in Mandarin for thank you. Underneath the Chinese was the word "*Merci*," and underneath that, the word "Thank you." The top corner of the card bore Canada's flag in colour, and the name of the federal department. On exiting the embassy car, he would hand out the cards to any Chinese in the vicinity. "See that?" he would say, "they love it!" And they did, but not quite for the reasons he thought. He did not know that the character for *Xie* is also a surname, pronounced in other Chinese dialects as *Jay* and *Der*. The Chinese who received the cards were amused to find they had met a Mr. Xie who had the strange first name of Xie and no middle name, but wait, he is foreign, so his name must be *Merci*, Thank you. Does he know his name in Chinese means thank you? The true depth of his preparations came out when he said, "You know, the minister wanted to meet with someone really important. Instead, all we got was this deaf old geezer, Kwo Moe Joe."

Anxious to prove the "breakthrough" nature of her trip, Sauvé, who later became Governor General of Canada, was ready to sign almost any agreement in sight with the Chinese. She was clearly annoyed when it was pointed out to her by the Prime Minister's Office that there had to be something left over for Trudeau. The Chinese continued to treat her well and on the eve of October 1, the national holiday, she was seated at dinner next to Mao's wife, Jiang Qing, whom she ignored. She took so little notice that when Trudeau's office, preparing to give Jiang Qing a gift of a northern Canadian parka, asked for some help in judging Qing's appropriate size, Sauvé was unable even to estimate.

As may be guessed from my reflections, I admit to a negative attitude toward this ministerial mission. It remains in my memory for the amount of time spent to insure the minister's deputy was never out of Coca Cola, which at the time was unavailable in China, and for a loud comment made at the ambassador's residence by a very prominent female civil servant and friend of the minister's who had come along for the ride: "What do you have to do to get a steak in this goddamned country?" The owner of the utterance, Sylvia Ostry, had been in the country only two days and was to leave for Ottawa the next morning, well before the mission was completed. As the embassy now scrambled to prepare for the prime minister's visit, to negotiate agreements in nearly all areas of the Canada–China relationship, each diplomatic officer went about their business with as much efficiency and speed as the short-staffed Chinese system, clogged as it was with reels of red tape, permitted. It was mostly serious work, but not always.

The world knows of the early 1970s as the era of Sino-American ping-pong diplomacy, but for Canadians it was not ping pong but pandas that kept us entranced. Few questioned how it was possible for the reddest of red regimes to succeed in promoting as its international symbol the cuddly black and white bear. Canadians watched with envy as Richard Nixon, George Pompidou, and Edward Heath each received a pair of giant panda bears as gifts from China to their people. The People's Republic of China had long branded the United States, France, and Britain as imperialists and class enemies, yet their leaders had been rewarded with pandas. Surely Canada, at best an adjunct imperialist, more of a running pup than a running dog, with assets such as Dr. Bethune and wheat sales, could expect no less a gift when our leader, whose diplomacy had opened up a fresh round of recognitions of China, came to call on Chairman Mao?

In July 1973, Trudeau was low in the polls. It was a time when a photograph in the company of Zhou Enlai, or Mao, was worth, perhaps, an additional five to ten points. Naturally, Trudeau would bring gifts, for example more mementos of Bethune. But in order to obtain a panda, something special would have to be proffered. Nixon gave musk ox, Pompidou, treasures from the French Renaissance, and Heath, so it was rumoured, offered Hong Kong, or was it Père David Deer? What could Canada offer? Well, it could keep to its tradition of following the American example and offer animals for the Beijing Zoo. But what kinds of animals?

What better than the beaver: *Castor canadensis*, dammer of rivers, felter of hats, prodigious breeder, and the symbol of Canada? Surely the Chinese, schooled in subtlety, would not fail to get the point. Cast your beaver upon Pacific waters, it was thought, and they will come back as pandas. Of course, we were offering one of nature's most prolific creatures, known to China since the days of Beijing Man, in exchange for one of nature's most reticent ones. But then, it was that sort of thinking that gave us the sixty-three-cent dollar.

On September 19, 1973, a telex arrived at the Canadian Embassy in Beijing. It was entitled "PMS VISIT ANIMAL PRESENTATIONS," and read:

> FOUR BEAVERS ARRIVING ON THE PMS AIRCRAFT WILL
> NEED TO BE FED. AS BEAVERS ONLY DEFECATE IN WATER...
> THEY SHOULD BE PLACED IN POOL OF WATER ON ARRIVAL

TO PROVIDE RELIEF AND PREVENT POSSIBLE CRITICAL
CONDITIONS EXPECIALLY AFTER SUCH A LONG FLIGHT.

This was all very interesting, but it was the final line that caught and held my attention. It stated, seductively, "GRATEFUL YOU DESIGNATE MEMBER OF EMBASSY STAFF AS BEAVER LIAISON OFFICER." My heart leapt. What an opportunity. I immediately wrote the ambassador:

Dear Ambassador,

I wish formally to apply for the position of Beaver Liaison Officer for the visit of the Prime Minister of Canada to the People's Republic of China.

Normally, I do not seek positions, but an opportunity such as this one has never before come within my grasp. To be appointed BLO to the PMO would be an honour yet undreamed of by the Evans family.

In case you have doubts about my qualifications for the position, let me point out that I grew up near a stream inhabited by beaver. As a child, I used to go down to the banks of the stream at night to watch the beaver cut down the remaining trees in the district. I always felt a certain pride in their dams, until the river became too polluted and the beaver were forced to move away.

Sincerely,

P.S. The nickel has always been my favourite coin.

There being no other applicants, I got the job, which, after all, was a cultural matter.

The next evening, I accompanied Maurice Copithorne to the Chinese Foreign Office to give them the wonderful news of the coming of the beaver. The sun was setting, a burnt-orange Frisbee hanging in the grey-black haze of a Beijing autumn sky, when we were shown into a reception room on the wall of which was a huge painting of two panda contentedly eating bamboo shoots. How serendipitous, we thought. Because it was late, a junior Chinese diplomat, who had once travelled to Canada and had eaten in the revolving restaurant atop the Chateau Lacombe in Edmonton, was pressed into service as the interpreter.

"The people of Canada," we began, "wish to give the people of China a gift."

"How very kind and thoughtful," came the reply.

"Canada wishes to present China with four beaver," we continued, our eyes fixed firmly on the panda still munching bamboo over the official's head. There was a pause while our words were translated into Chinese. Suddenly, the Mandarin melody was broken by the word "beaver."

"What," asked the acting interpreter, "are beaver?"

"You know," we said, "they have large front teeth..."

"Oh, an elephant."

"No, no," we protested. "They have large tails and swim under water."

"A whale."

We were at an impasse, the sort on which the very history of the world turns. We were stuck for the term in Chinese for beaver. What is more, we had obviously led our Chinese hosts to expect a gift considerably larger than the one we were actually offering. We retreated, making broad reference to the lovely panda picture on the wall and how much the Canadian people love panda. Careful to hit the right note, we did not go so far as to state that Dr. Bethune, had he survived, would have wanted the Canadian people to have a pair of panda. Later that evening, in the Great Hall of the People, at a banquet held for the prime minister of Australia, the acting interpreter called out to me down one of the long corridors, "Dr. Evans! *Shui ta*, beaver!" So there it was: Canada was giving the Chinese people four water rats.

In the days leading up to Trudeau's arrival, I was engaged in many other negotiations, but I did not neglect my BLO responsibilities. In fact, there were numerous telexes exchanged on the subject. I requested a copy of *"Everything You Ever Wanted to Know about Beaver But Were Afraid to Ask."* Trudeau had abandoned an earlier idea of having the beaver travel with him. They would have had to share space in the back of the plane with the press corps and Trudeau had too high a regard for our national symbol to subject them to that kind of treatment.[23] On October 9, the eve of Trudeau's arrival, the embassy received the following telex:

REGRET DELAY IN SENDING BEAVER. TENTATIVE AR-
RANGEMENTS TO SHIP BY AIR CARGO, PIA 752, MON-
TREAL, PARIS, ISTANBUL, ISLAMABAD, BEIJING. BEAVER

WILL HAVE HEALTH CERTIFICATES AND INFO ON CARE EN
ROUTE AND ON ARRIVAL.

To reassure Ottawa that everything was in hand, I replied:

BEAVER WILL BE MET BY BEIJING BLO AND OTHER RE-
SPONSIBLE MEMBERS OF CHINESE DEPARTMENTS CON-
CERNED. PLEASE WARN BEAVER THAT PIA 752 IS OFTEN
VERY LATE INTO BEIJING.

Almost immediately came final instructions, which read, in part:

ON ARRIVAL BEAVER NEED ONLY ENOUGH WATER AT
65–70 DEGREES F TO SIT IN. BEAVERS ARE HARDY AND
NORMALLY TRAVEL WELL. DESPITE INTESTINAL FORTI-
TUDE THEY MAY BECOME VEXED WHEN THEY LEARN PIA
752 LATE INTO BEIJING.

Well, it is hardly a state secret that nothing gets Canadian diplomatic blood
boiling faster than the knowledge that somewhere, some place, there is a vexed
beaver. Our instinct is to rush to the beaver immediately and to unvex it. It is an
obsession with us. After all, we are only human, Unvexing beaver is something
that all Canadian diplomats learn, I believe, at an early stage of their careers.
It is just one of those things that set Canadian diplomats apart from those of
other nations. We do not talk about it much—we just do it. But I digress. The
telex continued:

THEREFORE ADVISE HANDLERS KEEP CAGE BETWEEN
SELVES AND BEAVER WHEN FIRST OPENING AND QUOTE
WATCH TAIL AND TEETH UNQUOTE.

You will agree it does not take a rocket scientist to realize that if you are watching the tail and the teeth, you are pretty well watching the whole beaver. But
enough, the telex concluded:

CAGES WILL BE MARKED TO IDENTIFY MALES. (THEY
ALSO HAVE HOLES PUNCHED IN WEB REAR FOOT). YOU

MAY CHOOSE TO PUT ANY TWO OF OPPOSITE SEX TO-
GETHER. AS BEAVER YOUNG ENOUGH NOT/NOT TO HAVE
ESTABLISHED DEFINED MARITAL BEHAVIOUR ANY PAIR-
ING WILL RESULT IN MONOGAMOUS SITUATION.

And some still wonder why the beaver is our national symbol!

The beaver were now scheduled to arrive the evening of Trudeau's departure from Beijing. PIA 752 was due in at 8:00 in the evening, but of course no
one believed it—except me. The burdens of BLO-ing weighed heavily on my
shoulders. Although it was October 13, the third anniversary of Canada-China
recognition, and I would miss the farewell banquet, I headed out to the old
Beijing airport (replaced three times since 1973). Waiting for the plane were
one protocol officer, whose last assignment had been Poland, one customs
official, one health officer, one official and one deputy director at the Beijing
Zoo, and an airport official. PIA 752 was late, of course. We spent the first
hour of our wait exchanging documents and making small talk. We discussed
beaver mating habits and Norman Bethune, techniques for watching teeth and
tail, and Norman Bethune, and how much water a beaver needs to sit in, and
Norman Bethune. With PIA 752 nowhere in sight, we split up and pledged to
meet again when, and if, PIA 752 landed.

At midnight, it was rumoured that PIA 752 would be earlier than usual and
was expected in the next half hour or so. At thirty-five minutes past midnight,
the green and white Boeing 707 touched down and we boarded a little flatbed
truck, sent by the Beijing Zoo, to travel across the concrete apron to greet it.
The captain was standing in the doorway awaiting the arrival of some mobile
steps. I hailed him with the following well thought out diplomatic phrases:
"I am the Beaver Liaison Officer of the Canadian Embassy. Do you have any
Canadian beaver on board?" To which the flight captain replied, and I quote
it exactly as I heard it: "Oh goodness me yes, we are having beaver on board.
All the way from Paris we are having them."

In a brief but touching ceremony on the edge of the runway, at 1:15 in the
morning, I officially handed over the beaver to the deputy director of the Beijing
Zoo. My duty done, in conjunction with Minister-Counsellor Copithorne, I
filed my final report, as follows:

BEAVER ARRIVED 00:35 HOURS IN EXCELLENT, ALMOST
INSULTING CONDITION. RUSHED BY ZOO OFFICIALS TO

NEAREST SHALLOW PANS OF WATER, CLOSE WATCH
BEING KEPT ON TAILS AND TEETH. CUSTOMS, HEALTH,
PROTOCOL, PROCEDURES ACCOMPLISHED QUICKLY,
THERE BEING ENOUGH PAPERS FOR EACH OFFICIAL TO
HAVE ONE. ZOO AND CUSTOM OFFICIALS WILLING TO
TOLERATE BEAVER MATING HABITS, PROTOCOL OFFICIAL
LESS CERTAIN. CAGES STILL WELL MARKED, THEREFORE
NO NEED TO EXAMINE REAR FEET. HOWEVER, IN VIEW OF
YOUR ADVICE, ALL MALE EMBASSY OFFICERS HAVE HAD
HOLE PUNCHED IN SHOES![24]

The "beaver" correspondence ended up being sent to Mitchell Sharp. It gave him a laugh during what had turned out to be a tense time internationally, as the next chapter will show.

My year in Beijing provided me with a wealth of insights and information on contemporary China, much more than was provided in the then current studies on China. John Burns used to say that a walk down a Beijing *hutong* was worth more than most of the books on modern Chinese history. Although I would not go that far, I feel he was more than partly right. Despite travel restrictions, I managed to visit a number of Chinese cities and the countryside around them. I saw numerous communes, factories, schools, and universities, each of them attempting to apply the teachings of Chairman Mao as best they could. I visited Mao's birthplace at Xiaoshan, only to find that his childhood circumstances were much better than mine. I climbed the hills around Dazhai, the model commune, which was later revealed to have had special treatment and considerations from leaders of the Communist Party, and I observed study sessions held by Red Guards who had been sent to the countryside to reflect on the revolution and the "Thoughts of Mao." I spent a few nights in the caves of Yen'an where the Communist Party had set up its headquarters at the end of the Long March, its strategic retreat while under attack from Chiang Kai-shek's forces in the mid-1930s. And I roamed the *hutongs* of Beijing to see how average Beijingers lived, in contrast to the banquets in the Great Hall of the People and the receptions in the Beijing Hotel. The China I had come to know something about was light years away from the one I imagined in my childhood during the Depression and dirty thirties in southern Alberta.

SIX ★ ★ ★ ★

Basic Diplomacy and the
Many Uses of Norman Bethune

Within China, the political scene had been tense for some years leading up to Pierre Trudeau's visit, the first state visit ever to China by a prime minister of Canada.[1] The Cultural Revolution, begun in 1966, was declared over at a Communist Party meeting in May 1969, although in fact it lasted until 1976. It was said that all those ideals for which the revolution had been initiated: the establishment of a worker, peasant, soldier state; the honouring of the teachings of Chairman Mao; the creation of a new culture; and a new standard for selecting bureaucrats, teachers, and doctors based on "redness," rather than upon "expertness," had been accomplished. Out of the revolution had come so-called socialist newborn things (shoots) that had to be nurtured by leaders steeped in the teachings of Mao. But less than two years later, the leadership faced a major crisis. The defence minister, Lin Biao, a veteran of the Korean War and leader of the Cultural Revolution, named in the party Constitution of May 1969 as Mao's close comrade in arms and successor, was dead. According to the official story, Lin, too anxious to replace Mao, initiated attempts to assassinate Mao and to lead an armed uprising called Project 571. He failed. In September 1971, not long after the Canadian Embassy opened, he commandeered a Trident jet in an ill-fated attempt to flee to the Soviet Union. The jet crashed in Mongolia, killing all on board. Since Mongolia was favourable to the USSR, the Chinese could not examine the wreckage.

The Chinese Communist Party had a major crisis on its hands. How was it to explain why Lin turned against Mao? It took nearly two years to brief all levels of the party and by the summer of 1973 it was prepared, more or less, to face the Chinese people. A noisy procession in central Beijing the night of August 28, 1973, marked the close of the tenth meeting of the Congress of the Chinese

A welcoming crowd gathers at the Beijing airport for the arrival of Prime Minister Trudeau, October 1973.

Communist Party. The decisions made at that meeting were to plague China's domestic and foreign policies for the next three years. While it attempted to look united, the Chinese Communist Party leadership was deeply divided. Wang Hongwen, a very handsome young man from the northeast, a worker who had served Mao's cause in Shanghai to good effect but a virtual unknown, was made a vice-chairman of the Politburo of the Central Committee, ranking number three in the order of power after Mao and Zhou Enlai. Since his death, Lin Biao had been criticized within the party, but now the criticism had to spread to inform the masses. But, in order to make clear that Lin's failure was not that of the Cultural Revolution's, the campaign to criticize him would have a parallel one criticizing Confucius. The ancient thinker and educator Confucius? Confucius was a surrogate for Zhou Enlai, premier and leader of the modernizers in the party. Confucius, in the fifth century BCE, praised an ideal statesman called the Duke of Zhou. By January 1974, the campaigns were combined and dubbed *Pi Lin Pi Kung* (criticize Lin Biao criticize Confucius), after evidence was found, or manufactured, to show Lin Biao was an ultra-rightist and follower of Confucius. The campaigns were destined to befoul the very Canada–China relations Trudeau's visit, arranged before this fateful August meeting, was meant to promote.

Ambassador Small and China's Premier Zhou Enlai on their way to greet Prime Minister Trudeau at the Beijing airport.

TRUDEAU IN CHINA

On a bright, blue-domed day in early October 1973, a Canadian Forces Boeing 707 drew to a stop on the concrete apron of Beijing airport. As the plane taxied to a stop, a flock of pom-pom-waving youngsters in colourful costumes, and other Chinese well-wishers (cynically referred to by Westerners as a "rent-a-crowd") chanted and cheered. A bleacher at the edge of the tarmac accommodated Canadian residents in Beijing, with space for members of the press, who were onboard the plane but ready to rush out to cover the prime minister's arrival.[2] The airport terminal, a low brick and masonry building, had a small waiting/departures lounge, and an even smaller arrivals area. Boarding, after a walk across the concrete apron, was accomplished by mobile staircases pushed up to the doors of airplanes. Staircases were wheeled to the rear and front doors of the Canadian government jet. The rear door opened: two dozen or more press members ran down the stairs and across the concrete to the bleacher. There, cameras and notepads at the ready, they waited with members of the embassy staff, I among them. The front door opened, and Prime Minister Pierre Elliott Trudeau,[3] accompanied by Margaret (Sinclair), his pregnant wife, stepped out to descend the stairs to be welcomed by Premier Zhou Enlai, Foreign Minister Chi Pengfei, Ambassador John Small, and others.

Prime Minister Trudeau's Canadian delegation with Premier Zhou Enlai, Great Hall of the People, October 1973. The author and Margo are in the second row, immediately behind Premier Zhou. [Xinhua news photo, Beijing]

Trudeau's visit was deemed of major importance in Canada, at least among those who wanted to get access to the fabled Chinese market. As a result, a system to take advantage of the International Dateline was set up to insure Trudeau's activities in China would be ready for the evening newscasts in Canada. When Nixon visited China in 1972, he brought in his own satellite station to ensure direct contact with the US media, but this option was not open to Trudeau as being too costly. In order to get "live" coverage from Beijing to Canada, television reports filed by Canadian correspondents were flown to Canton (Guangzhou), taken by taxi to the Hong Kong border, handed to Canadian correspondents for sending via satellite (called "birding") to Canada, all in time to appear as the lead stories on Canadian television screens the evening of the same day. But this was all to no avail. Unfortunately, Trudeau's visit to China coincided with the outbreak of the Yom Kippur War in the Middle East, effectively removing it as the priority on Canadian evening news.

As with all state visits, a welcoming banquet was offered in the vast Great Hall of the People, located at the western edge of Tiananmen Square. Zhou gave a toast of welcome and Trudeau replied. His words were interpreted into Chinese by Gilliane Lapointe, the newly appointed consular officer at the embassy. She was so good that at my table, far from the centre of attention, one Chinese official commented, "I can't see who she is, but I am sure she comes from Shandong." Prior to the banquet, a group photo was taken. It included the official Canadian delegation, members of the embassy and their spouses, and their Chinese hosts, including Premier Zhou Enlai and Vice-Premier Deng Xiaoping. In posing with the group, Premier Zhou risked further criticism from his political enemies. Standing next to Zhou was Margaret Trudeau, a pregnant woman—albeit a foreigner—out in public contrary to Chinese tradition. More-over, standing behind him and beside me was Margo, whose white hair was symbolic of a demon in Chinese tradition.[4] The photo, published the next day below the fold on the front page of the *People's Daily*, was vague and indistinct.

The welcome over, the serious work of the visit proceeded. Trade, immi-gration, and cultural agreements were signed. After Trudeau and Zhou signed the breakthrough immigration agreement allowing for the reunion of family members in China with their children or parents in Canada, the Canadian delegation was invited to have lunch in one of the large provincial rooms of the Great Hall of the People.[5] Zhou was every inch the patrician host, charming and self-deprecating. He exuded the air of a confident, dedicated, and tire-less servant of the Chinese people. Little did we know that he was suffering from cancer. Although the Cultural Revolution was ever present, with Maoist slogans to be seen everywhere in the city, the walls of the room where we ate were decorated with traditional Chinese landscapes. In his short speech, Zhou drew attention to this fact. "Previously," he said, "these walls were adorned with sayings of Chairman Mao. One day I asked the waiters if they studied the sayings and they replied that they were always too busy. So, I said, if they are not serving their purpose, let's replace them with some art."

Before leaving Beijing, Trudeau had three formal meetings with Zhou Enlai, also in the Great Hall. Each sat facing the other in the middle of long narrow tables. Each was flanked by ministers and officials. I attended their final meet-ing, on the afternoon of October 13. It provided another opportunity to see Premier Zhou up close, as he summed up the official part of the visit. There was a slight tension in the air because it was the third anniversary of the dec-laration of recognition and Trudeau had not yet been invited to see Chairman Mao. Trudeau's schedule was already tight. After the meeting, he was to hold a press conference, then host a farewell banquet, before taking an evening train to the south. As the meeting wore on, it became clear that Zhou was killing time. He was frequently interrupted by Chairman Mao's grandniece, Wang Hairong, an official with the Protocol Office, who would whisper to him or pass him a note. Meanwhile, Zhou discoursed on the problems of modernizing production in China. He wondered aloud how it was possible for the people of Taiwan, fellow Chinese, to do so much better than his compatriots in China. At one point, he referred to his long underwear, which he could not get to fit properly. He pulled out the sleeve of the ones he was wearing to display it below the cuff of his jacket. No two pair were the same, he complained. He

MENU

Hors-d'oeuvre

Consommé à l'agaric blanc

Divers émincés veloutés

Poulet sauce salée et
poisson frit au beurre

Moutarde aux champignons

Canard à l'étuvée

Purée de châtaignes

Pâtisserie

Fruits

Menu

Hors d'Oeuvre

Consomme of Sponge Bamboo
and Quail Egg

Silver Agaric with Egg White

Fried Duck and Chicken Crisps

Haricot Beans with Mushrooms

Steamed River Shad

Sweet Dumplings with Orange

Pastries

Fruits

[Left:] October 11 banquet given by Zhou, menu in French.
[Right:] October 13 banquet given by Trudeau, menu in English.

always ordered a larger size because they shrunk, eventually becoming too small. As he spoke, one of his ministers began to grow red in the face because he was aware that by the end of the day he would no longer be the minister in charge of domestic industry.

Zhou next turned to comparing China and Canada. "What," he asked, "was the oil production of Canada this last year?" There were blank stares from the Canadian side when none of the Trudeau team could come up with the figure. In the end, Zhou supplied the answer. One Canadian official commented, in a low voice, "Perhaps we should exchange prime ministers." At this point, Mao's niece came into the room once again and caught Zhou's attention. He stood up and said he would like to adjourn the meeting in order to have a word in private with Prime Minister Trudeau. Trudeau joined him in a corner of the room while the Canadian group stood, awaiting the news. Shortly, Trudeau came back to be greeted by an anxious, "Well?" from Ivan Head, his advisor on foreign affairs. "Oh," said Trudeau with a shrug, "he asked me if I was free to visit Chairman Mao." "And?" asked Head, clearly frustrated. "Well," replied Trudeau with a wry smile, "I told him that I had a press conference and I could not keep them waiting." "What?" cried Head. "What did you expect me to say?" laughed Trudeau.

With that, the Canadians adjourned to a side room to sink into a circle of easy chairs. Trudeau sat with his back to the curtained entryway and began to quiz the group about the substance of the afternoon's meeting. It was not unlike a university seminar, but at least two members were not concentrating: Ivan Head and Ambassador John Small were looking for the hint that they could accompany Trudeau to see Mao at his residence in Zhongnanhai, the western section of the Forbidden City reserved for the homes of China's top leaders.[6] As the discussion proceeded, a Chinese official came up behind Trudeau and whispered something. Trudeau then got up and left, alone, to see Chairman Mao. There was no time for anyone else to even flex their knees.

Needless to say, Trudeau kept the press waiting and shortened the conference in order to host the farewell banquet. Later, at Beijing railway station, he encountered Chester Ronning, the old China hand and diplomat, who had just arrived from a visit to Datung. It was the second serendipitous meeting of the official visit. The first was an earlier "chance" encounter with Professor Paul T.K. Lin and architect Arthur Erickson at the Summer Palace. Trudeau and his party departed Beijing by train, accompanied not by the much sought after panda bear,[7] but by Vice-Premier Deng Xiaoping, a man who was condemned during the Cultural Revolution but rehabilitated six months prior to Trudeau's visit.

GETTING TO KNOW YOU:
CULTURAL DIPLOMACY DURING
A CULTURAL REVOLUTION

Planning for Prime Minister Trudeau's visit began with the hope for a thoroughgoing series of cultural exchanges between Canada and China. What was achieved, however, was a much-reduced program that had been leached away by the acid of ideology.[8] Among the cultural items and events linked to the state visit were an exhibition of paintings by the Group of Seven, as well as a visit by the Vancouver Symphony, a tour by a Canadian hockey team, and a visit by a delegation of university chancellors and presidents. In Canada, an exhibition of recent archaeological finds in China was to be held at the Royal Ontario Museum in Toronto. There was also the launch of the first official exchange of university students between Canada and China. This last item had been in the works for some time. Professor William Saywell had negotiated an exchange of six students, but the Trudeau visit increased the number to twenty, delaying the start of the exchange until late November. There was no shortage of students wanting to come to China, but there was a shortage of government budgeted funds. The extra places were thrown open to select pairs of universities to fund: Toronto/York, McGill/Montréal, UBC/Simon Fraser. Thus, the original six places were supplemented to make twenty.

Some of the exchange students, in anticipation of an earlier start to the program, were travelling in Asia, while others came directly from Canada. They gathered in Hong Kong late in November 1973. Margo and I went to Hong Kong to meet them and to accompany them through the border crossing and on the flight to Beijing. They were an interesting group with a broad range of interests, including poetry, traditional Chinese medicine, history, politics, and film. There were ten women and ten men, representing most regions of Canada and having a range of political views from conservative to Maoist. The Maoists had a mentor in the person of Professor Paul Lin of McGill. They expected to share accommodations in Beijing with Chinese students and to participate fully in the Cultural Revolution experience. Others expected to pursue their studies, hopefully in the free-ranging way they enjoyed in Canada. Alas, this was not to be, nor did the Maoists get what they expected. The *Pi Lin Pi Kung* campaign mentioned earlier had gathered strength, and with it the influence of the Cultural Revolution group under the state council in charge of education and the arts. It had the power to countermand the directives from the regular departments of government. Thus, previous promises made about the exchange program were ignored. The Canadian students shared rooms with each other in a converted geological sciences compound on the outskirts of Beijing, where foreign students from many countries were billeted. Their promised courses of study were cancelled and they were expected to take language lessons heavily laced with political teachings and to obey the strict rules and curfews of their student residence. Canadian students were considered by other foreign students to be special in Chinese eyes because of Norman Bethune, and so when they came back after curfew they always said they were Canadians. The months of December and January were particularly dreary: cold with some snow, and lots of dust. The majority of the students, however, seized the opportunity that had been given them and tried to make the most of it. Some managed some train travel and were astounded to see marijuana growing wild and unharvested along some of the railway lines.

Because the stipend given to each student by the Chinese government was very small by Canadian standards, the Canadian government supplied a small monthly supplement. Each month, I went to the Institute for Foreign Students, where the students were staying and where they took classes, to distribute the supplement, to gauge student morale, and to supply them with any information I could. In some cases I attempted to reinstate the special programs they had originally been promised, but with very modest success. On occasion, we had a meal together, along with Margo, in central Beijing. The Maoists remained aloof from these arrangements, fearing, I suppose, capitalist-imperialist contamination. One person very interested in the progress of the students was the journalist John Burns. Burns met the students when they arrived and openly expressed his scepticism at the solidarity and togetherness the Maoists said they would achieve. During the winter, Burns, along with members of the embassy, extended hospitality to interested students, enabling them to have a weekend away from the institute to enjoy the comforts of home like a bath and a Western-style meal. In the spring of 1974, Burns wrote a series of feature articles on the life the students experienced in Beijing. The articles were reasonably fair, although he had little truck for the Maoists, but they stirred interest in Canada and raised questions about the worthiness of the exchange itself, since the students had not been free to study the subjects they desired as originally promised. But the doubts were not sufficient to halt the exchange and the second year's crop of students was selected through a national competition, with no illusions as to what to expect in Beijing.

The student exchange program was not the only Sino-Canadian activity to be affected by the increasingly tense political atmosphere in China. Even after I made several visits to, and had many discussions with, the Association for Friendship with Foreign Countries and even after carefully vetting the program of the Vancouver Symphony—to perform anything later than Beethoven in China was too risky. In December, with no firm decision from the Chinese, it was decided that the visit by the symphony could not go forward in the first half of 1974, which was the only time the symphony had free in its schedule.[9] A similar fate faced the Group of Seven when paintings by Lawren Harris were deemed by the Chinese to be too avant-garde—too abstract—for the Chinese public. Meanwhile, Canadian authorities grew more and more concerned about the exhibition space and the lack of environmental controls, as well as the purpose of mounting the exhibit given the political atmosphere.

Some light relief came with a whirlwind visit to Beijing by a Canadian trade delegation in November 1973. Well, it was not really an official trade delegation. Rather, the CIA (Canadian Importers Association) was a delegation of Canadians who wanted to trade a bit and to see China. It was made up of business people, importers, hockey promoters, and newspaper columnists. The group sought to take advantage of the Canton Fair,[10] a twice yearly showcase of Chinese goods where foreign buyers came to make deals and place orders. It echoed the days before the nineteenth-century Opium Wars, when Western traders were confined to Guangzhou for trading and could not go to Beijing. Russians could go to Beijing, because Beijing was the closest cross-border city to their country. Europeans and North Americans, who came by sea, were assigned to Guangzhou as the closest border point.

Members of the CIA arrived in Hong Kong, and may or may not have taken into account the international dateline. In any case, they were pressed for time. They went by train to Guanzhou, but they were a day late. Nonetheless, they were convinced they were important enough to the future of the Chinese economy that a major Chinese trading corporation, headquartered in Beijing, would greatly benefit from their visit. They pressured their Chinese hosts in Guangzhou to provide them with space on an airplane to Beijing—done by bumping twenty regular passengers. They arrived in China's capital just in time for a late lunch. Their schedule included sightseeing, a meeting with the corporation, a cocktail party at the Canadian ambassador's residence, all before catching the night train to Guangzhou and an eventual return to Canada. They had about ten hours in Beijing: the equivalent of the famous five-minute tour of the Louvre.

I attended the CIA's meeting with the Chinese trading corporation, held in a large room upstairs in the old Beijing Hotel. In addition to the CIA delegation, there was a larger number of Chinese and a few hangers-on like me. The head of the CIA was supplied with an excellent interpreter, but for some reason, known only to himself, he chose to speak in broken—pidgin—English. The stunned interpreter attempted to cope. The overall scene came to resemble the Hollywood Western cliché of white men trading beads and guns with native Indians. The CIA leader introduced a leather-goods dealer named Barrington who had come to China in hopes of tapping greater supplies of excellent horse hides. He had sent an order to China by mail, but had heard nothing back. He had brought with him copies of his company's catalogue, on the cover of which was the likeness of a beautiful racehorse. The CIA leader grabbed a copy of the catalogue and, holding it up before his bewildered Chinese audience, said, "Him—him over there—him Barrington. Him want buy leather. Him want buy horsehides. You sell. Him buy. Him buy lots. You sell lots. You get rich."

The name for horse in Mandarin is *MA*. As the leader concluded his sales pitch, he displayed the cover of the catalogue to each quadrant of the room saying: "Horse." "*MA*," said the interpreter. And it went on like this for some time: "HORSE." "*MA*." "HORSE." "*MA*." "HORSE." "*MA*." Seated in the back row, a member of a Chinese trading corporation, a person in his fifties, with a PhD in economics from Fordham University, turned to me and said, "Dr. Evans, you are a Canadian. What is he trying to say?"

After the CIA's visit, I was directly involved in arranging for the first hockey exchange between Canada and China,[11] to occur in December 1973. It too had its lighter moments. The idea of the exchange had earlier been mooted during the summer of 1972, when Canada had staged a big trade show. Part of the entertainment during the trade show had been ice dancing by a number of figure skaters. It was August, and Beijing was passing through the period know as "Tiger Heat"—artificial ice was simply unavailable. Instead, the skaters performed on plastic sheets. The sight of young ladies in tutus and flesh-toned tops went far beyond the puritanical standards of the Cultural Revolution. The dancers made an enduring, or as the Chinese then were fond of saying, a "deep lasting" impression. Their performance had certainly caught the attention of Kuo Lei, the senior member of the Chinese Sports Federation who negotiated the hockey exchange. Perhaps in his seventies, with a far-away look in his eyes, the official said to me, "Now, you are absolutely certain that Canada will not be sending any more of those scantily clad young ladies who performed those shocking dances."

Initially, the Chinese Sports Federation had wanted the Toronto Maple Leafs as its exchange team. It had to be convinced this was an unreasonable request, given the NHL schedule and the fact that the players were highly paid professionals. For them to take two weeks off in early December to tour China was impossible. Canada offered instead to send a university team from the west coast, a highly skilled team that had a coach who would be very useful in advising the Chinese national team. Canada intended no slight by this offer.

In early December, the University of British Columbia Thunderbirds arrived. The overall delegation was led by Don Johnson from Newfoundland, an executive of the Canadian Hockey Association. There were certain Cultural Revolution rituals that leaders of foreign delegations had to observe. In sport, the slogan most used was: *Youyi di yi, Bisai di er* (Friendship first, competition second). Hardly a concept honoured in North American hockey. The Chinese always expressed a warm welcome to visitors in general and praised the skills and expertise of their country: in this case, Canada. They said they wanted to learn from the visitors. The leader of the visiting delegation was then expected to reply that they were overwhelmed by China's friendship and hospitality, they were willing to share what little knowledge and skills they had, and that actually, it was a question of learning from each other.

Given the nature of the expected diplomatic niceties, the visit by the Canadian delegation was not to pass with flying colours. Don Johnson knew hockey, but he had little appreciation for the rituals of China. He did, however, want to give the Chinese full value for their money. Johnson was a direct person, and when asked for an opinion, he gave it—straight. He had not taken to his briefing on Chinese politics too well, believing, like Chairman Mao, that experts make things needlessly complicated. The leader of the Communist Party, Chairman Mao Zedong, and Premier Zhou Enlai were each revered by the Chinese people and were referred to respectfully as Chairman Mao and Premier Zhou. Johnson, for reasons never shared and perhaps known only to himself, combined the two great leaders into one person he called, appropriately, Chairman Mou (pronounced MOE).

The first game between the Thunderbirds and the Chinese national team was played in the Beijing Capital Stadium and Johnson was seated with Kuo Lei. Because sports exchanges were so important to the diplomacy of China, the interpreter at the game, Liu Shih-chin, was a superb practitioner of the art. He edited the conversation between Johnson and the senior official brilliantly. The unedited version went something like this:

KUO: Welcome. Canada is a very good friend of China. Dr. Norman Bethune travelled thousands of miles and sacrificed his life for the Chinese people. The Chinese people will never forget him. Your prime minister, Mr. Trudeau, visited China last October and made a very deep impression upon us all.

JOHNSON: Thank you. It is a great honour to be here. Canadians are greatly impressed with the achievements of your great country under the leadership of Chairman Mou. I have read the works of Chairman Mou, and I am impressed by what he has written. Chairman Mou is a great man.

KUO: Canada is famous for hockey, but unfortunately in China it is in its infancy. We must learn from you. You must be our teacher.

JOHNSON: Yes, we do have very good teams and we beat those Russians. I think your main problem, as I understand it, is that your team is not prepared to be physical and to fight. You have to be physical in hockey.

KUO: We have a saying: Friendship first, competition second. It is in keeping with the teachings of Chairman Mao.

JOHNSON: Chairman Mou must never have played hockey. It won't work in hockey.

The conversation continued in this vein until it was time for the start of the first period. It was a complete mismatch and the eighteen thousand spectators laughed and cheered loudly when the Chinese players fell down, or were knocked over. They remained silent and seemingly indifferent as the Canadian team filled the Chinese net with pucks. Johnson took the opportunity to instruct his Chinese host in the finer points of goal-tending—with liberal references to "Chairman Mou."

From the point of view of scoring by the Chinese national team, the three-week tour was a disaster, but the coach of the Thunderbirds provided much needed coaching advice.[12] On the eve of the delegation's departure, at a farewell banquet, Johnson, who by now had grown to appreciate the skills of Liu Shih-chin the interpreter, was moved to tears at the prospect of saying goodbye to a good friend. He still spoke of Chairman Mou, but his parting compliment went untranslated: "I have grown so fond of Mr. Liu that I have invited him to my province to open up a Chinese restaurant."

The hockey tour did not receive a passing grade from the Canadian diplomats present at the banquet, but in a perverse way it was a success. Unsophisticated as some may have thought him, Johnson the foreigner had pierced and stripped away some of the meaningless rituals. Nearly a decade later, well after "Chairman Mou" had passed from the scene, and the Chinese had relieved themselves of the burden of paying lip service to his achievements, a Chinese basketball team participated in the 1983 Universiade games at the University of Alberta. The interpreter accompanying them was none other than Liu Shih-chin. I asked him what he had thought about the Thunderbirds' tour in China. "Oh, we learned a great deal and the tour leader, Mr. Don Johnson, became our great friend. He has been back to China a number of times since." I could not help asking about Johnson's offer to help Liu set up a restaurant in his home province. Liu replied, "I understand it is a beautiful place, but I am not such a good cook."[13]

BETHUNIANA

For Canadians living in China during the Cultural Revolution, Norman Bethune was both a boon and a burden. He was so politically correct at that time that mere mention of him brought a positive response and those with a connection to him were almost certain to find doors opened to them and to be guaranteed special treatment. He was what might nowadays be called "the Canadian brand." At the same time, the growing myth around the name Bethune placed unreasonable expectations upon ordinary Canadians and their behaviour.[14] No matter whether Canadian visits to China were official or unofficial in those days, Norman Bethune was an inescapable subject of conversation. Bethune was an exceptional person: an exceptional doctor, an exceptional surgeon, an exceptional Canadian. A hero. As I mentioned briefly in the previous chapter, he was also a Communist, and it is this fact that contributed most to his fame in China and to his relative obscurity in Canada. Bethune had gone to the Spanish Civil War, after an earlier career as a socially conscious young doctor in Montreal. In Spain, he developed a mobile transfusion service for use on the battlefield. After Spain, he returned to Canada and engaged in a lecture and fundraising tour in support of the Spanish cause. Early in 1937, he left for China to assist the Communist guerrillas fighting against the Japanese invaders. On the way to the mountain hideouts of the guerrillas, he stopped in Yan'an for a meeting with Chairman Mao Zedong. In less than two years, Bethune was dead of blood poisoning, the result of operating without rubber gloves.

Bethune's passing was noted in Canada where his memory was kept alive by his friends and fellow leftists. In China, however, it was a different story. Mao Zedong, on hearing of Bethune's death, wrote an essay praising the selfless internationalism of this Canadian doctor. Mao's essay was to become compulsory reading for young Chinese and during the Cultural Revolution, it was one of the three "most read essays" by all Chinese. Thus, Bethune and Canada became fixed in the minds of Chinese. It was a connection that made Canadians feel special when they went to the People's Republic of China. It also made us feel dumb, because few of us knew who Bethune was. Indeed, Bethune was but one of many Canadian doctors who had served the needs of the Chinese, but he had been particularly fortunate in his eulogist.

I was vaguely aware of Bethune when, in June 1964, I made my first visit to China. He was brought to my attention by a window cleaner in my hotel in Beijing. He asked where I was from. When I replied "*Jianada*," he grinned, gave me a thumbs-up and said, "*Baiquen, Baiquen.*" But it was not until I served as cultural officer at the embassy a decade later that I learned to appreciate the various uses of Norman Bethune. During the Cultural Revolution, official conversations with Chinese (there were very few of any other kind) followed a ritual. There was an introduction in which the history of the unit, institution, commune, or factory was outlined, with heavy emphasis on how bad things were before liberation in 1949, and how much better they were now, particularly under the leadership of the Communist Party and its "Great Helmsman" Mao Zedong, and the guidance of Mao Zedong thought. For Canadians, there was an added moment in which the memory of Dr. Norman Bethune was honoured in hushed tones and with reverence. "Dr. Bethune met Chairman Mao," it would be said with awe.

For Canadians on a short trip to China, these comments reminded them that when they returned home they should find out just who Bethune was. For diplomats and other longer-term residents, Bethune became a sort of burden. Not only were we constantly reminded of him but it seemed we were expected to follow his example. Not to die, but to show selfless sacrifice. With Chinese officials with whom we dealt almost daily, a sort of cynical or jocular tone was possible. But these were not times when we could go too far, in case such comments might be seen as reflecting badly on Chairman Mao. The Chinese were always a little surprised—sometimes more—that Canadians were not as aware of Bethune as they were. Those Chinese who travelled to Canada were perhaps saddened to see how little Bethune was present in the daily life of the average Canadian. To those Canadians anxious to trade and make deals with China, knowing about Bethune became essential and it was not long before commercial uses were found for him and his legend.

Canadian capitalists, drawn to China by the prospect of cheaply produced goods and non-union labour, were not averse to embracing Bethune. Books about Bethune were acceptable presents to give Chinese hosts, and many a Canadian businessperson took back to Canada a bust or small statuette of Bethune. When it came to hosting Chinese visitors in Canada, time was found to have a photo taken by the statue of Bethune in the small square at the corner of Guy and Maisonneuve in Montreal, or, more ambitiously, to arrange a side trip to Gravenhurst, Ontario, to see the house in which Bethune was born. Trips to Niagara Falls and other wonders in Canada were not approved of during the decade of the Cultural Revolution and those who took them could be subjected to great criticism. Bethune, a "Mao-approved" tourist attraction, was the safest of the safe.

The importance of Bethune was recognized by the Canadian Wheat Board a full decade before Canada and China exchanged official recognition. The big wheat sales to China, made during the John Diefenbaker-Alvin Hamilton years, brought home to the Canadian Wheat Board negotiators the importance of Bethune, and it was they who found out where Bethune was born and began the treks with Chinese officials to see the house. At the time, the house, a former United Church manse, was occupied, so only the exterior could be viewed. Once Canada recognized China and ambassadors were exchanged, something more substantial had to be done.

In August 1972 in Beijing at the large Canadian trade show, Mitchell Sharp, the minister in charge of the official delegation, promised the Chinese that something more would be done to raise the profile of Norman Bethune in Canada. The house where he was born would be purchased and a museum to Bethune established in it. Official efforts were then made to persuade the Historic Sites and Monuments Board of Canada to declare the house a historic site, but without success. One of the problems, apart from Bethune's controversial career, was he had not lived very long in the house of his birth, his father being called away to another parish shortly thereafter.

Nonetheless, a year later, in discussions held during Trudeau's visit, the Chinese were informed that the house had been acquired by the Department of External Affairs and that work would go ahead on the museum. The departments of International Trade and External Affairs knew the importance of Bethune to the Canada–China relationship and with the United States growing closer to China, Canada needed all the trading advantages it could get. Let everyone who went to China with trade and commerce in mind be thoroughly briefed on Dr. Norman Bethune. In China, Canadians regularly made trips to the tomb of Bethune, located in a large military cemetery in the provincial city of Shihjiazhuang, a few hours by train south of Beijing. Along with the Chinese pilgrimages in Canada, this made for an appealing symmetry.

As powerful a commercial tool as he was, Bethune was of little use in dealing with one of the more intractable problems following Trudeau's visit in 1973. The Exhibition of Archaeological Finds from the People's Republic of China began its European tour late in 1972. Originally a project of the London *Sunday Times*, which had persuaded the Chinese authorities to allow out of China a collection of recently discovered artifacts dating from prehistory to the twelfth century A.D., the exhibition was displayed at the Royal Academy of Arts in London in a traditional setting and using traditional descriptive chronology. It went on to Paris and eventually to Austria and Sweden. The jade suits sewn with gold thread and the flying horse balanced on the back of a swallow caught everyone's imagination, and China was urged to let the exhibition travel to the Royal Ontario Museum (ROM) in Toronto for the summer of 1974. An agreement to do this was signed in Beijing by Ambassador Small. Because the exhibition had already made several stops, it was just a matter of using the existing agreements as templates, making minor adjustments to fit the Canadian circumstances, and settle matters of venue, insurance, and transportation.

ROM curators began to prepare for the exhibition's arrival and ordered copies of the illustrated catalogue the British had prepared, emended where needed to suit the ROM. The catalogue represented a substantial outlay of funds. Unfortunately, no one could foresee the *Pi Lin Pi Kung* campaign and its implications for the exhibition. While the campaign was gathering strength in China, the exhibition continued on its European tour to Stockholm from where it was to travel to Canada. Negotiations for its Toronto visit were going smoothly until the Cultural Revolution Group under the State Council in Beijing became aware that a Confucian-related document was being displayed as part of the exhibition, and more horrifyingly, the exhibition was being shown in settings that did not reflect revolutionary China. The exhibition and its catalogue did not recognize the Maoist interpretation of history.[15] These issues came to a head in the spring of 1974 when the ROM had already invested heavily in exhibition design and in the catalogue. The Chinese threatened to withdraw the exhibition unless changes were made.

Matters were resolved through negotiations between the ROM, External Affairs, and the exceptional Chinese ambassador Zhang Wenjin, with minor

Statue of Norman Bethune at his tomb in the military cemetery
in Shijiazhuang, capital of Hebei province, 1974.

participation by me in Beijing. The offending artifact was withdrawn from the exhibit and another politically correct one was inserted. A new "official" catalogue was produced. It was a simple document mimeographed with a yellow cover (later, it was printed with the flying horse on a red background for its cover). The exhibition opened on schedule. Those who visited it were charged ten dollars for the new catalogue and given a free copy of the "offending" illustrated catalogue previously prepared in Britain. Face was saved all round.[16]

While of no use to the ROM, while at the embassy, and on subsequent trips to China, I called on Bethune in various ways. The first time was in 1973, on a searingly hot July day when I, and two companions, were out taking photographs of the *hutongs*, that maze of narrow lanes that connected the residential areas of old Beijing. Having wandered for some time, we ate lunch in a Muslim café, before ending up in a cul-de-sac leading to an old monastery. During the Cultural Revolution, Chinese citizens were encouraged to be very suspicious of foreigners. Moreover, large white foreigners just might be Russian spies. In the cities, street committees monitored the various districts. They were usually headed and run by women, and on that hot July day the head of one such street committee arrested us. What could be more suspicious than three foreigners with cameras in a cul-de-sac, not far from the Soviet Embassy? Each of us carried ID cards issued by the Public Security Bureau, but the street committee leader was not convinced of our innocence until we waxed eloquently about the exploits of Norman Bethune. She made a quick phone call and we were free to go.

In the summer of 1974, the Canadian Embassy suffered a minor crisis because of Norman Bethune. In July, a delegation of Canadian university presidents and chancellors arrived in Beijing. When it came time for the group to leave, the delegation leader, Nathan Nemetz, who was the chancellor of UBC, a judge, and a former leader of the Liberal Party in British Columbia, asked to stay on in China a little longer. In 1937, Norman Bethune had spent his last night in Canada in the Nemetz's family home and he wanted to make the pilgrimage to Bethune's tomb. I travelled with Nemetz to Shijiazhuang and the visit went very well. He was treated with the great respect befitting someone who had actually had contact with Bethune.

On our return to Beijing, Nemetz was received by some officials, including some medical doctors, on the evening before his departure by train for Guangzhou and Hong Kong. At the Beijing railway station, Nemetz gave an interview to John Burns of the *Globe and Mail*. He assumed Burns was interested in Bethune, but Burns was after a bigger story. There was a rumour that Zhou Enlai was ill. Had Nemetz heard anything about Zhou's health? Was it his heart? Not wishing to look uninformed, Nemetz more or less affirmed the rumour. Burns filed his story and Nemetz headed south by train. The story caused a sensation and to Nemetz's surprise he was met by a horde of reporters when he stepped off the train in Kowloon. He denied any knowledge of Zhou's state of health. Because I was present at the interview, I was called back from a brief seaside holiday to explain. In my view, Burns had enough of an assurance from Nemetz to reach the conclusion he did, but he should have given Nemetz more background as to why he was asking the question. The rumour about Zhou's ill health was indeed true, but it was cancer not heart problems that confined him to the 302 Military Hospital for most of the remaining eighteen months of his life.[17] Public comment on the health of China's leaders was forbidden. In a previous incident in 1973, John R. Walker of The Canadian Press, on leaving Beijing for a tour of other Asian countries, mentioned casually to his interpreter that he would not be back early unless "Chairman Mao dies." Because of this remark, he was nearly denied re-entry into China.

Even after leaving the embassy I was not free of Bethune. By late August 1976, the Bethune birthplace museum was ready for opening and I received an invitation to go to Gravenhurst to participate. It was a little perk for a retired BLO, but the ceremony itself did not come off without a little hitch or two. The house, located near Lake Muskoka, Ontario, with plenty of green lawn surrounding it, was closed until the official ribbon-cutting ceremony. Beside the house was a large tent to accommodate the post-opening reception. On the lawn in front of the house was a low dais with a lectern and microphones facing rows of chairs. The front rows, marked VIP, were reserved for the official party coming from Ottawa by bus. It included a delegation from the Chinese government, including officials who had served on the Chinese foreign office (*waijiaobu*), Canada desk, and their counterparts from the Department of External Affairs. It was a warm sunny afternoon and sitting in the shade of a tree near the dais were members of the press including a CTV crew. The program included brief speeches by both Chinese and Canadians prominent in establishing Chinese–Canadian relations. Chester Ronning, whose name was synonymous with China–Canada diplomatic relations, was one of the speakers. Otto Lang, a prominent Cabinet minister whose responsibilities included the Canadian Wheat Board, was to cut the ribbon. He arrived by government plane at a nearby airfield because he only had a "small window" for the ceremony.

As the time for the ceremony drew closer, the seats filled up and people sat on the lawn, preserving the ribboned-off VIP seats. A few moments before the ceremony was to begin, the filmmaker Otto Preminger, who was investigating the possibility of making a movie about Bethune, arrived with an assistant or two. Refusing to believe that he was anything but a VIP, he and his party appropriated some of the reserved seats. When the time for the ceremony arrived, but the guests of honour had not, the people who had been seated on the lawn took over the remaining VIP seats. By the time the bus with the official delegation had arrived, late because the driver had lost the way, there were no chairs left and the Chinese delegation had to sit on the grass in front of the front row. With Minister Lang anxious to catch his plane, speakers were encouraged to be brief. Chester Ronning, then eighty-two years old, had a tendency to extemporize on the history of China from the mid-nineteenth century to the present, a subject he knew from memory. As such, preparing a text for him to read had been essential to keeping things short. When it came time for Ronning to speak, the sun shone directly in his eyes and he could not see his text, so he launched at length into history.[18]

Once he had finished speaking, the minister, champing at the bit, declared the building open and fled to his plane, leaving Ronning, always a superbly gracious and entertaining host, to escort the Chinese guests through the museum. As the delegation entered the house for their private tour, the audience quickly occupied the refreshment tent, slaking the thirst that gripped them under the August sun. They fell upon the sandwiches and sweets with passion. The tent was picked nearly clean by the time Ronning and the Chinese delegation had emerged from the house. Hardship and hunger were things Bethune had learned to live with and in his spirit the Chinese guests accepted the circumstances gracefully.

During the Cultural Revolution and its immediate aftermath, resident foreigners were given a great deal of privilege. They had a separate form of currency called FEC (Foreign Exchange Certificates) and they had special shops in which to spend it. Transportation was cheaper for resident foreigners than for Chinese, and they always went to the head of a line. This treatment was probably the result of a mix of traditional Chinese courtesy to official guests and respect for the foreign currency that was exchanged for FEC. By 1981, however, this was beginning to change as more and more tourists came to China contributing hard currency. The pampering of resident foreigners was coming to an end, which led to the abolition of FEC, while the special "friendship" stores were opened to ordinary Chinese using regular currency. Foreigners had to fend for themselves for air and rail tickets, which were no longer a bargain. Even the Civil Aviation Authority of China was feeling some pressure to change. In its effort to encourage more tourists, both foreign and domestic, the government had to increase airplane capacity. It allowed the Chinese Air Force to enter the domestic passenger carrying market. They did not have regular schedules and their planes arrived and took off with no, or very little, notice. A traveller was foolish to believe the listings in the airline office downtown—it was necessary to be on the spot at the airport.

During this time (the early 1980s), pilots were very important people in China. Not only did they fly the planes but they decided when and where to land, and even got involved in the question of which passengers to let on board the plane. In July 1980, I had travelled with a friend to Guilin, whose Li River is perhaps the most famous of China's beautiful spots. The city was jammed with tourists from China and abroad and we did not have confirmed flights out to Guangzhou, which would enable us to connect with our flight out of Hong Kong to Vancouver. Following advice given to us on the street, we went to the airport to see what could be done. There were certainly more flights than those listed in the city. After a short wait—or was it long?—an Air Force plane arrived unannounced. It was on its way from Shanghai to Guangzhou with a brief stop in Guilin. I was told that if we wanted seats I would have to negotiate directly with the pilot. As far as they (the desk) were concerned, the flight was full, but the pilot always had a seat or two, if he could be persuaded. They pointed to a table where the pilot would shortly take a seat. I was second in line to see him and he was amused to see a desperate foreigner. Our conversation, in Chinese, went something like this:

"Do you have any seats left on your plane?"
"Perhaps."
"Perhaps, what does that mean?"
"There are seats, but I don't think you would like them."
"Try me."
"No, you are a foreigner and you will just criticize conditions in China."
"I am hardly a foreigner. I have lived and worked in China before, and I am impressed with how conditions have improved."
"No, the seats I have are not very good, too difficult."
"Come now, do you think that those of us from the land of Norman Bethune worry about hardship? Please, we would very much like the seats."
"Can I be sure you will not complain?"
"Did Dr. Bethune ever complain?"
"All right."

I paid him the money and my companion and I headed for the plane, feeling sorry for the last man in the queue, who also happened to be Chinese.

The plane was a British Trident. We boarded through the rear door and were led to the front of the plane where we were given the pull-down seats in the front doorway, usually reserved for flight crew, opposite the small galley. At least there were seat belts. Just before the rear door closed, the last man in the queue boarded. He was brought to the front of the plane and seated on a kitchen stool in the galley where he sat facing forward. On the counter before him was an unopened glass bottle of Coke. On an open shelf under the counter was a large watermelon. The pilot taxied the aircraft down to the end of the runway and then took off at a very sharp angle to avoid the mountains around the airfield. The watermelon rolled out of its shelf, headed for the floor. The man on the stool leaned forward to catch it, only to be struck on the head by the falling coke bottle. He seemed none the worse for wear and came up smiling. I made a mental note to be cautious in the future when speaking of Norman Bethune to pilots.

On another occasion, in July 1981, a Canadian friend, who had been invited to visit friends in Beijing, and I, being on my way to interview graduate students, found ourselves in a minor dilemma. We had stayed overnight in a huge hotel in Guangzhou and had to catch an early train north. We wanted breakfast in the morning, but there seemed little hope. The line-up for the dining room stretched as far as the eye could see, made up of couples who were waiting for a table. Out of the corner of my eye I saw another dining room where there was no line-up. We went over to investigate and were told that it was for groups only:

"But we are a group."
"No, you are not. You are a couple."
"What is your smallest group?"
"Three."
"Ah ha, we are Canadians, and everywhere we go, Dr. Norman Bethune is with us. So you see, we are actually a group of three."

Either fed up, or amused, the young lady showed us to a table and we caught our train in time.

Nowadays, the power of Bethune in China is waning. He is remembered most by those over fifty, and one is likely to be reminded of that fact by questions such as, "Didn't Dr. Norman Bethune come from Canada?" China's youth are now caught up with *Da Shan*, or Mark Rosewell, a Canadian star of Chinese stage and television who teaches English and Chinese. A big touring bus with his picture and name on it can regularly be seen in the streets of Beijing. Bethune has nearly had his day, so it seems. Evidence of this can be found if one goes to the city of Shihjiazhuang, to the military cemetery where he is buried. The cemetery is magnificent and well maintained by the army. At one end of a cross promenade stands a statue of Bethune, identical to the one in Montreal. Behind him are his tomb and a photo display. He looks down the promenade to the statue of Dr. Dwarkanath Kotnis, an Indian doctor who also died serving the Chinese people and who was the first director of the Norman Bethune Memorial Hospital. Near the far end of the main promenade that crosses at right angles to the one linking Bethune and Kotnis is a museum with displays illustrating the lives and contributions of the two doctors to China. A similar display can be found in the Norman Bethune Memorial Hospital in Shijiazhuang, the first of six hospitals in China named after Bethune that sports tall modern buildings. The only thing missing are tourists, Canadians who used to come as a matter of course to the tomb of Bethune. I have made four of these pilgrimages, which were very popular during the Cultural Revolution. Chinese students journeyed to see Bethune and to recount his deeds. Canadians could purchase (actually rent) a plastic wreath at the gate to lay at the tomb of Bethune. On a long visit to Shihjiazhuang in 1992, I visited the tomb and hospital. I was the only Canadian they had seen for some time, and the old plastic wreath had long been retired.

SEVEN

In the Hot Seat

China in the mid-1970s continued to be wracked by conflict among the top members of the leadership. The Cultural Revolution adherents pressed on with the *Pi Lin Pi Kung* campaign, but Zhou Enlai and the reformists continued with an agenda of reform, announcing a program of Four Modernizations in 1975.[1] To counter this, the radical left, with Mao's tacit support, launched yet another campaign, this time against "Bourgeois Rights," attacking the concept of allowing farmers to have private plots and other forms of material incentives. Meanwhile, Zhou Enlai's cancer limited his ability to keep pace as he worked from his bed in the 302 Military Hospital in Beijing. Mao's own health was at risk; he suffered from Parkinson's. Speculation among Western observers, who had previously assumed Zhou would outlive the older Mao, was now focussed on what would happen if Zhou died first. Lin Biao was long dead and Mao had not named a successor. Wang Hongwen, listed as number three in the leadership, was young and had no firm base within the Communist Party and among the people. Where was China going? All questions were answered in one year and with one name: 1976 and Deng Xiaoping.

"THE BEST LAID SCHEMES... GANG AFT AGLEY"[2]

A year as a diplomat in China did wonders for my reputation, academically and publicly. On my return to the University of Alberta in the fall of 1974, following my sojourn in Beijing, I was in demand as a speaker. I illustrated my talks with the many slides I had taken in China. A natural optimist, I was generally positive about the Chinese experiment. I felt reasonably certain that given a chance, China, led by Zhou Enlai and his modernizers, would not only win out but would be able to avoid some of the excesses of North American life, such as rampant consumerism and individual car ownership, and build a modern, freer, and more open society. For my audiences, I pictured a poor, idealistic, prudish, and at times heroic China. It was, of course, decades behind Canada in its development. I knew one thing. I was now hooked on the unfolding story of contemporary China and was keen to follow it. The federal Department of External Affairs put me on academic advisory committees charged with selecting young scholars to go to China and promoting Canadian studies abroad. I was also active in the Canadian Association for Asian Studies (CAAS) and served a term as its treasurer. In November 1974, Brian Heeney, vice-president at Trent University, asked me to organize a China Week at his institution. I called on some of the returned students whom I knew from Beijing. Our efforts met with enthusiasm and we formed a panel for the spring meeting of the Association for Asian Studies in San Francisco. The panel was well received. Nixon had opened a door to China and American scholars were thirsty for first-hand accounts of life in China.

A year in Beijing had greatly improved my understanding of modern China and furthered an interest I had in Canadian–East Asian relations, I hoped to the benefit of my students. In 1976, I took a year's leave to study China's cultural relations and cultural diplomacy, something about which I now had first-hand experience. I wanted to see whether China had a different cultural strategy country-by-country and to see what value selected countries placed on cultural relations. My project was funded by the Social Sciences and Humanities Research Council of Canada (SSHRC), and had the support of John Paynter, the desk officer for East Asia in External Affairs, Ottawa. The topic took me to Washington, Paris, London, Stockholm, Ottawa, and, of course, Beijing. Moscow was also on the list, but my visit there was delayed two years.[3]

I could not have chosen a better year for observing Chinese internal affairs. However, it bode ill for my topic that 1976 began with the death of Zhou Enlai in early January. This was followed a few weeks later by the dismissal of Deng Xiaoping; spontaneous demonstrations in memory of Zhou; the elevation of Hua Guofeng, a virtual unknown, as China's new leader; the death in early July of President Zhu De; the loss of 240,000 in a horrendously destructive earthquake at Tangshan in late July; and the death of Mao on September 9. It was truly the year of the Dragon.[4] With Mao's death I assumed went my chance for a visa. To my surprise, within hours of the news of Mao's passing, I received a call from the Chinese Embassy in Ottawa—my visa was ready, along with one for Margo.

My research plan called for a month in Beijing, followed by a brief stop in Hong Kong before leaving for London, Paris, and Stockholm. Margo took a

Mourning Chairman Mao Zedong, September 1976, Beijing.

month's leave from her work and came with me to China. Sadly, it was to be her last trip to the country she had grown to love. Her bouts of travel sickness were to get worse, to the point that, in the years following this trip, she could not tolerate being in any vehicle for more than fifteen minutes. When she attempted anything longer, she paid for it with fainting spells, nausea, and severe headaches. She insisted, nonetheless, that I continue travelling, taking a vicarious pleasure in my trips.

After flying to Hong Kong on October 6, we took the now familiar trains to the border and on to Guangzhou to connect with the northbound train for Beijng. China and the Chinese people looked worn out and downcast after the accumulated shocks of the first nine months of the year. Because of Mao's death and the mourning for the dead of Tangshan, there had been no celebrations on October 1 to mark National Day. There had been little to celebrate so far in 1976. Evidence of the effect of Mao's death was particularly obvious. As Margo and I travelled north from Guangzhou, we saw the whole of the countryside, towns and cities in mourning, with most buildings draped in white and black. In Beijing, I sat in on a meeting of the group of China-watchers drawn from a number of embassies. The foreign community was rife with rumours, many reporting that Mao's wife Jiang Qing—popularly despised—and her cohorts (the Gang of Four) were now in charge, with an equal number positive that the gang had been removed.

Demonstrators In Tiananmen Square, October 1976, following the news of the fall
of the so-called Gang of Four marking the end of the Cultural Revolution.

A few days later on October 21, speculation ended. The streets exploded with
noise and colour as workers, students, and soldiers marched along Chang'an
Avenue, passing through Tiananmen Square where large crowds had gathered
carrying red flags and banners denouncing the Gang of Four. At last there was
something to celebrate. Large trucks sped by with people in the back beating
huge drums, banging gongs, and clashing cymbals. Firecrackers of all sizes
filled the air with blue smoke. Joy was everywhere—for the first time in years,
ordinary Chinese dared to speak freely with foreigners.[5] A Chinese professor of
literature from the People's University I recognized, who only the year before
had lectured at the University of Alberta, rushed from the crowd carrying a
very large firecracker to set off in front of Tiananmen. We exchanged brief
greetings before he rushed back to join his ecstatic colleagues. In the square,
crocodiles of primary students marched, waving little flags shouting, "*Da dao
si ren bang*!" ("Down with the Gang of Four!") Cameramen from Chinese TV
asked them to look grim and angry for all the world to see. As they dispersed,
one little boy holding his mother with one hand while waving a flag with
the other shouted, "*Da dao Hua Guofeng*!" ("Down with Hua Guofeng!" [the
newly appointed leader]) as they passed me on a street leading from the square.
Clearly, he was caught up in the enthusiasm of the moment and did not appreciate what he was saying. Yet, as lively as the scenes were in the square and

Celebrations in Tiananmen, October 1976. Between the rain and the firecrackers, the air was blue.

along Chang'an Avenue, life, after the first day, went on quietly and as normal just a few streets and lanes away.

The demonstrations/celebrations went on for three days, defying rain and traffic congestion. Banners and cartoons depicting the gang as four rats caught by the tail could be seen everywhere. Crowds were good humoured and friendly, but with my high forehead I looked something like the cartoon portrait of Yao Wenyuan, one of the dreaded gang. Many a banner carrier did a double take as they passed me, only to laugh and shout their denunciations even louder. Margo was amused, although she had thought me perhaps a little foolhardy for mixing with the crowds, taking pictures and taping the sounds on a miniature Sony recorder. In public parks, such as Ritan (Altar of the Sun), we saw that the earlier photos showing the mass gathering of a million people in Tiananmen Square to mourn Mao Zedong had been replaced with a new set, airbrushed to remove the members of the Gang of Four. Under their blank spaces in the photos was written: xx, xxx, xxx, xxx. Everyone knew whose names these x's represented. In and around Tiananmen Square people smashed small bottles on the pavement in tribute to Deng Xiaoping, the mastermind behind the overthrow of the gang.[6] Street sweepers were busy cleaning up the glass and the spent firecrackers amid the din and wreaths of blue smoke.

On the fourth day, on Sunday, October 24, over a million people gathered in the square and along Chang'an Avenue to face the gate atop of which stood

Tiananmen celebration following the fall of the Gang of Four, October 1976.

the new leadership and the number one leader, Hua Guofeng, but everyone knew that Deng Xiaoping—yet to reappear—was running things. From our room on the upper floor of the Beijing Hotel, we, along with a few friends, watched, taking photos, as during the morning groups from institutions and organizations all over Beijing marched in designated order into the square to take up their positions as indicated by numbers written on the stone paving slabs. There they sat in the sun until the ceremony began, and then they all stood. Once the speeches were over, these thousands of people scattered like autumn leaves driven by a gale.

Indeed, change, like a high wind from the Gobi, swept through China. The swiftly changing party line caught many people off guard, including Qiao Guanhua, the Chinese Foreign Minister at the UN, who gave a speech on October 5, 1976, outlining Chinese foreign policy.[7] A very talented person, he associated himself too closely with the Gang of Four. He went to New York on September 21 as Foreign Minister but did not come back with the same title. The change also affected Canadian students studying in Beijing. Some of them were greatly impressed with Jiang Qing and could not believe her blackened reputation. They were moved to tears. Still another Canadian, Neil Burton, a long-time student of Paul Lin's, who had just landed a job with Radio Beijing, was caught off guard. He sincerely believed that the previous Maoist line would be maintained and he got into a long-distance argument by mail with a

Crowds in Tiananmen, October 1976.

famous French sociologist, Charles Bettelheim, who resigned in disgust from the France-China Friendship Association, claiming that Deng Xiaoping would re-ignite capitalism in China.[8]

Margo and I stayed on in Beijing for another dozen days and we were able to observe some of the changes occurring in cultural performances. We attended an evening of music and dance during which a number of songs and dances, banned during the Cultural Revolution, were performed to loud applause from the audience. What brought the house down, however, was the first ever public appearance in China of an electric guitar. In Hong Kong, following Margo's departure, I recounted our adventures and observations to David and Judy Bonavia. We discussed the implications of a new, more open China, and how unlikely it was that the new regime would allow much more freedom, even with the public display of relief marking the end of the Cultural Revolution. We agreed on one thing: Maoism had suffered a blow from which it was unlikely to recover. In December, David published a cover story in the *Far Eastern Economic Review* proclaiming the end of Maoism. He received some early ridicule from other China-watchers for his views, but they proved to be prescient.

After staying in Hong Kong for a week, I travelled to London, aware that the world of Chinese cultural diplomacy was now in hiatus on the cusp of a state of flux. In London, I interviewed Maggie Dean, a member of the British

Foreign Office who served in Beijing in the 1950s and who knew the famous "Two-Gun" Cohen when he went to China as an advisor to British arms dealers, anxious to use his connections with Soong Chingling, the widow of Sun Yat-sen, for whom he acted as a bodyguard in the 1920s.[9] It was clear from my talks with Dean that the British did not place great store in cultural exchanges. The heirs to the master opium merchants of old continued to regard trade as the be all and end all of relations with China.

I left foggy and wet London for a chilly, dark, and gloomy Paris, where I enjoyed the company and expertise of my colleague Patricia Prestwich who was on leave in the city doing research. The French, past masters at cultural diplomacy, documented their links with China very well. The government was not too concerned with the internal fights within France's China Friendship Association. Both in London and Paris, the impact of October's events was obvious on China Friendship organizations, separating the Maoists from the moderates and those who followed whatever Beijing propagated at any given point in time. The French envisioned a future of exchanges on high culture rather than the kitsch of the Cultural Revolution. Besides, the French had a particular interest in Deng Xiaoping because of his experience as a student in France in the 1920s; he had been warmly welcomed the year before in 1975 when he made a tour of France.

From Paris, I travelled by train and ferry to Stockholm. I found the Swedes to be less enthusiastic about cultural relations with China and they had few insights to share. They were still smarting from a tiff they had had with Beijing in 1974 over the Exhibition of Archaeological Finds from the People's Republic of China. Sweden had objected to the attempt at political interference from Beijing on how the exhibit should be displayed.[10] After a brief visit to Stockholm University to interview Professor Goran Malmquist, who had taught me at soas, I returned to Paris in time to fly back to Edmonton for Christmas.

My original hopes for my research were no longer realizable with the dramatic changes in China, to which other countries were adjusting. Moreover, I was unable to go to Washington until the next August (1977) and to the Soviet Union until October 1978. I was beginning to conclude, however, that cultural diplomacy reflected how much a given country emphasized culture domestically. In which case, France and China were natural allies. Perhaps it was no accident that their respective cuisines are widely regarded as the best the world has to offer. During the decade of the Cultural Revolution, the Chinese government used culture as an ideological weapon, distorting the traditional arts favoured by the aristocratic and scholarly elite by emphasizing the themes of the worker, soldier, peasant life, and attempting to use old art forms such as the opera, acrobatics, scroll painting, porcelain decorating, silk embroidery, and even paper cutting to carry the message of a new Maoist society. While this approach threw up some outstanding artists and performers, they commanded a narrow audience beyond China's borders, particularly in those Western countries in which the Willow Pattern was the abiding image of Chinese life. This was why the Exhibition of Archaeological Finds proved so popular in the West because it failed to convey the message cultural revolutionists in Beijing wanted. The fall of the Gang of Four would require both the Chinese and the rest of the world to adjust their views.

CULTURAL DIPLOMACY, ALBERTA-STYLE

My research unfinished, and in effect derailed by the events of October 1976, I took up a three-year term (1977–1980) on the University of Alberta Board of Governors as an elected academic member. In those same years and beyond, I was to become part of an exercise in cultural diplomacy at the provincial level and as an individual in China as the modernization process began to gather speed. My time on the Board coincided with the final years of the presidency of Harry Gunning and the first year of that of Myer Horowitz.

Harry Gunning came to the presidency directly from the chair of the Department of Chemistry. He had a great reputation and was credited with building the Chemistry Department into one of the top dozen or so in North America. As president, however, he proved less able. The university had democratized to a great extent, and one of the challenges for the president was to chair General Faculties Council (GFC), which, under a newly revised Universities Act, was given considerable power. Its members included representatives from all segments of the campus, especially students. It had an executive committee, which a president could use to help formulate policy. Gunning admired China and was a little impatient with democracy; he favoured direct action. He was know for not reading documents and "winging it" by assuring all those assembled that he had studied everything thoroughly. He was fortunate in his vice-presidents, Henry Kreisel and later Myer Horowitz, who knew the university well and were generally well liked.

Gunning was capable of spontaneous actions. For example, he ordered that university flags be flown for a week at half-mast in mourning for Mao Zedong. But it was a statement he made at a meeting of the GFC on March 6,

1978, that caused him; Eric Geddes, the chair of the Board of Governors; Burt Hohol, the Minister of Education; and Premier Peter Lougheed a great deal of embarrassment. At the time, the students were very angry at a fee increase of fifty dollars. As on a previous occasion some years earlier, they proposed to march across the High Level Bridge to the legislature to confront the minister. They brought the proposal to the GFC. Gunning, sure of his ground, boldly said that he would march with the students if the GFC voted in favour of cancelling classes so everyone could join the march. Perhaps like Mao with the Red Guards, Gunning felt he was in control of the youth. Much to his dismay, the GFC voted in favour of the cancellation of classes on March 15, the day of the march. The government was faced with the spectre of the president of the largest university in the province leading a protest against it. Emergency meetings were called involving, among others, Lougheed, Geddes, and Gunning. At a hastily called meeting of the Board of Governors, I defended the president's right to march with the students, but the matter went to a tie vote, broken by the Board chair in favour of the president not marching. A face-saving compromise was reached. Gunning would see the students off the campus and then join the Minister of Education on the legislature steps to greet them. This he did, standing beside the minister while the students chanted, "Burt sucks for fifty bucks!" It was a demonstration unlike any to have been seen in China or indeed, France. Nevertheless, Gunning enjoyed a good rapport with the Lougheed government, which saw him as an administrator with a broad vision.

The Lougheed government was also broad in its vision when it came to the initiatives it pursued in Asia. The province was already linked with Kangwon province in South Korea and Hokkaido in Japan when in 1979 the Chinese ambassador in Ottawa suggested that Alberta and Heilongjiang province in Northeast China might make good partners. The Alberta government thought the idea worth exploring and in October 1980 despatched a small delegation led by Hon. Dick Johnston, Minister for Federal and Intergovernmental Affairs (FIGA), to Harbin, Heilongjiang's capital. The delegation included Johnston, his wife Janice, his Executive Assistant Nancy Betkowski,[11] his Assistant Deputy Minister Wayne Clifford, Akira Nawata from Alberta Economic Development, and me. In China, the delegation was accompanied by Jean Duval, an extraordinarily talented interpreter on loan from the federal government, and in northeastern China by John Higginbotham from the Canadian Embassy in Beijing and Herb Pickering, the agent for Alberta in Hong Kong. Johnston's

Tourists and school children in the Forbidden City, October 1980. Following the return to power of Deng Xiaoping in 1979, emphasis was placed upon the foreign tourist trade. Monuments and historic sites were refurbished, many of which had been destroyed or damaged during the Cultural Revolution.

Deputy Minister J. Peter Meekison, on leave from the University of Alberta, had suggested I be included in the delegation.

I had travelled to China twice since 1976, once with a Friendship Tour in April 1978, and once with the first official tour of Canadian academics under an agreement with the Chinese Academy of Social Sciences in late June-early July 1979. On these two trips I had seen some of the changes taking hold with the reappearance of street vendors and increasing numbers of foreign tourists, many of them Americans. Tourists had much to learn about China, and the Chinese had to get used to tourists. On a visit to a hospital just outside Shanghai, I was present with some American tourists, one of whom asked if the portraits of Marx, Engels, Lenin, and Stalin hanging on the wall in the reception room were of former surgeons at the hospital. To travel with the official Alberta delegation was an opportunity to see more of how the "new" China of Deng Xiaoping was progressing. After visiting China, the minister was to open a new Alberta Government office in Hong Kong and to make a visit to Governor Naohiro Dogakinai of Hokkaido in Sapporo, Japan.

When the delegation arrived in China, it was apparent that matters were continuing to change. The atmosphere was more laissez-faire. China was showing a

Suzhou (the "Venice" of China), famous for its gardens, prepares for a wave of tourists beginning in 1981.

new openness to the West, notably American-style clothing. Tourism, a quick source of foreign exchange, was one of Deng Xiaoping's early priorities, and historic sites damaged or destroyed by the Red Guards were being restored and rebuilt. New hotels were thrown up, old ones refurbished, and once exclusive guest houses pressed into service. The People's Liberation Army Air Force branch was asked to supplement the services of the overtaxed national airline Civil Aviation Authority of China (CAAC). Private restaurants were emerging and efforts were made to improve the standards of service in hotels. During the Cultural Revolution, the state-run hotels and restaurants,[12] as well as CAAC,[13] were assigned staff recruited from the sons and daughters of Communist Party members anxious to avoid the hardship of working in the countryside. Generally, the service they provided ranged from indifferent, through sullen and rude, to surly. In the period of early modernization, with better opportunities opening up, they found themselves stuck where they were, and standards sunk even lower. In one case, at least, foreign tourists staged a sit-down strike for better service. China's more conservative leaders, who opposed the new openness, railed against such "poisonous weeds" that would contaminate Chinese culture. Initially, only the film *The Sound of Music* was acceptable to them, while rumours persisted that many business deals were sweetened with a copy of *Deep Throat*. Also, the return of peddlers to the streets of China foretold the beginnings of Deng-style capitalism, which the conservatives dreaded.

The Alberta delegation experienced some of the changes during its travels. Nonetheless, the trip began well with a warm welcome by our hosts in Harbin, followed by serious negotiations. A draft agreement on a partnership, called "twinning" at the time for exchanges and co-operation in the fields of agriculture, oil-well technology, education, medicine, sports, and culture, was reached quickly in a straightforward fashion. Each province had much to offer the other and each had reinforcing similarities of climate, topography, and resources. Dick Johnston had a sharp intellect augmented by wit and quick humour. The delegation's host, Wang Jun, the vice-governor of the province, was a gracious lady who easily saw the humour in life. Heilongjiang province had willingly joined in the Deng Xiaoping modernization movement, unlike parts of the neighbouring Jilin province that had pockets of diehard Maoists still in control. The delegation was treated royally, staying at the very comfortable Provincial Guest House reserved for heads of state. The long history of Russian influence on Harbin was visible in its architecture and in its restaurants. Russian-style salads were served, but local delicacies of Moose nose and bear's paw, though offered, did not prove a hit. However, iced coffee—hot coffee with ice cream in it—was. There was an evening theatre performance by acrobats and dancers, and later a train trip to Daqing, an oil-producing town made famous during the Cultural Revolution by the Maoist slogan: "In Industry learn from Daqing, in agriculture learn from Dazhai."[14] There, in honour of my forty-eighth birthday, we had a cake tasting of dust, with pure butter for the icing.

A highlight of the negotiations was the presentation of gifts, an aspect of cultural diplomacy that interested me. The minister's executive assistant organized a wide range of artwork representative of Alberta, mostly paintings, sculptures, and wall hangings. The minister had not seen them all, and before the trip began there was no way of telling which piece of artwork would be appropriate for which occasion. This was decided on the spot, with the minister making the presentation and his executive assistant feeding him descriptive information, line by line, interleaved with translation. This process worked well, until the minister was handed a small framed work that cried out for a more detailed explanation. It clearly bore no relation, even in the abstract, to the beautiful scenes of mountains and plains that were prominent in the gifts already presented. It was the first time the minister presented a piece of art executed in this traditional manner. His words were prompted by Nancy Betkowski, and translated by Jean Duval:

"It is my pleasure to present you with this picture from my province," said Johnston.

    ("It is made of birch bark," whispered Betkowski.)

"It is made of birch bark."

    ("It was created by a ninety-two-year-old artist.")

"It was created by a ninety-two-year-old artist."

    ("A lady.")

"A lady."

    ("She is a member of our Native community.)

"She is a member of our Native community."

    ("She employs a special technique.")

"She employs a special technique."

    ("She chews it.")

Johnston's hands began to quiver. "She chews it."

    ("But because she has no teeth...")

"But because she has no teeth..." He was now beginning to tremble.

    ("She uses her gums...")

"She uses her gums..." Johnston began to shake with repressed laughter.

    ("The design you see is the imprint of her gums...")

Now he was struggling. "The design...the design...the design, you see, is the...the...the imprint of her gums..."

Tears were now rolling down the minister's cheeks as he presented the gift to the grateful, but perhaps a bit confused, recipient. Gusts of merriment whirled through the room directed at the minister, but not at the art that was examined with growing fascination. Only half a dozen years before, cultural affairs representatives of the Maoist government had declared the paintings by Lawren Harris problematic, being too abstract for the Chinese people. Times were certainly changing.

The formal visit over, the delegation was invited to see something of China in the company of Heilongjiang's Vice-Governor Wang Jun. There were to be stops in Beijing, Shanghai, and a cruise on the Li River at Guilin before our departure for Hong Kong.[15] At Harbin airport, the vice-governor learned her office had not confirmed the travel arrangements—there were no seats available and the plane just leaving for Beijing was the last one of the day. It connected

Hon. Dick Johnston, Minister for Federal and Intergovernmental Affairs, leader of the Alberta Government delegation, presenting a special piece of art to his hosts at a banquet in Harbin, Heilongjiang, October 1980.

to our Beijing-Shanghai flight the next day. The vice-governor, a well-known national politician, worked the phones calling in some favours. After an hour, she reported that a plane was being sent for us from Beijing. A couple of hours later the plane arrived—and what a plane. It was one of the eighteen Boeing 707s reserved for members of the top party leadership. But it was not just the plane of any old top leader: it was the plane of *the* top leader, Hua Guofeng, the equivalent of US Air Force One. It was rare, indeed, for foreigners to see inside such a plane, never mind fly on it. The front of the plane was made up of a suite: a bedroom, bathroom, kitchen, dining area, and meeting room. In no way was it opulent. It was functional and modest, much like the leader, who was not known for his ego or for drawing attention to himself. At the time of our flight, it was less than a year before he completed his five-year term as supreme leader and was replaced by Zhao Ziyang, a person of Deng Xiaoping's choosing. Hua would retire into relative obscurity,[16] probably unaware of how grateful we were for the ride we took on his plane.

The travel glitches at the Harbin airport turned out to be the norm. There were no confirmed flights for the rest of our trip either, and the vice-governor spent hours on the phone making arrangements and contacting old friends. She and Johnston enjoyed an easy relationship, but she spent a great deal of time making ongoing arrangements. We flew by Air Force jet to Shanghai,

Hon. Dick Johnston (right) and John Higginbotham of the Canadian Embassy in Beijing, aboard Chairman Hua Guofeng's private Boeing 707, October 1980. Hua succeeded Mao Zedong as Chairman of the Communist Party of China, becoming the country's leader after Mao's death in September 1976.

where we were joined by Sandra Poohkay, an Alberta student studying in Nanjing, for a cruise on the Wusong River (Suzhou Creek) and a water tour along the famous Bund area in the city, but it was our exit from Guilin that proved once again to be very difficult. We were accompanied on the Li River cruise by a woman strictly known as Mrs. Lin, one of the top members of the local branch of the China International Travel Service (CITS). She took us to eat in the local street restaurants where we tasted snake soup and drank the local firewater, which had little effect on Mrs. Lin but considerable effect on us, me in particular.

The plane from Guilin to Guangzhou connecting to Hong Kong was very small and already fully booked. By pulling rank, and by emphasizing that important foreign guests should be given preference, the vice-governor saw that we were given seats, which local Chinese passengers had been encouraged to give up. There were other foreigners on the plane, namely a group of Americans making a brief tour of southern China. The vice-governor had one more hurdle to jump: finding room for our luggage. The baggage handlers removed select pieces of American tour luggage and replaced them with ours. I pointed this out to my seat companion, one of the American tour group, but she expressed little concern as she continued to talk enthusiastically about the Li River and the fine treatment their group had received. Much later, on the twentieth anniversary of the agreement in 2001,[17] Vice-Governor Wang came to Alberta and was received like an old friend. She made sure to confirm her reservations.

After leaving China, the Alberta delegation's travels in Hong Kong and Japan were of a different order. Every move was well planned and executed on time, and, in Japan, quite formal. We spent Thanksgiving in Hong Kong with members of the Canadian expat community who seemed to us to be beleaguered. Many of them had little appreciation for things Chinese and could not wait to move on. The delights of Hong Kong appeared to have worn thin, and they had grown weary of short-term visitors telling them how lucky they were to live in Hong Kong. This was understandable perhaps because there was a limited range of activities Westerners found attractive: horse racing, picnics on the Peak, sailing, and shopping. Mr. Herb Pickering, Alberta's Agent-General in the new office in Hong Kong, had had an earlier career with the Jasper Park Lodge. He later became Chief of Protocol for the Alberta government. He was a brilliant choice for the new office, located in the Admiralty Centre on Hong Kong Island. He made friends easily and influenced people on behalf of Alberta. He did good work on behalf of the university advancing the interests of the university effectively.

In Hokkaido, Japan, the delegation was in the hands of another excellent Alberta Agent-General, Ivan Bumstead. Bumstead was married to a Japanese woman and knew the subtleties of Japanese government, business, and culture. He too furthered the interests of the university in later years, both in Japan and in Korea. In Hokkaido the delegation was taken to the provincial museum for a formal signing of an agreement renewal document by Governor Naohiro Dogakinai and Minister Johnston. Dogakinai was a strong, handsome man, an Olympic bobsled athlete in his earlier life. The histories of Alberta and Hokkaido are similar, and their provincial museums reflect it. Both are frontier provinces, each was settled in the late nineteenth and early twentieth centuries, with railroads playing an important, even vital, role. Each has Native peoples whom the settlers displaced and who were relocated into separate areas. At times, the Hokkaido provincial museum could have been the Alberta provincial museum with different nametags.

After the delegation's return to Alberta, and the formalization of links with Heilongjiang the following year, the Lougheed government provided funding for educational and cultural exchanges in what were seen as the building blocks of good friendly relations. These were ground-breaking exchanges in fields such as agriculture, medicine, pharmacy, education, and physical education in the very early years of the opening of China to reform and modernization. All of Alberta's universities in nearly every discipline were to benefit from these twinning arrangements with China, as well as those formed with Japan and Korea. In addition, working within provincial and federal agreements with China, an enterprising group of Albertans launched a project called Ex Terra, on whose Board I served, linking paleontologists in China and Alberta in preparation for a major exhibition. *The Greatest Show Unearthed* opened in Edmonton in 1993 and toured North America for two years. There were also archaeological exchanges between Alberta and Heilongjiang.

Another aspect of cultural exchange with China involved the training of Chinese scholars. Beginning in 1979 and for the next five years, the University of Alberta, among others in Canada, received scholars whose careers had been made stillborn by the Cultural Revolution. They were not seeking higher degrees but were looking for a chance to upgrade their knowledge to enable them to go back to teach in Chinese universities that were now being freed from the ideological straitjacket of Maoist thought. They were charged no fees and they worked with experts in their fields. It is one of the greatest unsung goodwill gestures made by Canada to China as it began to upgrade and to modernize its universities. Friendships made at this time have endured and blossomed into linkages between Canadian and Chinese institutions. These scholars were followed by regular graduate students seeking higher degrees. Many of these students were angry with their own government once they discovered that the Dickensian conditions they had been told were rampant in the West were nowhere to be seen. They felt they had been deliberately misled and lied to. While the majority won their degrees and returned to China to help in its modernization, a number did not. This was a risk Deng Xiaoping was prepared to take.

Students and scholars in the sciences predominated among these early arrivals, but in the spring of 1982, on behalf of U of A, I hosted a scholar from the Institute of World History at the Chinese Academy of Social Sciences, Beijing. It was my effort at personal cultural diplomacy. Zhu Guisheng,[18] in his mid-fifties, was an undergraduate during the last years of Nationalist rule.

Because of the hyperinflation at that time, he invested all of his money into a gold ring. Each year he filed enough off it to pay for his fees and lodging. He became an expert in American diplomatic history but, because of the Cultural Revolution, was frustrated in his study of the Chinese classics and calligraphy. His English was good, but in private conversation he spoke the old-fashioned way with his hand cupped before his mouth, sometimes making him difficult to understand. He delighted in being driven around the city by my graduate student at the time, Mary Jo Hague. She drove him to Sylvan Lake to pay his respects to my ninety-seven-year-old father.

Zhu's Canadian stipend was limited, so he was billeted with different professors. He stayed for weeks with my friends Dad and Vindu Prithipaul, famous for their hospitality, and later he stayed with me. Dad Prithipaul, a senior professor in the Department of Religious Studies and a product of Mauritian colonial education, had studied at Benares, the Sorbonne, and Harvard before coming to U of A in 1968. A brilliant scholar, he relished his discussions with Zhu. The longer Zhu stayed, the clearer it was that he was decompressing from the Cultural Revolution. He was able to indulge his passion for calligraphy and the Chinese classics. Together we purchased books to send back to his institute in Beijing. Because I was planning to be in Beijing in early June, we agreed to meet again in Beijing.

THIS END UP, HANDLE WITH CARE

During the winter of 1981–1982, prior to Zhu's visit, I decided to plan a trip to China to take advantage of China's new academic and cultural openness, It was to be a holiday, but academically useful as well. It would include my first visit to Shandong province, the birthplace of Confucius, and the locale of Mount Tai and the coastal resort of Qingdao. Professor Zhu urged me to visit him at the Institute of World History in Beijing before I began my holiday. While in Beijing, I was to stay with my friends John and Michele Higginbotham who were on a second posting at the Canadian Embassy. It was also an opportunity for me to see another old friend, David Bonavia of the *London Times*. The China phase of my holiday was to end with a train trip from Beijing, via Ulan Bator and Irkutsk, to Moscow, before taking a flight to Paris for a brief visit with friends and my return to Canada. Prior to leaving Margo, who urged me to take a holiday because she was having to devote more of her time to looking after her mother, I collected travelling supplies and purchased some lightweight blue trousers to keep me cool during the heat of an approaching

North China summer. As it turned out, I was giving the trousers a lift back to the land of their birth.

Although China was opening quickly, it was still not possible to fly directly to Beijing, so I flew to Hong Kong, arriving the evening of May 30 and staying at the Hong Kong Hotel, an establishment of impeccable reputation. The next afternoon, I boarded my Civil Aviation Authority of China (CAAC) flight to Beijing. It was a hot muggy afternoon with dyspeptic thunderheads standing guard on the horizon. I was assigned seat 18D: CAAC never gave you a choice.

As I mentioned earlier in the chapter, CAAC was special, a student of Russia's Aeroflot. Which airline in the world kept eighteen new Boeing 707s on standby for the country's top political leaders? Which airline allowed its planes to make unscheduled stops because the pilot was hungry and knew of a good restaurant in a town en route? Which airline studiously encouraged its passengers not to observe safety regulations, while admonishing them to leave any radioactive materials they might have with the flight crew? Which airline allowed passengers to pile luggage and parcels in the aisles and in the open overhead racks? Why CAAC, of course. It follows that it would be foolish to ask passengers to buckle their seat belts. They had to be free to dodge falling objects. And which airline counted on its sick bags to do additional service as in-flight reading material, spittoons, and ashtrays? Which airline kept a refrigerator full of drinks and snacks for the crew, handily blocking the rear exit? Which airline gave gifts of key chains, address books, fans, and pens but relied on the distribution of bags of hard candy, rather than an announcement, to indicate the plane would be landing in fifteen minutes? Why CAAC, of course. It was this same airline that assigned me seat 18D, into which I pressed my damp, jet-lagged body, encased in its newly purchased blue, Chinese-made trousers. Merely through force of habit, I fastened my seat belt.

In those days, with limited radar at Chinese airports, the weather at the point of landing was of greater concern to CAAC pilots than the conditions at takeoff. On the final day of May 1982, conditions were clear in Beijing, so the pilot directed our plane straight at the towering thunderhead at the end of the short Kai Tak runway, flew into it, and started to climb sharply. The former MiG pilots,[19] whom CAAC employed, always enjoyed a challenge. It was to be nearly half an hour before those of us who had fastened our seat belts felt it was safe enough to undo them. During that time, I became conscious of a burning sensation in that region of my anatomy that interfaced with the seat cushion of 18D. At first I thought I was being Canadian and overreacting, but as the sensation grew more intense, hot, and painful, I fled to the washroom at the end of the plane to survey the scene. But, despite what the *Emmanuel* movies of the day encouraged one to believe, the washroom was much too small for me to catch a glimpse of the affected area. In an attempt to reduce the burning, I stuffed some paper inside my trousers and returned to 18D. This measure had little or no effect, and the burning sensation was soon unbearably painful. I fought it by concentrating on the delights of the holiday I planned and the joy of seeing my old friends.

On my arrival in Beijing, I found it very difficult to stand, but I attributed this to the fact that I had gripped the seat with my legs throughout the flight. As usual, I was let through customs without formality, but perhaps it was the grim look on my face and my stiff-legged walk—perhaps mistaken for imperialistic smugness—that prompted the customs officer to call me back and to subject me to an excruciatingly long and thorough search of my luggage. Now in some agony, I exited customs to find David Bonavia waiting for me. He was assigned by the Higginbothams to take me back to their apartment and ply me with strong drink until they returned from the embassy. I told him nothing of the pain, which I was still hoping to be just a temporary inconvenience. Gin and tonic and the Higginbothams' soft sofa improved my condition remarkably. Bonavia departed and I was soon seated at dinner with my hosts and their two young boys Matthew and Ian. Later we went for a walk, but I could barely move. Convinced that all I needed was a hot bath and a good night's sleep, I begged off, claiming jetlag and general fatigue.

Indeed, the hot bath that night was wonderful, but as I exited the bathroom I noticed, in a convenient mirror, that I appeared to be wearing a flag of Japan behind me. But not to worry, a good night's sleep would set things right, or so I thought. At two in the morning I awoke, as one does with jetlag, to find that the rising sun was now embossed with quail's egg-size welts. Sitting was impossible and standing gave me the sensation that my tailbone was attached to my Achilles tendons by short pieces of fishing line.

June 1 is celebrated in China as International Children's Day, and I had promised John and Michele some weeks before to take Matthew and Ian to the festivities. At 6 a.m. I heard John in the kitchen making the dark black coffee of which he is inordinately fond. Like a willow-waisted Chinese beauty on bound feet, I teetered out of my room to tell him I would be unable to keep my promise to his boys. A true Canadian diplomat, John was trained to trust, but also to verify. "My gawd!" he exclaimed after one glance, "It looks like a pizza!"

Three hours later, I was flat—well, that is an exaggeration—on my stomach in the back of a Canadian Embassy station wagon on my way to the Capital City Hospital.[20] Michele, fluent in Chinese, accompanied me, delaying her morning's teaching. With her help, I struggled up the stairs of the hospital, and stood by tentatively while she approached the young doctor on the emergency desk—foreign section. The doctor was reading a novel. "My friend is in great pain," she said in Mandarin, "would you please attend to him?" "Yes, yes," he said, "when I finish this chapter."

A second, more insistent, plea got him, reluctantly, to turn his head toward what he clearly assumed to be just another hung-over foreigner wanting to have his stomach pumped. But after one look at me he ordered my immediate transfer to the foreigner's section of the hospital, in the old part formerly known as the Rockefeller wing. It had thick walls and a high, cool Chinese-style tiled roof. I was placed face-down, naturally, on a bed in a room equipped with a refrigerator, a desk, a gooseneck lamp, two moderately easy chairs, and a closet. It was a private room. Across the hall was the bathroom. A short while later a male nurse arrived with calamine lotion to paint the offending area of my torso. The flag of Japan became a pure white flag of surrender. To dry the lotion, the nurse rudely shoved the base of the gooseneck lamp under my hips in order to focus the bulb about two inches above my delicate condition. The rest of the day I played the "gooseneck lamp game." I would push it away and the nurse would push it back down on his hourly rounds. It was true what they said in those days: "Foreigners always received the best treatment."

Telephoning Canada was difficult in those days, but thankfully the Higginbothams phoned Margo to tell her of what had befallen me, and to convey my assurance that she was not to worry. I was not to learn until my return to Edmonton late in June that Margo had more immediate worries and stress. Her mother died suddenly in the first week of my hospital stay in Beijing.[21] Meanwhile, word of what had befallen me spread quickly through the foreign community and among my Chinese friends. Diplomats, booked on CAAC flights, approached their assigned seats carrying sheets of plastic and cardboard. On all flights, seat 18D remained empty. Bonavia wove my tale, so to speak, into a story for the *Times*. Rumours multiplied: I was the victim of sabotage by Taiwan Guomindang (Nationalist KMT) agents; I was the victim of Mainland Chinese wanting to provoke an incident to embarrass their own airline, for it was not just foreigners that CAAC offended mightily.

But the rumour that I sat on a seat soaked in cleaning fluid was dismissed out of hand by a German nurse: "Impossible," she protested, "Everyone knows CAAC never cleans its planes."

When my friends discovered where I was being stored, they drifted by. A former Consul-General of Japan, once stationed in Edmonton, visited bringing a huge bouquet of flowers. Bonavia brought several bottles of Great Wall white wine to stock the fridge for those long June afternoons when he sought refuge from the oppressive Beijing heat. A fellow sinologist Bernie Frolic from York University, who succeeded me at the embassy in 1974–1975 and who was in Beijing doing research, stopped by to see if it was all true, and Professor Zhu Guisheng from the World History Institute came to offer sympathy. Although there was a temporary restriction on Chinese officials fraternizing with foreigners, another old friend came by in defiance of the ban.[22] Ever resourceful, he brought his boss with him on a mission to offer me an official apology on behalf of the people of China. His boss understood no English, so after he delivered his message, my friend was able to give me some of the latest Beijing gossip. The Higginbotham family came down one evening armed with a cake to celebrate John's birthday. Although I was never in a position to look any of my guests in the eye, I was finding life in the Beijing Capital City Hospital to be quite a social whirl.

My friend John suggested I take some sort of action. "Why don't you sue CAAC?" he suggested as he finished a piece of birthday cake. "You're not doing anything and lawyers have just been reinstated in China. You can probably get one cheap. I'll get you one."

The next day a lawyer came by. He had a brush cut and wore a short-sleeved white shirt, with two pens in its pocket, sandals, and dark-blue trousers.[23] From what I could see, he looked very much like a CAAC employee. Meanwhile, his clerk looked like a member of the Communist Party. During our initial conversation, I came to the conclusion that he was less than likely to become my staunch advocate. After making sure I knew his fee (150 yuan, about C$30), and asking me what I wanted to do, I explained to him that I wanted to sue CAAC for my injury that had caused me to cancel my holiday in China. He was less than enthusiastic:

"How do you know CAAC is responsible?"
"Because it happened on their plane from Hong Kong."

"You will have to prepare a detailed statement. Leave nothing out."

"I will have it for you tomorrow, but it will be handwritten and in English."

"For what amount do you wish to sue?"

"I need your advice, but I want a refund for my airfare, the cost of my hospital treatment, compensation for time off work, and some recompense for my missed holiday—about 13,000 yuan (C$2,600)."

"But you are here and you can still go on your holiday. Isn't your university paying you? And don't you already have your air ticket? Shouldn't your university pay your medical bill?"

After explaining that the U of A did not pay me to lie in the hospital while it was CAAC's fault, I felt I had to double-check by asking, "Besides, aren't you my lawyer?"

After he left, I settled down to a routine of calamine coatings and Chinese food, with a little white wine in the afternoon. Saturday morning, at the close of my first week in the hospital, I awoke to see two people entering my room, one of them carrying a lamp. The second phase of heat treatment, I thought. The male nurse appeared and pulled back the covers to allow the cameraman with his fancy strobe light to take a few pictures for CAAC. My case was becoming serious. Later that afternoon, the Embassy of Canada, having heard what was going on, despatched the consular officer, camera in hand, to complete its file, thus giving a new meaning to the term "mug shot." This was all too much for Bonavia, who insisted that he would lose face with the *Times* if he did not have a photo as well.

On Sunday, I was visited by a doctor from the hospital. He was the first I had seen, but he was not there to discuss my treatment. He was there to discuss my pants. "Your statement says that you were wearing Chinese trousers," he said. "Why do you say they are Chinese? Are you criticizing the Chinese people? How do Chinese trousers differ from those from other countries?" I told him that I had been asked to describe the incident in detail and that I had not been passing any judgement. He continued his line of questioning:

"What was the colour of the underwear you were wearing?"

"Blue."

"Blue? Are you sure they were not red. It is a well-known fact that red dye causes a rash."

"Sorry, but they were blue."

In the course of this cross-examination, I told him I had been wearing talcum powder on the plane to reduce chafing, after which he issued a smug "Ah-ha!" and asked, "Have you not seen the reports from the United States about how talcum powder can cause severe swelling of the face when used after shaving?" I felt I had to tell him that the risk of chafing had been in an area where I had never felt the need for a shave. After that, blame was directed at a toilet seat in the Hong Kong hotel, where I had obviously picked up my condition. Although a medical man, he had taken it upon himself to legally defend China and CAAC.

Later that afternoon, I had a visit from my lawyer who continued to prove a champion to my cause. "Your demands are difficult," he said. "It is not the money, but CAAC does not want its reputation damaged." I pointed out that it was a little late for that, given their reputation was not exactly unsullied before I had threatened to sue them. Then he brought up the evidence. "Without a statement from the hospital, you do not have a case," he said. I replied that I believed the doctors were working on it. My confidence buoyed by his visit, he then left.

The next day, I found myself in for a taste of traditional Chinese medicine. As I contemplated my upside-down world, I noticed a silver-haired lady standing in the doorway. The male nurse, who came to readjust the gooseneck lamp, invited her to take a seat. She was carrying what I took to be a small aluminum lunch box, a common sight in those days. I closed my eyes, attempting to eavesdrop discreetly on their conversation. But she had not come to gossip or eat lunch. She was invited to inspect my condition, after which she opened her lunch box, took out a bottle of peanut oil, and began to apply it to my injury. Resorting once again to her lunch box, she took out a scalpel and quickly, with great skill, began to rearrange my assets—to reconfigure my bottom line, as an accountant might say. "Let me know if it hurts," she said. The word for "pain" in Mandarin Chinese is a homophone, with different tones for the words "soup" or "sweets." As I gripped the bars of the headboard, periodically crying out *Tang!* passersby could be forgiven if they thought I was just complaining about something missing from my lunch tray.

During the next few days, as I had my barnacles scraped, I began to think that I might just be able to walk and sit again. After two weeks in hospital, with still no report from the doctors on the cause of my problem, I asked Professor Zhu if he could get a car to take me to see my lawyer. It meant checking myself out of the hospital.

My lawyer's office was typical of lawyers' offices "the world over," or so, in my pain, I initially assumed, because I had managed to reach the age of fifty without ever having been in one before: a bare wooden floor, whitewash on the plaster walls, and a portrait of the current national leader as the sole decoration. My lawyer was seated behind a three-foot-by-four-foot desk of super-glossed varnished wood, on the end of which was stamped the state requisition number in white. There were two wooden chairs for clients. On the windowsill was a Thermos of hot water and a tin cup and, in one corner of the room, a dirty mop and pail. A single, bare light bulb dangled from the ceiling. (He is just like every member of his profession, I thought, squandering his fees on costly overheads to impress his clients.) I asked him what my chances were, and he told me they were 60/40, if I had a statement from the hospital. "And without?" I asked. Thirty-seventy came the answer. I asked him when we could go to court and was told October, and of course I'd have to bear the travel expenses myself.

"Well, what is your advice?" I asked.

"Drop the case."

"What do you mean?"

"Sign a statement that you do not hold CAAC responsible."

I turned to Professor Zhu. Clearly, I was in no physical condition to hang around Beijing and now that I was out of the hospital I was anxious to board a plane for Paris. "Okay," I said, and my lawyer produced a sheet of paper from his desk drawer. In Chinese it said: "Because there is no evidence that my injury was caused by CAAC, I am dropping all charges against CAAC." Professor Zhu stopped me and advised, "Don't sign that." Taking out his pen, he wrote: "Because the hospital has not provided a report on the causes of my injury, I am unable to pursue my case against CAAC."

On the way to my lawyer's office, I had gone to a bank to change money. I paid my legal bill and returned to the hospital to pay the equivalent of C$414 for two weeks in a private room with treatments. Along with my receipt, I was handed a report. It concluded that my condition was caused by a severe reaction to something, possibly cleaning fluid, from an unidentifiable source. During the remainder of the day, thanks to Professor Zhu, I purchased a ticket for Paris on an Air France flight leaving the next evening and did some shopping before he dropped me at the Higginbothams' apartment for my last night in China. I acquired a cane to help me balance when walking. Early in the evening, I received two phone calls: one from friends in Paris wondering where in heaven (or was it hell?) I was, and the second from Robert Hurst, the CTV correspondent in Beijing. He wanted to interview me about my experience. I told him that my backside was of no interest to the people of Canada. "On the contrary," Hurst said, "you are a seasoned China traveller. Canadians should know what can befall even the most experienced visitor to this country."

Eighteen years before in Beijing, I had turned down an opportunity to be interviewed by Patrick Watson from *This Hour Has Seven Days* about my opinions on the condition of China—something I was not prepared to do since I had only been in the country for about five days. He had offered to conduct the interview on a boat in the middle of Beihai Lake, but back then, as on that last night of my trip to China in 1982, I felt I had nothing to say that would be of use to Canadians. And I was feeling fit back then. Hurst and I haggled and finally, with his promise that my face would be blacked out so I would not be recognized, I agreed.

Immediately, I regretted my decision. The Higginbothams and I spent that evening thinking up what sort of responses I might give to the questions Hurst might ask. We agreed that if I went about it properly, by emphasizing key information, the interview would never hit the air.

Hurst and his cameraman arrived in the late morning and sat me in a chair with my back to a brightly sunlit window so that my face would be obscured. As I recall, the interview went something like this:

"You are a frequent visitor to China?"
"I come here at least once a year on average."
"Can you tell me what happened to you this trip?"
"I planned a holiday in China, but on my flight from Hong Kong to Beijing, I received a severe burn that put me in hospital for two weeks."
"Would you mind telling me just where and how you were burned?"
"I believed I was burned when I was sitting on the plane."
"I understand that you have attempted to sue CAAC."
"Yes, at first I considered turning the other *cheek*, but I thought that one should really get to the *bottom* of the matter."

"You hired a lawyer?"

"Yes, but clearly he thought I was giving CAAC a *bum* rap and he tended to argue a *posterior*ori. At times, I had the impression he was fighting a *rear*guard action, not for me, but for the airline."

While a bit frustrated, Hurst and his cameraman were also beginning to come unglued, so I pressed on:

"My lawyer clearly thought my charge was *ass*inine and that I didn't have a leg to stand on. I spoke to him *stern*ly, but he insisted I had only a *rump* of an argument and I was just making CAAC the *butt* of my anger. My case came to a *dead end* because I did not have the *ass*ets to continue it."

Hurst then asked, "What advice do you have for other travellers? You are known as a friend of China. How do you feel about it now?" I answered him, "*Bas*ically, I don't believe that my *tale* is *fundament*ally different from that of others. I have no hard feelings toward China. Quite the contrary, they are rather *tender* at the moment. It's just their airline that I have had problems with. The incident hardly ranks among the *anna*ls of Sino-Canadian relations." Hurst decided to give it one more try: "But hasn't your trip been ruined?" I ended the interview on a high note: "I came to see friends and to have a few days of holiday. I have seen my friends, but as for my holidays, it's *wrecked-'um.*"

With that, Hurst and his one-person crew packed up and left. I was confident the interview would never reach Canadian TV screens. And on the off chance that it did, no one would recognize me. That evening, John took me to the airport, accompanied by Professor Zhu. Zhu was unable to get beyond the final barrier, but John, being a diplomat, was able to escort me to the very desk where the People's Liberation Army officer stood ready to administer the exit stamp to my passport. Beyond him I could see the Air France jet, that shiny aluminum tunnel of delights through which I would pass from Beijing to Paris. I could see the beautifully coiffed and attired cabin attendants waiting to welcome me. But as I gazed toward my future, I did not hear the pleasing "chunk" of the date stamp hitting my passport on which my immediate present depended. I turned to see the officer staring at my visa, his hand hovering in the air. "You cannot leave," he said. "Your visa has expired."

It was true. I had overstayed my visa by two days. The proper way for me to leave now would be for me to be expelled, but that would take a few days to organize. John began to question the officer and to attempt to persuade him to let me pass, but this appeared to make matters worse. At this point, Professor Zhu beckoned to the officer from where he was standing behind the barricade. Eventually, the officer went over to him. They spoke briefly, and then the officer returned, shut his eyes, and stamped my passport. I was free to leave for France. Once the flight attendants had heard my story, I was coddled and cosseted all the way to Charles de Gaulle Airport.

Meanwhile, back in western Canada some days earlier, at her mother's funeral attended by some of my colleagues, Margo had been asked where I was. She replied that I had been burned in an accident on a plane and that I was in hospital in Beijing. That was sufficient grist for the academic rumour mill. Two nights later, the interview appeared on CTV news, introduced by Lloyd Robertson.[24] It seems I had been wrong about its suitability for the airwaves. I had also been mistaken in thinking my identity would pass unnoticed thanks to that sunlit window. Far from being anonymous, I was easily identified by friends and colleagues from Halifax to Victoria. Blissfully unaware of all this, I returned to the university in late June to be greeted by some as though I had returned from the dead, and by others, as the greatest "sit-down" comic since the days of silent film. When I ran into Terry White, U of A's dean of arts, he looked at me and said, "You poor chap. How wonderful to have you back among the living. Someone told me that they saw you on TV and your face was burnt nearly black."

"But," I interjected, "you've got the wrong end of the story..."

"Say no more. I know all about it," he said, touching me on the arm before he walked away. "How terrible it must have been." He has since gone on to other institutions and up to now I have been unable to tell him the true story. When the subject comes up, and he tends to raise it, he says, "Remember when you burned your face in China that summer?"

"Yes," I have taken to responding, "and the Chinese are so conscious of face."[25]

SOUTH OF THE CLOUDS[26]

In the almost ten years since my posting to the embassy in Beijing, I had witnessed the unravelling and disintegration of the Maoist system as it began to take on the look of "Socialism with Chinese Characteristics," a euphemism for increased capitalist enterprises and material incentives. Maoists were being replaced by Dengists who looked to pragmatism and modernization as the solution to China's problems. The Chinese transformation was smoother and less hectic than the collapse of the Soviet system that I witnessed a decade later, but in both cases there was a spiritual vacuum. In China, traditional culture and Confucianism began to re-emerge, while the ballets, plays, operas, paintings, and poetry of the Cultural Revolution were abandoned. China's cultural diplomacy that I had begun to study in 1975 was unrecognizable half a decade later. China ceased to attempt to win converts to its socialist system and was instead looking for assistance in transforming its economy and society.

Deng's modernization of China put paid to my research on Chinese cultural diplomacy, but it re-opened the door to me as a nineteenth-century historian. I was at last able to do the research I had originally hoped to do in 1967 and do further research on the life of diplomat Chester Ronning. I looked forward to making a visit to Yunnan province in the fall of 1984 where Margo and I had originally hoped to go in the spring of 1968, but the edge was taken off my anticipation by the death of my father. In the thirteen years since my mother's death in 1971, my father had taught himself to type and wrote three books: two memoirs and a history of the Celts. Although, statistically, his income was below the poverty line, he owned his own house, where he lived until his death, and even saved money, which he used to buy presents for his children and thirteen grandchildren. He retained his incredible memory and was physically active right until the end, but he lost his interest in politics when Pierre Trudeau retired. He died shortly thereafter, late in July 1984. I believe he willed himself to death.[27]

By the fall of 1984, I received permission and funding to return to China on a research trip. My costs were underwritten by a Social Sciences and Humanities Research Council (SSHRC) grant for China exchanges. I planned to go to Yunnan province in southwest China to see the towns where the Panthay (Muslim *Hui*) revolt of the late nineteenth century originated, and to visit Fancheng, Hubei province, where Chester Ronning was born in December 1894 and where he taught school from 1923 to 1927.

In preparing for my trip, I had the invaluable assistance of my doctoral student, Dai Xianguang.[28] In October 1984, on the eve of my departure for Beijing, Dai gave me a letter of introduction to Mr. Huang Hua, Deputy Chairman of the National People's Congress. Huang had had a charmed career. He had been the official in charge when the Communist forces took the Nationalist capital of Nanjing in 1949 (Chester Ronning had been the interpreter for the foreign community). During the Cultural Revolution, Huang was ambassador to Egypt, the only Chinese representative not recalled to Beijing. He was China's first ambassador to Canada and its first ambassador to the United Nations. On his return to China, he served as Foreign Minister (1976–1982) before being elected Vice-Chair of the National People's Congress. He and Ronning had remained friends over the years. Coincidentally, the very eve of my departure for Beijing was also the time that I received a telegram from SSHRC in Ottawa to say that the trip was off because the Chinese Academy of Social Sciences (CASS) could not receive me. I suspected it was because the subject of the Panthay revolt was still sensitive. At the time the rebels had proclaimed a separate state and offered to place themselves under British suzerainty.[29] I strategically chose not to have received the telegram and caught my plane twelve hours later. There was no one to greet me at the airport on my arrival in Beijing, a good indication that CASS assumed that I had received the word not to come in plenty of time.

Once I was in central Beijing, I went to the Academic Hotel where I was half-expected. That evening I dropped the letter of introduction to Huang Hua in a mailbox. The next day in the afternoon, having had no contact whatsoever with CASS, I received a phone call to ask if I was free to see Mr. Huang the next day. He received me in the Great Hall of the People. He shared with me his memories of Chester Ronning, someone he clearly admired and with whom he remained in contact.[30] The interview over, he asked about my plans and wished me well. From then on, my trip was pure magic.

On my arrival in Kunming, the capital of Yunnan province, I was received by the Minorities Institute where I met scholars and talked freely about my topic. A couple of days later, I was driven to Dali in the southwest of the province. "Driven," is too bland a term. I was provided a Toyota Crown and the top driver in the province, a Korean War veteran. Just as well, because the route to Dali from Kunming involves navigating the Burma Road, a series of ascending and descending switchbacks through breathtaking mountain scenery. The main traffic consisted of heavy trucks and a few buses. Every truck driver in China is also a trained mechanic, there being no garages en route. It was common to pass trucks being administered to by their drivers. On the mountainsides were vehicles whose brakes had failed, or for some reason were unable to make a turn.

Dali City is a glorious sight. Located beside a deep blue mountain lake, it is famous for the two white pagodas that shimmer against the bright blue sky. It was the seat of the Muslim (*Hui*) rebel government in the 1870s. The city is small and surrounded by high walls. In the years since the rebellion it has

Entry gate to walled city of Dali, Yunnan province, October 1984.

suffered major earthquakes. The then mayor, when a small child, was rescued from the rubble after a disastrous earthquake in the 1920s. He showed me the site outside the city walls where some twenty thousand massacred rebels were buried in 1873. The next day, I was taken over the mountains on narrow winding roads to the two villages where the rebellion originated. The villages, called Da Weigen and Xiao Weigen, are the subject of a local joke. *Da* means "big," and *Xiao* means "small," but Xiao Weigen has outgrown Da Weigen, so in reality small is larger than big. Told of my interest, the villagers invited me to a public meeting at the Xiao Weigun mosque where they brought me documents and told me their family stories. It was as though the rebellion had taken place only the day before. Later, I was shown the homes of the rebel leaders and the mass graves of their followers. It was an unforgettable experience.

Later, back in Dali, I was treated to a lunch in one of the "private restaurants" that were just beginning to flourish throughout China under Deng's new freedoms and modernization policies. It was a room with a dirt floor, but with an opening in the roof to let sunlight in and smoke out. Wooden stools surrounded a low table. In my honour they served a local delicacy—the meat of an animal that is best described as a cross between a badger and an armadillo. As much as I like Chinese food, I have always been nervous about being the guest of honour and the responsibilities that go with it:

Site of mass grave of Hui (Panthay) Muslim rebels suppressed in 1873.

"Do you often eat like this?" I asked the mayor.

"No, but we did last month when we had a special guest. He was a Canadian too."

"Do you remember who it was?"

"He said his name was Trudeau. Do you know him?"

"Not really,[31] but I certainly know who he is. He is very fond of China."

I enjoyed my trip back to Kunming, conscious that I was travelling in the style of retired prime ministers. I could not help but think of the opposite case of the Muslim rebellion and how when it was crushed in 1873 the leader's head was detached from his body and preserved in honey for transportation to Beijing—a rather gruesome show and tell. It did not end up making the trip. We stopped at the spot, not far from Dali, where it had ended its trip. It was breakfast time and each of us was given a washbasin-sized helping of "crossing the bridge noodles,"[32] a famous Yunnan dish, before proceeding on our way to Kunming.

From Kunming, I travelled to Hankou, the city that forms part of the modern-day city of Wuhan that bestrides the mighty Yangzi and that served as a foreign concession treaty port during the late nineteenth and early twentieth

Mosque in Daweigen village, Yunnan, October 1984.

centuries. It was there six years earlier, fresh from a trip through the Three Gorges, that I stepped off a Yangzi river cruise ship to be accosted by a wild-eyed woman who screamed, "There he is—a foreign devil. Kill him!" I froze, only to relax when the crowd began to laugh. She was clearly known for such antics. From Hankou I was driven to Fancheng to see the school that Chester Ronning's father had founded and where Chester had taught in the 1920s. In the courtyard of the school is the tomb of his mother. I was extremely well received by the mayor and I gained a first-hand appreciation of how much the memory of Ronning is ever present in the thoughts of the citizens. Chester Ronning is someone about whom many stories can be told, but the one that came to mind at this time was of a visit he made to his birthplace a decade or more before. Because he spoke the local dialect so flawlessly, it was sometimes confusing to the residents. One elderly lady looked at him and said, "You sound

Chinese Muslims gathering for a meeting with the author in Xiaoweigen, Yunnan province, October 1984.

Chinese, but you don't look Chinese." "Ah," replied Ronning, "that's because I have lived abroad so long that I have begun to look like them."

I exited China at Guangzhou (Canton) airport, congratulating myself on a superb research trip. However, before I left I was stopped by the customs officer. I was carrying the manuscript of a book about the Muslims written by a member of the Minorities Institute in Kunming. It was seized as forbidden fruit from the tree of academia. Clearly, the freer atmosphere I had sampled had its limits as far as Chinese intellectuals writing on sensitive topics were concerned. Notwithstanding the incident at customs, I left China filled with the success of my trip and the freer intellectual atmosphere. I told my friends David and Judy Bonavia in Hong Kong all about it. Later, when Judy, who among other things is a writer of outstanding travel guides, went to Dali and asked to see the historic evidence of the *Hui* (Muslim) Rebellion, she was told that none existed. But as excited as I was about my research, the next time I saw Deng Xiaoping's China it was as a university administrator.

The decade of the 1980s in China is known as the Deng Xiaoping era, but like most eras it began a few years before, when Deng returned to government and party positions following the death of Mao. By any measure, Deng was truly remarkable. Born in Sichuan in 1904 of peasant stock, he went to France at the age of sixteen to study and work. His experience working for a pittance in the Renault factory opened his eyes to the evils of capitalism. In France, most likely in Paris, he joined the Chinese Communist Youth League in 1921 and the Communist Party three years later. He returned to China in 1927 after a period of study at the Sun Yat-sen university in Moscow. He had gone to France to garner Western knowledge to save China, but he returned armed with Marxist-Leninism and his personal experience of capitalism. In France he also gained a mentor, Zhou Enlai, an older fellow student-worker.

Deng enjoyed a stellar career in the party and the army, becoming a very popular figure in the aftermath of the Great Leap Forward in the late 1950s when he assisted President Liu Shaoqi in bringing the economy back from the brink of disaster. He paid for this during the Cultural Revolution when he was a target of Red Guard criticism—he was demoted, humiliated, and his family was harassed to the point of rendering one of his sons a paraplegic.[33] In the spring of 1973, he was called back to serve as Vice-Premier in the wake of the Lin Biao treachery. With Zhou fighting cancer, Deng took on more duties, among them escorting Prime Minister Trudeau and Margaret Sinclair on their southern visit that October.

Following the death of Zhou, Deng was once again driven from office in April 1976, only to out-manoeuvre his political enemies to emerge the power-holder after Mao died. In 1981, he succeeded in replacing Hua Guofeng with Zhao Ziyang as premier and appointing Hu Yaobang as party chairman. Both of these men were reform-minded. From Mao's death until his own in early 1997, Deng was the driving force behind the transformation of China from one of Maoist shared poverty to one where to get rich is glorious. He piloted an assessment of Mao Zedong, finding the Great Helmsman 70 per cent good and 30 per cent bad. He encouraged the development of Special Economic Zones and negotiated the return of Hong Kong and Macau under the rubric of "one country, two systems."[34] He never occupied any of the highest government or party offices, yet the modernized China created under his stewardship was breathtaking to behold. It was to be seen most dramatically in the cities where skylines moved upward at a rapid pace. Buildings of twenty storeys and more were completed in eighteen months, while new highways, bridges, and railways were constructed with amazing speed. The material transformation of China was truly amazing to those familiar with the country under Mao.

EIGHT

Greet, Meet, and Eat

The 1970s saw a number of important developments in Canada's foreign policy and international outreach. The most dramatic foreign policy initiative was the recognition of China, but equally, if not more important, was the expansion of Canada's overseas development assistance administered by two agencies: CIDA (Canadian International Development Agency) and IDRC (International Development Research Centre). CIDA was by far the larger, undertaking projects throughout the developing world, in Africa, Asia, and Latin America, with IDRC sponsoring strategic research projects to assist in these same areas of the world. Both agencies, along with other world aid organizations, were shut out of China until the country was opened up by Deng Xiaoping. Previously, Mao had concentrated on building a country that was completely self-reliant. Many of China's revolutionary leaders, conscious of what foreign powers had done to China in the previous century, were wary of outside countries bearing gifts. Deng broke with this thinking, arguing that the People's Republic, as a member of the United Nations, should reap the advantages of membership relating to development assistance. Furthermore, in 1981 and 1982, CIDA and IDRC signed umbrella agreements with Beijing to operate in China. Ivan Head, whom Pierre Trudeau had appointed as director of IDRC, negotiated the arrangement for that agency.

In their global outreach, CIDA and IDRC sought the active participation of universities, eliciting academic staff members to undertake projects overseas. Most in demand were academics in the disciplines of agriculture, business, education, engineering, home economics, and science who were willing to apply their expertise to assist developing countries. At first this touched only a few universities, those that were large enough or specialized enough to enable staff to undertake overseas assignments. It did not take long for universities to seek compensation from the aid agencies for this service, and to undertake the management of small projects on behalf of CIDA and IDRC. Aid money, in the form of overhead compensations, began to seep into university budgets. Overseas development work, however, posed a problem for university staff desirous of budgeting their time to best advance their individual careers. Much of the work that CIDA projects demanded was applied and was not considered noteworthy in faculties where research and publications were essential for progress up the ladder. IDRC projects, because they were research-based, were generally acceptable, but CIDA work, arguably, was not. The question of academic credit for development work remained an unresolved issue between CIDA and universities.

THE GLOBE AND THE "U"

In 1979, the University of Alberta chose a new president to replace Harry Gunning. Myer Horowitz, previously vice-president academic, was a proactive and dynamic administrator. He proved to be adept, popular with both students and staff. He was sometimes criticized for never saying no, but he had a vision of the president as the conductor of the institution, drawing the best from its component parts. Staff members who presented him with ideas they thought worthy of pursuing, expecting him to undertake them, were urged to take the initiative themselves, to develop the concept for presentation to the university. In this way he separated the doers from the doodlers, assuring that initiatives with firm support came forward. It was in his first year as president that the Department of East Asian Languages and Literatures was approved, a development he had watched grow as vice-president academic.

Horowitz served for two five-year terms as president. During his first term, his vice-president academic was George Baldwin, the former dean of arts who had proven to be an administrator's administrator. For his second term, Horowitz was joined by J. Peter Meekison, who gave up his position as a deputy minister in the provincial government to return to the university. Then and now Meekison exudes humanity and calm efficiency. While others get excited and rail against circumstances, Meekison sets about repairing any damage. As vice-president academic he shared with Horowitz a profound interest in international affairs. They both thought that the university should be more engaged with the world.[1]

In the 1970s, after the creation of CIDA and IDRC, the U of A began to undertake international projects, following early efforts by the Business School in Kenya and the Faculty of Education in Thailand. The growing federal support for overseas projects and relationships was matched, in the case of Alberta, by the Lougheed government's many international initiatives that included its partnerships in Asia. The province encouraged its universities to embrace these new relationships and provided funds for cultural, scientific, and educational exchanges. Out of this came summer schools for U of A students in China and Japan, and summer schools for Japanese and Korean students at U of A. In addition, the Alberta government established its own development fund to which members of the universities could apply for matching funds to undertake preliminary soundings for projects abroad, to conduct individual research, or to bring overseas scholars to the university.

Within the university, the Faculty of Education, Department of Educational Foundations, established a Centre for International Education and Development under Professor Kazim Bacchus, and began a series of projects overseas with CIDA assistance. Also an International Centre for international students was established. The university welcomed an increasing number of international students who were charged a differential fee by provincial government regulation. Horowitz directed this extra money into services for international students, and the International Centre flourished as a result. By the early 1980s, it and an international projects office (later called Alberta International) were growing in importance under the care of the dean of students. Under President Horowitz, an emphasis was placed on international involvement and the number of overseas projects increased.[2] For example, in the early 1980s, the Business Faculty joined in CIDA-sponsored linkages between Canadian and Chinese business schools. The University of Alberta linked with Xi'an Jiaotong university, a relationship that has endured.

Under Pierre Trudeau, international development projects flourished, drawing more and more upon the resources of educational institutions. At the University of Alberta, administering the growing amount of international work was placed on the shoulders of Amy Zelmer, an already overburdened associate vice-president academic. In 1985, Horowitz decided that the international function of the university should be dealt with separately. The question was should it be looked after by a vice-presidency newly created for the purpose, or by an associate vice-president attached to the VP academic. The latter path was chosen and the position of associate vice-president (academic) international affairs was advertised.

At this time I had returned to full-time teaching and was an informal advisor to the Alberta government on Asian matters, having regular lunch meetings with Dr. Morris Maduro, who was in charge of East Asia in the provincial

Department of Federal and Intergovernmental Affairs (FIGA), and with Dr. Ron Micetich an adjunct professor of pharmacy who was dedicated to launching, with Japanese help, a company in Edmonton to carry out the research and production of new pharmaceuticals. Micetich was frustrated, unable to get the support he needed from the university. He required access to a high-ranking university official to help convince his Japanese partners of the seriousness of the project. The three of us, Micetich, Maduro, and myself, called a meeting to discuss the university's international needs. Like all ad hoc meetings, it raised more questions than it answered. It did emphasize to the president, however, that the current system was overloaded with obligations it could not meet, hence a search for a new associate VP.

I was invited to apply for the job by Horowitz and was subsequently interviewed by Meekison and Zelmer in July 1985. I did not take it too seriously, but a week later the president called to say I had the position. It was then that I suffered a major attack of cold feet, convinced that people thought I knew more than I did about international matters. Yet it was clear to me that the hidden force behind university international involvement was the opening of China, our growing ties with its institutions, and the increasing number of graduate students coming from China to study, science in particular.

At the time, Margo and I were in the midst of upgrading her parents' old house with an eye to enlarging it in some fashion to consolidate our goods. The opportunity this new assignment provided was great, but it would mean a full-time commitment of my time, thus delaying, or at least slowing down, our private plans. As always, Margo was enthusiastic about the offer given to me and was willing to put our plans on the backburner. Unfortunately, the plans grew rather cold because I was involved with the university's international outreach for the next ten years.[3]

My job as associate vice-president (academic) international affairs, which I started in mid-July 1985, was to attempt to co-ordinate, as much as possible, the university's approach to international involvements and to encourage faculties to participate and to internationalize their curricula. Some faculties resisted what they saw as a power grab by the central administration, while others, the Science Faculty in particular under Dean John McDonald, who also happened to be a fellow graduate from Taber High School, thought their subjects were internationalized already and there was little a central administration could do for them. My office in University Hall was just a few doors away from where I had worked on the *Gateway* more than three decades earlier. My assigned secretary, Florence Plishka, was an excellent choice. She received international visitors well. Moreover, she had worked for some time in the provincial government where she had retained good contacts. In addition to a secretary, I was given charge of the international development office, and I became chair of the Board of the Alberta Summer Institute for Petroleum Industry Development (ASIPID).

Shortly after I took up my new tasks, I received a congratulatory call from the associate director of McGill International, Ginette Lamontagne, a leading person in university international development in Canada. We became friends and collaborators over the next decade. In January 1986, after a tour of the more internationally active universities of Toronto, Guelph, and McGill, it became clear to me that McGill was the leader, largely through the skills of Lamontagne. To be sure, McGill had a well-established international reputation long before CIDA was formed, having been frequently called upon by the Canadian government to undertake overseas work. It had a research station in Barbados and was active in the Caribbean, Central and South America, as well as in Asia and Africa. McGill had other advantages over an institution like the University of Alberta. It was close to, within two hours' drive of, CIDA headquarters in Hull, and was in the same time zone. In addition, it was becoming a bilingual institution, enabling it to compete for both anglophone and francophone projects. The trick for getting a university involved in CIDA projects was to know what the current trends were in that organization and to know your home institution well enough to see the opportunities. Lamontagne was superb in both these areas, thus McGill's lead over the others.

Politics also played a role and was sometimes a key factor in the assignment of CIDA projects once they got to the minister's desk. Huge projects required political lobbying, often at both levels of government—provincial and federal. Sometimes it worked, sometimes it backfired. As I mentioned in the previous chapter, the province of Alberta is twinned with the province of Heilongjiang in northeast China. In 1983, the latter was looking for help in reforming its state farm system. A project called the Black Dragon River was assembled involving U of A's Agriculture Faculty, Olds College in central Alberta, and Guelph University in Ontario. It was a huge project and required major political lobbying on the part of the dean of agriculture, Roy Berg, and the director of the project, Peter Apedaile, also from the University of Alberta, along with the direct intervention of Premier Peter Lougheed. The project was nearly ready to go when I took up my appointment. All I had to do was sign the contract, an act that was to come back to haunt me a few years later.[4]

An example of political lobbying backfiring came later when I called for political help related to ASIPID. When Petro-Canada refused to let ASIPID bid on a contract for training people from Africa in the petroleum industry, and instead awarded it to a Montreal business school, I cried foul. I enlisted the support of our local MP Jim Edwards, a member of the Progressive Conservative Party under Prime Minister Brian Mulroney. Edwards made a blistering attack in the House of Commons on Petro-Canada, and wrote an equally strong letter to Petro-Canada in support of our case. The result was the suspension by Petro-Canada of funding for ASIPID on the grounds that it needed to be rethought as a joint effort with the University of Calgary. It took the intervention by another Progressive Conservative MP, the Right Honourable Joe Clark, to get the talks going. In the end, ASIPID was made arm's length from both universities and subsequently it cut ties with both institutions.

Another project that was to engage me for the whole of my time as associate VP began simply enough. In May 1986, a loquacious Welshman with a project to reform agricultural, business, and economic management in Africa arrived in my office. Terry Mackey is in fact of Irish parentage, but he was born and raised a few doors away from where my father grew up in Wales. As a result, I could understand his accent. A Labourite and a university teacher at City University, London, England, Mackey had trade union experience, as well as development experience in Africa. His wife Margaret, originally from Newfoundland, had family in Edmonton. A persuasive speaker, he has a tendency sometimes to use salty language of the sort not often heard from university representatives. But he was determined and the project proved to be of interest to a number of faculties on campus. We decided to pursue it. The trail was long and hard, with numerous visits to Ottawa and to the Washington offices of the World Bank. A major problem with the project was that it was not conceived in house at CIDA, nor at the World Bank, so it took some effort to convince both organizations of its merits. Only when we managed meetings with people at higher levels did we make progress. Eventually, the African Management Project (AMP), involving the U of A, World Bank, and CIDA, was approved and Mackey moved his family to Edmonton. AMP endured until 1996 and one of its final meetings, held in Ivory Coast, was my last international trip on behalf of the university before I retired.

The University of Alberta was engaged with CIDA through many faculties, departments, and individuals. There were separate U of A development projects in Indonesia, Thailand, Kenya, Bangladesh, Brazil, the Caribbean, and China. In addition, there were innumerable exchange agreements and projects with institutions in China, Japan, South Korea, Ukraine, the United States, and Western Europe. In keeping with the office, I travelled to many of these places representing the university.[5] I enjoyed a great deal of international air travel, not to mention travel to and from Ottawa. It more than fulfilled my childhood dream of being a pilot. Fortunately, my travels took place well before the introduction of heightened security measures following 9/11.

Before I was offered the position of associate vice-president academic, I had agreed to lead a university-sponsored group along the Silk Road. I was able to honour that obligation from mid-May to early June 1986, which included stops in Lanzhou, Dunhuang, Turfan, and Urumuchi in the far northwest Muslim area of China. After the tour was over, I stayed in Asia to accompany President Horowitz on visits to our sister institutions in China.[6] The tour was not without incident. China was continuing to implement the economic reforms proposed by Deng Xiaoping and matters were, at times, chaotic. China's universities were caught up in the changes. I met Horowitz at Shanghai's Hong Qiao airport, which consisted of a small building with all the day's flights listed on one little board. From Shanghai we flew to Harbin, Edmonton's sister city, arriving earlier than our hosts had planned. Horowitz, a patient and good-humoured traveller, "enjoyed" the waiting room of Harbin airport until, at last, we were enthusiastically greeted by our hosts. We stayed at the White Swan Hotel, one of the first modern hotels in the city. When the elevator up to our rooms stopped halfway between floors, we should have been alerted, but we were not. President Horowitz would later turn on the taps in his bathroom basin to find that there was no drainpipe and the water cascaded directly onto the floor and his shoes. For me, things got better, so to speak.

As a precaution, and unbeknownst to me, Horowitz had informed our hosts (through the Alberta government) that he was strictly kosher. Actually, he was not strictly kosher, but he thought it would be a polite way for him to refuse dishes he did not like. For some reason, during our visit our hosts assumed that I was the kosher one, so I sat hungry and bewildered as my favourite dishes were deliberately not offered to me, while the president noshed happily away. At Harbin University we met with students who had spent time at U of A and were taken by the president for a private lunch in a small dining room in the university garden. The room was decorated with a large calendar open to a picture of the Muttart Conservatory pyramids in Edmonton, identified underneath as being Cairo.

We then travelled to Beijing, where President Horowitz signed a memorandum of agreement with Beijing Aeronautical University. Afterward, the university's upper administration held a banquet for students who had studied at U of A. Later, we had discussions at the Canadian Embassy with Ambassador Richard Gorham, whose brother was a professor of botany in Edmonton.

From Beijing we flew to Xi'an, where we had meetings with the president and dean of business of Xi'an Jiaotung, whose faculty is linked with the Business Faculty at U of A. There was time to visit the terracotta figures of the Qin warriors being unearthed across the river from the old walled city. At each stop on our trip we gave and were given gifts. At Xi'an, we each received a reproduction of a Tang horse, lovely, large, and a challenge to pack. I decided to carry mine on the plane, but when I went to Horowitz's room to help him with his luggage, I was mystified as to where he had packed his. Was he taking a chance on it being smashed in his checked bag? No. After a couple more questions, he agreed to show me how he, determined to travel light, had solved the problem. He lifted the cover of the toilet tank in his bathroom so I could see the submerged horse. I suspect we were well clear of China before the Horowitz design for a low-flush toilet was discovered. In the years since our trip to China, I have not heard President Horowitz express any burning desire to go back to reclaim his horse.

In addition to direct university business, I travelled as a member of provincial and federal delegations to Ukraine, Russia, and Siberia. Moreover, as a member of the Southern Africa Education Trust Fund (SAETF), I travelled twice to South Africa. SAETF, an effort to undermine apartheid, was established by the Mulroney government under External Affairs Minister Joe Clark to bring black South Africans to Canada as students and professional trainees. Originally chaired by Archbishop Ted Scott of the Anglican Church, and later by John Harker of the International Labour Organization,[7] the committee was a mix of political practitioners and academics.[8] I owed my own SAETF appointment to the 1985 Ontario election. When the committee was proposed, I was asked for an opinion on who should be on it. In my opinion, the committee need not have been of the "representative of Canadian geography" type. I thought it important for the committee to contain good people, even at the risk of them all being from Ontario. And indeed the original committee was struck with a university representative from the University of Toronto. But before the committee met, David Peterson won the Ontario election, taking into his Liberal government the person from the U of T. I was asked to fill the gap.

On my two journeys to South Africa in February 1990 and March 1993, I was able to see apartheid in practice and to meet with people who were active in undermining it. They included white professors at universities, union organizers, and others. I toured Soweto outside Johannesburg where its black citizens were contained. It was in no way a slum like the ones marring the outskirts of Nairobi, Kenya, or in the barrios of Salvador de Bahia in Brazil. Instead, the small shack-like houses were laid out in neat rows and individual houses showed evidence of the pride and care of their inhabitants. In contrast, also in Soweto, was the area where black professionals, doctors, and dentists lived in handsome modern houses, and where Archbishop Tutu lived in his walled-off home. All of them were forbidden to dwell in the main city because of the colour of their skins. The atmosphere in Johannesburg was tense and even more so on my second trip. Foreigners, foolish enough to wear or display jewellery, handbags, and the like, were regularly mugged and robbed even in the close precincts of the best hotel. In contrast, I was taken to nightclub bars where blacks and whites mixed freely. Cape Town was much calmer, perhaps due to the influence of its superb location and scenery. It was there that I witnessed the rapturous demonstration of February 11, 1990, that welcomed Nelson Mandela back from his incarceration on Robben Island.[9]

In addition to travelling, a major part of my responsibilities included the meeting and greeting of international visitors to the campus. My job used to be summarized as greet, meet, and eat. Visitors to the campus included a Thai princess, government ministers, ambassadors, university presidents, and church leaders such as the head of the Coptic Church of Africa. In addition, there were delegations travelling across Canada on information-gathering missions and delegations to conferences being held on campus. Early in my term, through the good offices of Ivan Bumstead, the head of the Alberta office in Japan with responsibilities in Korea, a link was formed between Yonsei University in Seoul and the U of A. Annual conferences were held on themes relating to comparative policies and practices in Korea and Canada. The conferences alternated between Seoul and Edmonton, followed by a brief post-conference excursion. It was after one of the meetings at the University of Alberta in July 1989 that I accompanied our Korean visitors to Jasper and Banff.

Even though it was a short trip, I was, as usual, uneasy in the mountains. A true son of the Prairies, I have always looked on mountains as unnecessary barriers to a good view. I have called them God's leftover ironing, and badly expressed prairie. My views were definitely *not* shared by our Korean guests to whom mountains have a special appeal. It was particularly important to them to be photographed in front of every beauty spot. Our van was driven by a colleague, Charles Burton,[10] a post-doctoral fellow in political science with whom I chaired a seminar on modern China. His cousin happened to operate a teahouse high up on a mountain overlooking Lake Louise. Nothing for it, we climbed up for tea. It was on the way down that the mountain got its revenge for my negative thoughts. In my haste I stepped on some loose pebbles and broke a bone on the side of my left foot. It was the first and only time for me to break a bone, so far at least. It confirmed my gloomy view about mountains.

As a result of my injury, I needed a cast and crutches for nearly two weeks before I was able to get around with a cane and a bandage. My left foot, though bandaged and swollen, fitted into a half-Wellington boot, fashionably matched to the slip-on Oxford on my right. Shod in this fashion, I undertook a trip to Indonesia in late August 1989 as part of a University of Alberta–CIDA rehabilitation medicine project led by a very dynamic professor, Sharon Britnell. It was an ideal time of year and the meetings were held outdoors; the air around Solo, Java, was redolent with the scent of cloves. The trip went remarkably well and our hosts were discreet about my footwear. Even a visit with the Minister of Health for Indonesia went off smoothly. It was not until I was at Jakarta's airport, preparing to depart for home, that anything happened. Because of a minor problem with my ticket, I was invited upstairs to the airline office to straighten it out. As I sat waiting my turn, a young airline executive approached me. He was Chinese, dressed in a beautifully tailored blue suit, silk shirt, and tie. His shoes shone like headlights beneath his trouser cuffs. "Excuse me sir. Are you aware that your shoes do not match?"

I was stunned and amused. I mumbled something about it being very early in the morning, and gazed at my feet before giving him a grateful, "Thank you." I fancied he had a spring in his step as he walked to his office.

My years as associate vice-president international provided me with opportunities to return to the Soviet Union/Russia. As I detailed in previous chapters, my first visit had been in 1968 when Margo and I crossed from Vladivostok to Moscow on the Trans-Siberian railway. I then returned ten years later in October 1978 as a scholar on an exchange to investigate Soviet studies on China in light of the Sino-Soviet dispute as part of my research on China's cultural diplomacy.[11] My return ten years later in 1988 on behalf of the university was to a changing USSR. Mikhail Gorbachev had proclaimed Glasnost and I was accompanying Professor Bodan Krawchenko,[12] the director of the University of Alberta's Canadian Institute of Ukrainian Studies (CIUS), to Kiev and Lviv. Because of Glasnost, we were free to deal directly with institutions in Ukraine without seeking approval from Moscow, unlike China where we had encountered no such restrictions from the central government. At Lviv, we signed the first independently negotiated institution-to-institution agreement between a Canadian and a Soviet university. Our purpose was to give U of A scholars direct access to archival and library facilities in Ukraine. The agreement called for a scholarly exchange. The president of Ivan Franko National University clearly held his position more for his politics than for his learning. I suspect he thought the same of me as I signed for the University of Alberta.

Apart from the new relaxed policy regarding university agreements, there were other aspects of life in the Soviet Union on display. On the trip I forwent the opportunity to buy brassieres offered on the domestic flight from Moscow to Kiev, even though the solidly built flight attendant modelled them for her customers. It was not long after the Chernobyl disaster and that, along with Gorbachev's policies,[13] was unsettling. Thanks to Krawchenko, one dark night I met some of his dissident academic friends who, despite my lack of language, conveyed to me an air of hope for a better tomorrow. Krawchenko and I attended a wedding at the Wedding Palace in Kiev. We helped celebrate the nuptials of Bodan Klid, one of our graduate students on an exchange. Although the wedding ceremony was far from traditional, the joy and warmth that accompanied the feast afterwards certainly were.

Three years later, I was back in Kiev as a universities representative on an Alberta government mission that was exploring educational links with Ukraine and the Soviet Republic of Russia. The tour included Kiev, St. Petersburg, and Moscow. Our hosts in Moscow were from the government of the Russian Republic. Life under Gorbachev was clearly much more relaxed, but there were signs that the machinery of the state was starting to break down. On the tour we stayed in university dorms in Moscow and St. Petersburg, where obliging cats spent the night on rodent patrol. Cats seemed to be everywhere. In St. Petersburg, at the opera, an obliging feline chased a mouse across the stage during an aria. While travelling, we were entertained royally in private homes. On our return to Moscow from Kiev, after midnight on a much delayed flight, our hosts met us with bottles of champagne, shouting welcome to us from the airport's observation deck, which they had managed to keep open.

In less than two years, I was once again in Moscow. In 1993, the Soviet Union had come unglued and Yeltsin was now the leader of Russia. I was one member of a three-person federal government delegation to Yakutsk in eastern Siberia, on the Lena River. The delegation leader was Brian Long from the Department of External Affairs and the third member was Doris Sherwood from the Association of Universities and Colleges of Canada (AUCC). We were accompanied out of Moscow by Georgi Arbatov, a director of the United States and Canada Institute of the Academy of Sciences. I had known Arbatov for years, since 1968. He was a frequent visitor at U of A, as he travelled throughout Canada and the United States each year on a fact-finding tour. A charming man, whom Americans generally thought to be a spy, at Canadian universities he was considered just an academic visitor, although a very highly placed one. The purpose of our delegation was to discuss exchanges relating to northern studies and to be present at the formation of a new centre of Canadian studies. It became clear very early on in our trip that the old system of bureaucratic privilege was coming apart similar to what I had witnessed in China in the early 1980s.

In July, I was attending to university business in Africa prior to the tour so I joined the delegation in Moscow. I broke my journey in Paris, where I picked up a couple of bottles of cognac and two rounds of Brie. I arrived in Moscow around ten in the evening. Our flight to Yakutsk left at midnight from another airport nearly an hour's drive away. I made it in time, in fact, more than time, because our plane was delayed. The airport was crowded and the passengers snarling. Arbatov took us to the VIP lounge, but all the chairs were filled with "ordinary" passengers. Around 2:30 a.m., our plane arrived and the crowd surged across the runway to climb the steps. "Don't worry, stay back," said Arbatov, "we are VIPs with reserved seats." Eventually, we climbed the stairs only to join a line of people standing in the aisle where a desperate flight attendant was telling people to get off as there was no more room. VIP status, it seemed, no long existed, and only after some sharp words from Arbatov were we shown to seats scattered about the non-VIP cabin. It was a wonderful sight inside the airplane. Aeroflot had no restrictions on transporting animals or birds, so our flight was a mix of fin, fur, feather, and cloth-covered passengers. Brian Long, a tall man with heft, was squeezed into a middle seat. On his right was a lady with a bird in a cage on her lap, and under the seat in front of him was a tray of newly hatched chicks.

Once everyone was settled and the excess passengers decanted, the plane prepared to leave. Instructions to those passengers who remained were brief and uninformative. Just as well, because shortly after takeoff, people fell asleep with little expectation of service. I have never been able to sleep on planes and this one, a speedy Soviet jet, was launched on a six-hour nonstop flight to Yakutsk. At about 4:00 in the morning I walked to the end of the plane to the bathroom. I entered and locked the door. The light came on to reveal an interior devoid of paint and decoration. This really did not concern me, but my inability to unlock the door did. I began to knock loudly, and then to shout, with no result. After a time, I accepted I would probably be there until we landed, but to my great relief the door was opened by a blonde attendant. She was cooking the evening meal of chicken and peas. When I say "cooking," I mean frying. There was no such thing as a microwave on board and the chicken, for over one hundred passengers, was being fried one piece at a time. Just after 5 a.m., the passengers were aroused to eat "supper." We then learned that our table trays were exactly that. They had three hollows in them. The attendant dropped a piece of chicken in one, some peas in another, with a piece of rough brown bread on the side. On arrival at Yakutsk airport, we were treated, as promised, as VIPs and taken to the state guest house, which Boris Yeltsin was expected to occupy after our departure.

The city of Yakutsk and its people are enchanting. Located on the right bank of the Lena River, which looked as broad as an ocean, in a region rich in diamonds and minerals, the city is built on permafrost with all of its utilities above ground. It boasts a museum devoted to the study of mammoths, with the remains of one in its original location, in the basement of the exhibition hall. The city is also proud of its museum dedicated to the mouth harp, known in my youth as the "Jew's harp." The state guest house was located outside the city and we were driven around in a van with a huge interior heater set at right angles to the dashboard. After visits and discussions on co-operation in northern studies with university and government officials, we attended the meeting called to elect the executive of a newly formed Canadian studies centre. Canada deemed it important that the director be a native of the region, fluent in the local language, and not a member of the Communist Party. We were there to observe but not to interfere in the election. Needless to say, the person elected was a Russian, a member of the Communist Party, and he did not speak the local language.

In contrast to the newly elected director of the Canadian studies centre, the members of the local government we met in Yakutsk were native to the region, young, and enthusiastic. They had already forged links with the Northwest Territories and the Yakutsk Minister of Culture sported a baseball cap issued to commemorate a papal visit to the NWT. But like the rest of Russia they were fond of alcohol. Over the twenty-five-year span of my visits to the Soviet Union, the ravages of alcohol were always evident: Yakutsk was no exception and to which I contributed.

One Sunday during the visit we were treated to a cruise on the Lena River. As soon as we boarded, well before noon, it was clear that at least one of our guides was drunk. I contributed one of the bottles of cognac I had bought in Paris for the day's festivities, but it was drained even before the boat had left its moorings. After about an hour, we were invited to disembark to participate in a conducted tour of the wooded park. En route we encountered, "by accident," a choir that performed for us in anticipation of an invitation to tour Canada. Further on, we examined old style huts that early pioneers used. Around noon, we came upon a very long picnic table of rough wood, large enough to seat two dozen people—the size to which our group had grown. I sat at one end of the table while skewers of horsemeat and plates of blood sausage were prepared. I thought it an opportune time to circulate the two rounds of brie and the remaining bottle of cognac from France. The cheese made it up my side and partway down the other, but the cognac failed to make the turn. I tasted neither, but was told by those who did that both the cheese and wine were very good. On our return trip up river, we paused for some swimming. Ordinarily, I do not find drunken men funny, but this day was an exception. One would-be swimmer emerged from the river and began the first of many staggering attempts to put both his legs into one pant leg, before teetering up the boarding plank to the boat in a vain effort to reach the cruiser without falling into the river. When, later that afternoon, we reached our departure point, our host, dead drunk, had to be carried off into an awaiting car. He had meetings early the next morning when, it was said, he would be bright as a button.

VIP status deserted us again on our return flight to Moscow. The plane, a Russian-built jet, was generally devoid of seat belts. Arbatov considered me lucky because I had half of one. We were seat companions on the flight and he confided to me that Gordon Lonsdale, the SOAS spy I have written about earlier in the book, had indeed died picking mushrooms. It turns out that he and Lonsdale had lived outside Moscow in adjoining *dachas*. Back in Moscow, I was heartened to see Russian–Chinese relations had improved to the point that the lone Chinese restaurant had re-opened, featuring Peking duck flown in daily from Beijing. Unlike the roast duck restaurants in Beijing, however, the Moscow establishment featured belly dancing. I missed my flight out of Moscow, not because I was late but because the airport was plugged. The rouble had collapsed and items, particularly antiques and artworks, were dirt cheap. The airport check-in lines were full of people pushing carts piled high with treasures.

TIANANMEN SQUARED

In 1989, there was a wave of unrest throughout the communist regimes in Poland, Czechoslovakia, East Germany, and China. The year is remembered most for two events: the fall of the Berlin Wall in November and the demonstrations in Tiananmen Square, Beijing, which lasted from late April to June 4. The latter ensnared the University of Alberta. In May, as was customary every other year, a group of U of A students left for a six-week summer language school in Harbin. Chinese literature Professor Chen Yu-shih, a senior scholar known for her charm and determination, was in charge. The students faced a full program of classes and cultural visits, but as events drew to a climax in Beijing, parents of the students began to worry, putting in calls to their MLAS and the university, wanting to know about the safety of their children. They were assured by Professor Chen that all was quiet in Harbin, and the students were proceeding with their program without interruption. But after the night of June 4, when tanks entered the square in Beijing, such an explanation was no longer good enough. Parents demanded that the students return immediately.

As the demonstrations had escalated, Canadians were leaving Beijing and the embassy was inundated with requests for information and assistance. Canadian Ambassador Earle Drake was under great stress, working with his staff long hours to meet the emergency. He really did not need a recalcitrant professor on top of his other problems, but Professor Chen refused to accept his advice, or respond positively to the strong requests from the Alberta government and me that the students return home immediately. Ultimately, the ambassador and the professor refused to speak to each other. Harbin remained quiet and Professor Chen saw no reason to interrupt the intellectual development of the students because of the events in Beijing. She assumed her assurances would suffice. The Alberta government, most notably Minister of Advanced Education Jim Horsman, requested the university to recall the students. The government chartered a plane to meet them in Dalian for a flight to Hong Kong.

Sonja Arntzen, chair of the East Asian Studies Department, in the midst of an afternoon Kabuki performance at the Edmonton Citadel Theatre, phoned Professor Chen with the message, but Professor Chen remained adamant. Eventually, through the good offices and intervention of an Edmonton businessman active in Harbin, the students were sent by train to Dalian. Sometime later, an unrepentant Professor Chen returned to Edmonton, as did the students, some after more travels in Asia.

The plight of the U of A students drew national attention, including interviews with Barbara Frum of the CBC. As a consequence of Professor Chen's actions, the Alberta government hinted that the university might be called on to pay for the students' charter flight home. Ironically, about a week following the Tiananmen incident, on a provincial radio, noon-hour, phone-in show on which I was asked to participate, the overwhelming number of callers supported the Chinese government's actions. They were of the opinion that if Canadian students had occupied Parliament Hill and refused to obey martial law, as the Chinese students had done, the Canadian government would be required to employ force. I was not overly surprised by this because I had written a letter, published in the *Globe and Mail* on June 4, predicting that the Chinese students were to fail as the government, once martial law had been imposed, could define those who persisted as rebels. I felt the students were naive to assume the regime that they were criticizing would risk its modernization program by showing weakness.

Following the events in Beijing, the Canadian government offered refugee status to Chinese students studying in Canada. This caused a hiatus in the flow of new Chinese students to Canadian universities, as the Chinese government, angry with the Canadian government's action, refused to grant exit permits. Stronger actions against China were demanded in some quarters. The Department of Foreign Affairs and International Trade called a meeting in late June 1989, to which I was invited to attend, to discuss the matter. The meeting, which included representatives of government, business, the Chinese community, academics, and others, concluded that the government of Canada should halt all of its high-level visits and curtail displays of approval of the Chinese government, but that people-to-people contacts should be retained. It would be three years before matters returned to normal, but students who had accepted refugee status and later returned to China found the Canadian Embassy in Beijing unhelpful to them.[14]

In 1989, President Horowitz's second term was drawing to a close and a search was made for his replacement. Peter Meekison was the strong favourite as the internal candidate, but the Board of Governors decided to employ a headhunter, Janet Wright, to conduct the search. The final choice was between Meekison and Paul Davenport, a vice-principal at McGill. Originally from New Jersey, Davenport had made his home and his name in Montreal. An economist by training, he was also bilingual in French and English. The decision was close with Davenport winning out. Meekison agreed to stay on as vice-president academic for the time being.[15] International affairs were not a priority of the new president and he was encouraged in this by the Board of Governors. Meekison resigned a few months later, and the new vice-president academic, John McDonald, the former dean of science, had little enthusiasm for internationalizing the university. Shortly after the transition was completed, and under pressure from the president, McDonald reorganized his office, eliminating the international functions of the position I held. Anxious that U of A not lose its achievements and continue to meets its obligations in international affairs, I stayed on as a co-ordinator of international affairs (1992–1994) outside the central administration's organizational chart. I continued in this position for the remainder of Davenport's five-year term.

Late in 1993, the Board of Governors decided not to renew President Davenport for a second term without an open competition. Ironically, a major criticism of Davenport was that he failed to engage the university internationally. My relations with Davenport had been proper but reserved. Shortly before the end of his term, he called me to say that he had been wrong about international affairs. It was a call I did not expect, but it raised my opinion of him to a high point. In retrospect, my opinion of him rose even higher when I learned of how testy his relations were with the chair of the Board, Stanley Milner. From the beginning there had been a struggle between the Board chair and the president over who ran the university. The president lost, but went on to an outstanding tenure as president of the University of Western Ontario.

Meekison was once again a candidate for president, but once again the Board made an outside appointment of Rod Fraser, a vice-principal of Queen's University who himself was passed over for an outside candidate for principal. Following a University Senate report from a commission on the university's international mission chaired by Chancellor Sandy Mactaggart, Fraser was enjoined to make international affairs his priority. He re-established the position of associate vice-president (international affairs) and immersed himself in relations with China. At this point in 1994, having been involved with the university's international outreach for a decade, I took a year's leave prior to a return to full-time teaching and a slightly early retirement in 1996.

My involvement in the university's international programs provided me with some of the most interesting and exciting times of my career. I was fortunate to have the support of colleagues at all levels within the university and in particular from deans such as Bob Paterson of education, Fred Otto of engineering, Eloise Murray of home economics, Ed Tyrchniewicz of agriculture, and Roger Smith of business, whose faculties were leaders in international education and development. In addition, in the half-dozen years that I was in University Hall, I enjoyed not only a close working relationship with Peter Meekison but also with Brian McDonald, associate vice-president (academic administration), whose sense of fair play and legendary sense of humour made him the ideal person to deal with matters related to academic personnel. Along with international affairs, I had responsibilities dealing with promotion and tenure appeals, and investigations into complaints brought by one academic staff member against another. It was on these issues that I grew to appreciate McDonald's open-mindedness, balance, and fairness.

I left the realm of university upper administration conscious of the fact that my views on university governance were in eclipse. The use of headhunters and of outside appointments at top levels was destined to drive a wedge between the administration and the academic community, to test the goodwill that had existed when the top-level appointees were people who knew the university, warts and all, and who themselves were well known, warts and all, to the academic community. As much as I respected members of the Board of Governors, from my years as one of them, I have concluded that they are not equipped to run the day-to-day operations of the university, nor should they regard it as part of their mandate to do so. On top of this, the core group of governors are partisan political appointees who find it difficult to comprehend the workings of what some might regard as a minimum-security mental institution. Issues such as tenure, and mandatory retirement,[16] have traditionally driven Board members to despair, bringing them into open conflict with academic staff. Under such circumstances, it is difficult for them to appreciate the old adage: "One can catch more flies with honey than with vinegar."

When I was in mid-career, I could not conceive of leaving the University of Alberta. "They will have to drag me out kicking and screaming," I was fond of saying. But when the time came for me to retire in 1996, I did so with alacrity, because I felt I was not so much leaving the university as the university was leaving me. I enjoyed teaching and research,[17] and I maintained these two activities during my years in administration. What I found most disturbing during the final decade of my career was the rapid adoption by the university of a corporate model of governance. This trend had been evident in universities across Canada for some time, but it accelerated when government policies sought to place more of the costs of higher education directly on the shoulders of the students, and, in addition, put pressure on university boards and administrations to seek major funding from non-public sources. These policies were traceable to the initiatives of Margaret Thatcher, Ronald Reagan, and to the rising influence of neo-conservatism. The gist of the argument is that higher education represents a private, long-term gain for the individual who receives it. The taxpayer should pay only a portion of the costs of what really enriches the individual. It is also argued that universities and the private/corporate sector are natural partners. Corporations want to develop products and techniques to benefit society as well as to enrich their stockholders. Rather than corporations having to set up their own research arms (although some, of course, have), their needs can be met by contracting with universities. They can also be encouraged to donate funds to universities to build research facilities and to provide scholarships. While on the surface this appears to be a benign and fruitful relationship, it is fraught with potential conflicts for universities that come out of a tradition of seeking truth and speaking it no matter the consequences.

Slowly, but surely, universities have begun to cut the truth to fit the cloth supplied by their funders. Moreover, the university's top administrators have become high-level panhandlers, going from corporate door to corporate door seeking largesse, while professors are increasingly judged by the money they manage to generate. More and more time is taken from basic research and teaching while university professors prepare grant proposals for external funding. God forbid that anyone in the university should engage in criticism that might endanger funding. From the early 1990s onward, the University of Alberta Board of Governors, always dominated by government appointees, became the prime force in directing the university's future. Gone was the creative tension between the academic needs of the university and the government's agenda, between professors and students and lay Board members. Boards now hired presidents—CEOs—willing to do their bidding. There was a near moratorium on public criticism by the university of the provincial government. The central administration of the university became like Russian space station Mir, floating high above the university, with little concern for its core day-to-day activities, but at the same time requiring expensive maintenance.

A tragic outcome of the fund-hungry university is a decline in the rigour of assessing student achievement. As student fees rise, and international student fees rise even higher, cash-strapped institutions offer courses that will "draw" students. Those courses that do not are threatened with extinction. Universities are tempted to cater to popular tastes rather than to ensure that students receive a thorough and basic understanding of a discipline. Having paid their high fees, students feel they are entitled to success no matter what effort they have expended. Grades are not accepted as the professor's considered assessment of the student's level of achievement but are regarded as an opening offer in a bargain that has to take into account the student's career goals. This approach has corrupted the attitudes of some of even the very best students. Meanwhile, research-based universities scour the globe for good students to fill their graduate programs, often to work on projects favoured by corporate funders.

The University of Alberta where I took my first degree and in which I spent most of my academic career was of the old sort. University education was regarded as a public good and not just a private prize. Fees were low and high academic standards were rigorously applied. Tenure for professors fostered open discussion and debate, particularly within the faculties of arts and science, the traditional heart of a university. Truth was debated, not fudged. Then again, perhaps such a time never really existed during my years at the University of Alberta, but at least the illusion of it remained strong well into the 1980s.

NINE ★ ★ ★ ★

My China

Each of us has a vision of China. It may be benevolent, threatening, benign, mysterious, magnificent, maddening, intriguing, or even boring, depending upon our experience and understanding. In my case, the word "benevolent," "magnificent," and "intriguing" dominate my vision, although the others have at times been present to varying degrees. Having pursued China for over seven decades, and led readers along my path, I think it only fair that I describe my China, the China that I have come to inhabit physically and intellectually.

GOOD FOOD MAKES GOOD FRIENDS

China began for me at 8:55 in the morning on Tuesday, September 5, 1939, when I met Herbert How. With Herbert and his family, my view of the Chinese was set. They were kind, generous, and prosperous, much more so than my economically stressed family. Consequently, I have a problem with those stereotypical views of the Chinese as crafty, indolent, clannish, and cold. A year or so later I was introduced to authentic Chinese food, fresh from the wok, as prepared by Herbert's mother. A quarter of a century would pass before I encountered real Chinese food again. In the interim, my taste buds grew accustomed to chow mien, chop suey, lemon chicken, sweet and sour pork, egg foo yung, wonton soup, spring rolls, fried rice, and fortune cookies, common fare on the menus of Prairie cafés. Recipes for these dishes appeared in local newspapers and everyone learned how to "cook Chinese." Just take one tin of Chung King chop suey vegetables, heat, and pour over a tin of crispy Chung King chow mien. Cut up two pork chops into small squares, fry, and when well done, remove from the pan to a dish that contains a sauce mixture of tomato ketchup, orange juice, sugar, and vinegar. Anyone could be a Chinese chef. It is amazing that the British Empire, containing a colony called Hong Kong, could allow such a cruel joke to be played on its far-flung populations.

But then, what could one expect when the empire's shock troops were eaters of Scots haggis, Welsh rarebit, Irish stew, and toad in the hole?

Not until the late spring of 1964 did I encounter authentic Chinese food again and on a daily basis as I ate my way through Hong Kong on a line to Guangzhou, Beijing, Shanghai, and back. From dim sum, garlic shrimp, beggar chicken, gailan, bak choy, mustard and pea greens, pea pods, twice-fried beans, steamed ginger fish, to Mandarin fish, ma po dofu, "crossing the bridge" noodles, Peking duck, hot and sour soup, fish-flavoured eggplant, jiaotz, guotieh, steamed bread, five-spice beef, soft-fried pork, dry-fried Sichuan beef and hotpots, my taste buds were reprogrammed. I came to pity the sweet-and-sour-pork-and-lemon-chicken eaters of Canada who had not yet been handed the keys to paradise.

I developed a passion for Chinese food that remains unrequited, and although some might scoff, I am never happier than when I am in a Chinese restaurant—if there is a religion that guarantees a heaven full of Chinese restaurants, I might consider becoming a convert. China in the twenty-first century is a gourmet's nirvana, filled with restaurants from the tiny to the majestic, from the drab to the glitzy. I am eternally grateful to Charlie How, his family, and their Cameo Café for introducing me to Chinese food and for starting me on my pursuit of China. I make it a practice, no matter where I am in the world, of seeking out a local Chinese restaurant. I fear that not all countries are well served and like Prairie Chinese chefs, cooks have adapted their menus to suit local, non-Chinese tastes.

My China, of course, is made up of more than restaurants, good food, and good chefs. It contains millions of wonderful people, a few of whom I have befriended and who have taught me to appreciate Chinese culture and to understand better China's history. Locally in Edmonton, I have enjoyed good relations with the Chinese community. Like all immigrant communities, it is made up of layers—each layer is the result of different times and sources of immigration. The foundation of the community is composed of those who trace their Canadian roots to before World War II and represents the descendants, and in increasingly rare cases, the survivors of the early Chinese settlers in Alberta dating back to 1880. Following the horrible years of exclusion from 1923 to 1947, their ranks were later supplemented by post-1950 arrivals from Taiwan and Hong Kong, or those fleeing the Communist Revolution in China. Other layers were added after the establishment of Canada–China diplomatic relations in October 1970, or with the arrival of "boat people" from Vietnam in the late seventies. Throughout the years, others have arrived from Chinese overseas communities in Southeast Asia and Latin America. Many came first as students and then decided to seek permanent residence and citizenship. Like most ethnic groups in Canada, the Chinese community embraces the policy of multiculturalism that frees them of any lingering feelings of second-class citizenship. Organizations within the Edmonton community link the layers through common bonds of clan, surname, home village, or special interests. But they are not exclusive—I am an honorary life member of the Lee Family Association and the Chinese Benevolent Association.

My connection to the Lee family in Edmonton started with Ned Lee, whom I first met in 1957 when he ran a small grocery store and I was home briefly from England. He had left China in 1950 to join his family in British Columbia and worked in restaurants in Vancouver, before moving to Edmonton. Our friendship blossomed in the l960s when he opened the Bamboo Palace restaurant and began to promote an understanding of Chinese food, particularly dim sum, in Edmonton. A superb restaurateur and chef, at one point he operated three restaurants at the same time until ill health caused him to cut back. Through Ned, I was invited to join the local branch of the Lee Family Association, which is connected with other branches throughout the world. As an honorary Lee, I am welcomed at any of the associations' branches.

The Chinese Benevolent Association, founded in British Columbia in 1884, is one of the oldest community organizations in Canada. My membership is in the Edmonton branch and was given to me by a former student when he was head of it. His name was Kim Hung, who along with another of my students, Lawrence Lau, began the Chinese Library Association at the University of Alberta. As I have mentioned in earlier chapters, I became involved with the Chinese Library Association and later with the Chinese Graduates Association, in which both of them were also active. Kim Hung went on to head the Chinese Benevolent Association in Edmonton and was the catalyst that brought the community together to establish a multicultural centre and the first elders' mansion, a multi-storied group home for the elderly. Tragically, Kim died very young in 1996 at the age of forty-five, but not before he left a major legacy. Ten years after his death, his contributions to the city were recognized by his induction into the City of Edmonton Hall of Fame. His work, particularly in liaison with the university, was carried on by Daisy Cheng, a former TV personality from Taiwan and a writer of novels and poetry with whom I worked closely for a number of years. In due course, she left for Vancouver, but my contacts with the community are maintained through a network of good friends, many of whom I continue to meet at my thrice-weekly visits to the Dynasty Century Palace, a large-capacity restaurant owned and operated by my good friend Chi Wang who hails from Hong Kong. His day chef, a woman,[1] is one of the best dim sum chefs in western Canada.

FOOD FOR THOUGHT

There are over fifty thousand citizens of Chinese ethnic origin in Edmonton. Many of them are graduates of the University of Alberta, while numerous others are studying there. Members of Edmonton's Chinese community have for years served on the U of A's Board of Governors, but the university has not involved the local Chinese community as much as it might have. The Department of East Asian Studies and the China Institute were established with little direct participation from the local community, in contrast to the development of Ukrainian studies and the Canadian Institute for Ukrainian Studies, which were co-operative efforts involving the university, the local community, and the provincial government. This can be partly explained by the make up of the local community and the nature of China studies at the university. Although it is changing, the local community is made up primarily of immigrants from Guangdong province. They speak Cantonese or one of its many local dialects. The university, on the other hand, concentrates on studies using Mandarin, reflecting the official language of China and the dominance of northern capitals in recent centuries of Chinese history. By the same token, the provincial government's partnership with Heilongjiang in northeast China and Edmonton's twinning with Harbin engaged the interest of few within the local Chinese community.

Nonetheless, the Chinese community on a regular basis has called on members of the university as resources for its civic and cultural activities. It has also been active in funding scholarships. Only in recent years, with the university, city, and provincial government linking with institutions throughout China, has the local community found a place. In the summer of 2010, the university for the first time in a substantial way reached out to the local community through an exhibit emphasizing the lives of the early Chinese pioneers on the Prairies.[2]

Retirement did not end my direct involvement with China. Indeed, my personal contacts with China increased and deepened. Shortly before I retired, through my friend and former colleague Charles Burton of Brock University, I met a group of Chinese scholars from the Chinese Academy of Social Sciences (CASS) who were linked with the Royal Society of Canada in the Democracy Project.[3] Two of the scholars, Chen Qineng and Jiang Peng from the Canadian Studies Centre of the Institute of World History in Beijing, became my close friends. Professor Chen and his wife Professor Cao Tejin were part of the first wave of Chinese students to study in the Soviet Union during the period of Sino-Soviet friendship in the early 1950s. They studied in Leningrad before returning to positions at the World History Institute in Beijing. With the coming of the Cultural Revolution, Chen was considered suspect because of his Russian contacts. He spent six months literally locked in his office at the institute and was later sent to a farm in the countryside, which turned out to be a good time to breathe fresh air, eat good plain food, exercise, and regain one's health. After Mao's death and the opening of China, Chen eventually returned to his former position and has since worked on many projects promoting the understanding between China and other countries. He served as president of the Chinese Association for Canadian Studies (CACS). Now in his seventies, well past the normal retirement age for Chinese academics, he continues to organize conferences, and write and edit books. He is eccentric and learned in the tradition of great Chinese scholars.

My other friend from CASS, Jiang Peng, was young enough to be a Red Guard during the Cultural Revolution, but she lacked the proper class background of worker, soldier, or peasant. Even so, she did indulge in destroying some family artifacts that reflected Western influence. She too is active in Canadian studies, co-authoring with Chen books on Canada as well as co-editing series on world culture and civilizations. She has a sharp incisive mind and a quick wit.

A third Chinese scholar who has become a close friend of mine is Liu Guangtai, a historian from Hebei Normal University in Shijiazhuang, the capital of Hebei province. In 1992, Liu came to U of A on a one-year research grant from the Canadian government to study Canadian history. He then returned to the university in 1994 for a shorter research trip to complete a biography of Chester Ronning that he later published in Chinese. Liu comes from a peasant background and is the only member of his family to have graduated from a university. He is a serious student of Canadian history and along with the biography of Ronning, he has published works on Trudeau's foreign policy and the Canadian health care system. Like Chen and Jiang, he is an independently minded scholar and a thorough researcher—a genuine bookworm.

I am happy to number among my friends two other Chinese scholars who obtained PhDs in Alberta. Wang Bing of Liaoning University holds a doctorate from the University of Calgary. He was a genuine Red Guard and participated as an enthusiastic teenager in one of the million-strong rallies of Red Guards in Beijing reviewed by Mao and Lin Biao. Like all Red Guards, at the close of 1968, at Mao's urging, he was sent to the countryside to work. In his case it was to Inner Mongolia where he spent the next decade. Because of his Alberta experience, he is not only a student of Canadian education practices but a proponent of multiculturalism, Canadian-style. Zhao Yifeng was my last PhD student who did a brilliant thesis on Ming history before returning to China as a Canadian citizen to take up a position of dean, and associate editor of the press, at Northeast University in Changchun, Jilin province. He spent a lonely and isolated time during the Cultural Revolution making ends meet by raising rabbits. Like Wang Bing, he is very much a self-starter who has contributed a great deal to provincial university development in China. Each of my friends faced hardship during their student days and academic careers. Like Chinese scholars of old, they have risen above their difficulties with a stoic dedication to learning and the dissemination of knowledge.

The transformation of China since the early 1990s has been on a scale never before witnessed in history.[4] Nowhere is change more palpable than in Chinese universities. China has a long history of a close association between scholars and government. Traditionally, government officials were scholars, selected by a rigorous system of examinations. The very best often became members of the Hanlin Academy, a type of think tank for the emperor. China's rulers have always been very sensitive to the opinions and ideas of the country's scholars and scholars have often suffered for their contrary views. In 1898, in an effort to modernize Chinese education, the emperor created the first Western-style university. Beijing University, commonly known as Beida, was first located close to the Forbidden City. It had a shaky start, but early in the twentieth century a reform-minded president recruited excellent professors to the institution.[5] Today, it remains the premier university in China.

During the first fifty years of the twentieth century, the growth of Chinese universities was greatly influenced by colleges founded by Christian missionaries, and by the American model of a liberal arts institution. When the Nationalist government of Chiang Kai-shek withdrew to the island of Taiwan in 1949, professors and students faced a choice: either go to Taiwan to build new universities under the continued influence of America and Christian missions, with prospects of study and links with the United States, or remain on the mainland to help build a new China, to face Marxist re-education with prospects of study within the Soviet Union and the Soviet block.[6] Thus, the academic community of China was divided. Within China, the Soviet Russian model of institutional structures—theoretical studies separate from applied learning—was influential until 1960 when Beijing and Moscow split over the issue of communist doctrine.

In 1964, through a socialist education movement, Mao sought to place his imprint on educational institutions at all levels. Scholars were enjoined to combine work with study, particularly the study of his thought. There were to be no more long fingernails on the hands of scholars showing their Confucian distain for manual labour. More was to come two years later with the launch of the Great Revolution for the Establishment of a Proletarian Culture. Universities and university professors were prime targets, particularly those educated abroad in America or the Soviet Union. Many were persecuted and hounded to death, or sent to the countryside to reform their thinking. The universities were closed and their students were free to roam China to make revolution. When the universities re-opened in 1970, they did so under new Cultural Revolution guidelines. Professors and students were to be selected on the basis of their revolutionary—worker, soldier, peasant—heritage and their knowledge of Mao Zedong thought: Redness trumped expertise. To provide work experience for their students, universities were linked with industry.

Not until Deng Xiaoping consolidated his power following Mao's death in 1976 did matters change. Deng abolished the class background system that fixed children in the class of their fathers and grandfathers: once a capitalist, always a capitalist, once a class enemy, always a class enemy. Expertise was once again valued. Deng's new priorities were illustrated in a poster of the time. During the Cultural Revolution, a popular poster pictured a worker, soldier, and peasant resolutely facing the future. Now the posters included a bespectacled intellectual with a roll of plans under his arm. The experts were back. By 1980, Deng launched a program to send Chinese scholars overseas. To hasten development, a number of universities were designated as key institutions to receive more resources to build their capacities to raise the standards of university education.

This agenda was followed with success, but not everyone was happy. In December 1986, students in Anhui province demonstrated ostensibly against conditions in their dormitories, but there were deeper issues related to post-university opportunities. Hu Yaobang, a reformist associate of Deng's and

One of the many posters used to launch the one-child policy in 1978. The billboards featured female children.

secretary of the Communist Party, dealt with the issue not fully to the students' satisfaction but too leniently for the conservatives in the Chinese leadership. Hu was demoted. The student issues remained unresolved, and on the death of Hu Yaobang in mid-April 1989, students gathered in Tiananmen Square to mourn him. To their grievances over living conditions were added cries for reform and an end to corruption.

At that time, graduates of Chinese universities had little hope of getting any of the top jobs in the country. These went to the sons and daughters of the party and government hierarchy who were educated abroad, usually on scholarships provided by America's top universities. The student demonstrations gathered strength as the seventieth anniversary of the May 4th Movement and the visit of Chairman Gorbachev to China approached.[7] The students disrupted both, and in early June those who remained after the declaration of martial law on May 20 were driven from the square by tanks, resulting in a number of dead and injured. The exact numbers and exact locations remain in dispute.

After Tiananmen, Chinese universities were once more in crisis and put under close scrutiny. At the same time, more resources were given to them to meet the students' material complaints. In the two decades after June 4, 1989, key universities were transformed into large, dual-campus, modern centres with new libraries and high-tech infrastructures, filled with first-rank professors and students chosen by countrywide competitive examinations. At the outset of the twenty-first century, Chinese students, the majority of them from one-child households, have never had it so good, materially. Their studies have become more challenging and competitive, keeping pace with rapid technological change and with the transformation of the Chinese economy and society that has opened up more employment opportunities.

In the first decade of the new century, Chinese refurbished universities are full of bright, fresh-faced young people, the majority of whom are female and only children. They were, at best, infants in 1989. There has been a deliberate revival of the Confucian values of respect for age, learning, and harmony, but they are also anxious to learn English, even to the extent of watching *Desperate Housewives* on the Internet. Few of today's students have first-hand information on the Maoist period and its immediate aftermath, although they do have some curiosity about the past. Their parents and grandparents are reluctant to relive the harshness of those times. They are more interested in making sure their only children study hard, do well, and get a good job. They are content to let their children believe that the Cultural Revolution was a fanciful period and that Mao was very much like the fat jolly image of him that dangles from the rearview mirrors of taxis.

However, I, a foreigner who has witnessed the transformation and who saw some of the revolutionary leaders up close, can provide these young students with glimpses of those earlier times.[8] As an invited lecturer, I find a ready audience when it becomes known that I lived in China during the Cultural Revolution, met Zhou Enlai, and witnessed the events following the fall of the Gang of Four. The students love and admire Zhou, greatly respect Deng, but are indifferent to Mao. Jiang Qing (Mao's last wife) fascinates the young women because their sexist male classmates conclude that the four women in Chinese history who wielded central power all ended badly. Although my lectures are usually on Chinese immigration to Canada, the history of Chinese settlement in Canada, and the nature of multiculturalism, question periods inevitably drift into a discussion of China's modern history and development.

Unlike their own revolutionary past, American or Western culture draws this new generation, as well as their universities, like a magnet. Both young men and young women display a naive view of America as a land where people of their age can do anything they want without restriction, without parents and grandparents telling them what to do and how to behave. As only children they are spoiled, as Chinese children have always been, but unlike their predecessors, they are not faced with making sacrifices to assist siblings. They want and expect to be able to do things their way. Chinese university presidents, emulating their Western counterparts, have become fundraisers, evident by the number of buildings named after prominent overseas Chinese donors, including "Superman" Hong Kong businessman Li Ka Shing. Canadian and Chinese universities face similar problems of funding and student recruitment. Administratively, they are growing in a similar way as well. The governing boards of Canadian institutions following the corporate model have asserted greater central control over the lives of students and staff. At the same time, Chinese universities are experiencing an easing of government control and direction—their students and staff are beginning to enjoy more freedom of expression. The universities on either side of the Pacific may soon become indistinguishable from each other in their style of governance.

A PERSPECTIVE ON CONTEMPORARY CHINA

In the decades since my first visit, I have watched China undergo a transformation not unlike that experienced by western Canada during my lifetime. My childhood and early youth were spent during the Depression, the dirty thirties, and World War II. In that time, the economy in my part of southern Alberta changed from one heavily dependent upon animal power, natural gas, and steam to one addicted to gasoline and the internal combustion engine in all of its forms. It converted from kerosene lamps, outdoor plumbing, prairie trails, and horse-drawn wagons and sleighs to electric lights, flush toilets, gravel and then paved roads, tractors, half-ton trucks, and private automobiles. The horse, outside cattle ranches, was relegated to recreation and entertainment, while the coal-fired, steam-powered iron horse gave way to diesel. Individual phone lines replaced the party line, with a devastating impact on the quality of local gossip. We all yearned for the war to end when everything we ever dreamed of could be achieved. Each of us would be well off and secure, the Depression and the war just memories. In today's terms, during the first two decades of my life, southern Alberta made the transition from the status of underdeveloped to developed. Since then, it has gone on to become an integral part of the modern, high-tech, pill-popping, gadget-crazed, Google-eyeing, consumer-driven, debt-ridden Western society that we all love and hold so dear. The Alberta of my childhood, which nurtured three-quarters of a million souls, has more than quadrupled in population. It is within this context that I have assessed my China.

In my opinion, 1976 is crucial to the understanding of contemporary China. It is the year China rejected Maoism and took the first steps on the road to wholesale modernization. Up until then, the Chinese were a people on standby, waiting to be told what to do. Pummelled by political campaign after political campaign, the average Chinese knew there was no room for private initiatives and one's life was governed by the criticism of, and by, others. In 1976, all that changed as the seeds for the remarkable transformation of China were sown. By the summer of 1977 Deng was back in government, but it took a couple more years before he could introduce major reforms from his position as deputy premier. Two famous sayings are attributed to him: "Who cares if a cat is grey or white as long as it catches mice?" and "To become rich is glorious." The first saying meant to the average Chinese that the Communist Party would get off their backs. Political indoctrination would thereafter be confined to members of the party. Gone were the endless meetings featuring self-criticisms, readings from the "Little Red Book," and groupthink.

And just what would the average Chinese do with their new spare time? Well, they could give some thought to Deng's second aphorism and improve their material well-being by, for example, growing some vegetables for private sale on the small plots of land they were now allowed to own. In 1978, I saw two of these budding capitalists on a street in the beautiful garden city of Suzhou. One had some surplus berries he was selling for his own benefit. The other had set up a weigh scale on the sidewalk. One could step on it for a couple of cents. I think of these two men when I visit the new Suzhou, or the unbelievably modern Shanghai. Through his modernization policies, Deng unlocked the energy of China and launched it on a decades-long journey of unprecedented growth.

Keys to this growth are the Special Economic Zones (SEZ) that Deng sanctioned, and which India is now copying. When the West invaded China in the nineteenth century, it established treaty ports, both inland and on the China coast. They were microcosms of Westernization. Shanghai, the most important treaty port, became a training ground in the rudiments of industrialization and modernization, as well as a haven for dissident Chinese. Maoists rejected treaty ports as relics of imperialism; Shanghai was allowed to wither. Later, Deng embraced them as a model. The SEZs are in essence treaty ports, but with one major difference: this time, the Chinese are in charge. The two most successful are Shenzhen, on the border of Hong Kong, and Pudong, across the river from Shanghai. Deng knew Western capitalism could not resist the lure of cheap labour and the vast China market. He built a better mousetrap and the world beat a path to China's door.

If 1976 marked the end of Maoism, then June 4, 1989, marked the end of Communism. Once again, Deng's role was pivotal. Although he had unleashed the energy of China, his policies were not without their critics. Cultural conservatives and old-line Communists criticized the unchecked invasion of China by corrupting Western influences. What were the limits? The cultural conservatives and the old guard continue to lose out, but they appeared to triumph briefly in 1989.

I was not in China in the spring of 1989,[9] but I wrote a letter to the *Globe and Mail*, which was published, coincidentally, on the morning of June 4, saying that the students were bound to fail and to face suppression. It was my view then, and it is now, that it was the result of tragic misperceptions, particularly on the part of the Chinese students and on the part of Western media that gathered in Beijing to witness the visit of Gorbachev and the reconciliation of the USSR and China. The students were encouraged in their protests by their professors and by the events that took place earlier in the year in Eastern Europe. They received additional encouragement from schoolmates overseas. Thinking that they were in a strong position with international support, the students sought to embarrass the government, but not particularly Deng, by disrupting Gorbachev's visit. Nonetheless, what was to be Deng's great international triumph now became a triumph for the students. As I mentioned earlier in the chapter, the government split on how to handle the students and their demands. They adopted what appeared to be a good cop, bad cop approach and then declared martial law on May 20 to re-establish control. But the students persisted, buoyed by their Western encouragers, their friends overseas, and the growing number of sympathizers in Beijing.

Although Premier Li Peng has received most of the blame for Tiananmen Square,[10] Deng took the decision to send in the army with tanks, effectively ending the Communist Party in all but name. One of the reasons for enforcing martial law so harshly was that the student movement was spreading to other cities and to other sectors of society, notably to workers. The protest was no longer one of naive idealistic students but of elements key to the base of the party's power. Things could get out of hand quickly, particularly since the Chinese media was following Western examples and reporting events without the party spin. Some have speculated that Deng was also influenced by his own experience in 1968 at the hands of rampant Red Guards when he was frog-marched through the streets with a dunce cap on his head and his student son was pushed out of a dormitory window. I think it more likely he felt his reforms were threatened by what could have developed into major civil strife. People who were close to Deng at the time say that along with the decision to use the army, he ordered that the students' basic demands be met.

But by sending in the tanks Deng violated basic dogmas of the Chinese Communist Party—slogans such as "Serve the People," and "The people are like water and the army is like fish." He was sacrificing decades of the carefully nurtured image of the good and kind soldiers helping the poor and the old, placing the welfare of the people above their own well-being. All that went by the board that night early in June. It became clear that the party was determined to retain power no matter what. It was a return to an earlier saying of Mao's: "Political power grows out of the barrel of a gun," but with an emphasis on the power. In doing so, the party risked losing a key constituency, the youth, on whose enthusiastic dedication it has always counted. Deng, true to his style, judged material incentives to be a more powerful human motivator than dogma.

Perhaps because of this, Tiananmen looms larger in the West than it does in the People's Republic. It is kept fresh on Western television screens; the image of the lone man facing a line of tanks is too compelling not to use at every opportunity. Deng, the hard-headed pragmatist, who the Western media had cast in the role of a democrat, largely because he wore a white Stetson and played to the crowds in Texas during a tour he made of the United States in January–February 1979, has been recast as a bloody repressor. But in China, the memory of Tiananmen is receding,[11] as is the history of the old Communist Party and its accomplishments. The vast majority of Chinese were unaffected by the events. Because the demonstrators were in defiance of a declaration of martial law, the government has been able to argue they were rebels encouraged from abroad. In any case, since June 1989, most Chinese have become less interested in politics. They are caught up in the new consumerism that Deng's reforms accelerated—what he called "Socialism with Chinese Characteristics," and with the triumph of the 2008 Olympics.

But my Chinese friends over fifty years of age are concerned about what sort of China will be shaped by the young. They miss very little from the old Maoist days except for one thing: the sense of purpose. Mindless consumerism is not their style. Escape through television is useless. Heirs to a civilization of such great cultural traditions, they long to be part of something uplifting and creative. The government realized this and tried to find something to fill the spiritual void. Falun Gong,[12] the result of an early government effort gone awry, is now banned as a cult, but it continues to flourish because of its simple appeal to the poor and unemployed in particular. Christianity is growing, and Buddhism has large, but unknown, numbers of adherents. For lack of anything better, the government has resorted to reviving Confucius, emphasizing his doctrine of harmony. Confucius, once the anathema of the Communist Party, has been recruited as a guru for the new China of "Socialism with Chinese Characteristics."

Despite the post-Mao, post-Deng leadership's failure to bring a sense of purpose and spiritual fulfillment to the general populace, it has, nevertheless, achieved some remarkable things. Never in history have so many people been raised out of poverty and in such a short period of time. China has gone from a generally underdeveloped country to one with pockets of development unmatched in the world. What took my small patch of southern Alberta seven decades to achieve, China has done in less than three, and on a grand scale. The problems are, of course great. How does one feed, clothe, and house nearly 1.3 billion people? Is meeting this challenge more important, as the Chinese leaders argue, than instituting Western-style democracy and human rights? These are perhaps ideas that are more attractive to a small but rapidly growing middle/entrepreneurial class than to the much larger population of struggling farmers. And how does one administer justice and assure fairness during a prolonged period of boom and industrial expansion when the pace of such expansion outstrips the government's ability, at all levels, to monitor it?

Some observers have compared what is happening in China to the last decade of the nineteenth century and the first decade of the twentieth in North America when capitalists ran roughshod over the interests of lesser mortals. China is a centralized state, nearly the size of Canada, with forty times the population, fifty-five minority ethnic groups, and provincial governments with strong local interests. Just how swiftly can a problem on the southwest frontier with Myanmar be brought to the attention of the central government, and how much time does it take to solve it? Needless to say, this gives local authorities considerable leeway and opportunities to be corrupt. Chinese land and property developers are likely no more corrupt on average than those in Canada, but the current phase of unbridled capitalism is providing more opportunities. The Chinese government admits that it has major problems with corruption and Westerners frequently turn this self-criticism against them, while overlooking what happens in their own countries. Taking into account the size of its population, the country, and the speed of change, levels of Chinese corruption are perhaps not much above world averages. China, however, executes the worst offenders. The higher the level of corruption, the more likely the death penalty will be applied, although more recently the Chinese have reduced the length of the list of crimes subject to capital punishment.[13]

In addition to its levels of corruption, the Chinese readily admit to major problems in relation to the growing gap between rich and poor, between urban and rural prosperity, and between the numbers of men and women, along with pollution and environmental degradation, water and power shortages, and AIDS. But the government has become less forthright on the matter of local unrest, much of which is the direct result of the actions of corrupt local officials. China has millions of unemployed, many the result of the collapse of state enterprises. There are also large numbers of migrants from the countryside moving to the industrial cities and SEZs seeking an improved standard of life, but often with a devastating impact on families. They come from the relatively unpolluted countryside to the cities wreathed in industrial smog and the smoke from stoves still using soft coal. Modernization brings even more pollution, some of it from outsourced foreign industry. How to reconcile this with the rising expectations of the average Chinese? Just how quickly can a country of this size and population cleanse its environment using new technology when it has the world's largest reserves of coal, and it has increasing demands for energy? Apart from the pollution generated by its product, the operations of the coal mining industry in China are an ongoing scandal. Thousands of miners die each year due to nonexistent safety standards and limited regulation. Indeed, government allows the mine operators themselves to investigate and to report on disasters. Even worse, many of the accidents take place in mines not even licensed or sanctioned by the authorities.

China also has problems with its minorities. The current boundaries of China are more or less those established in the seventeenth century by the last great imperial dynasty, the Qing. At that time, Tibet, Xinjiang, parts of Mongolia, the Qing homeland of Manchuria, and Taiwan were brought under the rule of Beijing. Beginning in 1895, Japan occupied Taiwan for fifty years. After the 1911 revolution, Tibet broke away and Russia, both the czarist and Soviet regimes, made efforts to detach Xinjiang, then known as Turkestan, and Mongolia. These areas lie outside the traditional homeland of the majority Han Chinese population and, along with a strip on China's southern boundary, are the home of most of China's fifty-five-plus ethnic minorities. Clearly, the minorities live in very sensitive areas and Beijing has to tread carefully. It has followed policies that allow minorities to retain their languages, cultures, and customs, and to be exempt from the one-child policy. But generally, the minorities remain apart from the mainstream. The Chinese are seriously studying Canada's policy of multiculturalism.

The most troublesome minority area is Xinjiang, the Muslim Uighur homeland. There, the Chinese are faced with an independence movement encouraged from across the border by sympathetic Muslim states. The events of 9/11 were a godsend to Beijing because it was able to declare the independence movement as terrorist and place it on the United Nations' list of terrorist organizations. The Chinese are also aware that Western countries, which are critical of their policy in Xinjiang, are active just across the border from Xinjiang in Afghanistan, attempting to suppress Muslim terrorists called the Taliban.

Rivalling Xinjiang is Tibet, which was given heightened attention by outsiders during the Olympic year, 2008. The Chinese have made genuine efforts to improve life in Tibet, but until the Chinese leadership in Tibet is purged and one instituted that is more beholden to the Tibetan population, they are unlikely to win any sympathy. (A similar problem exists with the administration in Xinjiang.) The approach taken to date only exacerbates the problem. It has become too easy to blame the Dalai Lama, who, after all, has rejected Tibetan separatism.

Abroad, China rarely receives sympathy for its problems. Often a double standard is applied. Many Westerners assume China is controlled by an all-powerful central government and therefore, if something nefarious happens in China, it must have been sanctioned by Beijing. It follows that this all-powerful government can easily decree the establishment of democracy, human rights, and the rule of law. This attitude echoes the Jesuit approach to China in the sixteenth and seventeenth centuries. The good Fathers thought if they could convert the Chinese emperor to Catholicism, all the people of the empire would follow. Then, as now, the nuances and intricacies of the Chinese system fall outside mainstream Western experience.

THREE THREADS IN
CANADA–CHINA RELATIONS

China has preoccupied me for most of my life, and I have spent my professional and retirement years attempting to promote Canada-China understanding. It is said that one either writes a book about China after a three-week visit, or after thirty years of its acquaintance. I missed both these deadlines, conscious of the fact that we each fashion our own "China," whether we have been there or not. To a historian, everything depends upon context, both from the perspective of the historian and of the time and place being studied. Because of changing contexts, China appeared differently to Western observers at the beginning of the nineteenth century than it did at the end of it. That century began with China still greatly admired as an inspiration for the European Enlightenment and ended with it being despised as sick, weak, and a part of both the "white man's burden" and the Yellow Peril. During that century, China changed very little in how it ran its government and how it looked at the world—it was the West that changed, giving it a new standard of judgement. In the next eight decades, China went from being the world's burden to a wartime ally and friend, from a Cold War enemy to an economic saviour, from a potential threat to a sort of "frenemy." In this case, both China and the West have changed their ways of doing things, China perhaps more dramatically than the West.

Canadian–Chinese relations have developed against this background. Today, by most objective standards, Canada–China relations are moderately good. Each country is keen on trade and commerce, and in general, we seek mutual understanding and a non-threatening harmony. From a historical perspective, three threads stand out in the fabric of Canada's relations with China. The dominant one is trade. It goes back long before 1867 to exports of wild ginseng to China from Quebec in the last half of the eighteenth century. Then, as now, Canadians sought to prosper through sales of goods to the vast China market. This thread was frayed by wars, hot and "Cold," and economic depression, but manifested itself anew in the early 1960s with the major wheat deals negotiated by the Progressive Conservative government of John Diefenbaker. Trade was a major driving force behind formal recognition of the People's Republic of China in 1970 as Canadians hoped to beat Americans to the China market.[14] It continues to power relations today at all levels of government.

The second thread is a twist of ideology and culture. This was rooted in the first wave of Christian missionaries sent from Canada to Sichuan in the last quarter of the nineteenth century. It then morphed partly into the anti-communism of the Cold War, and partly into socialist sympathy, which one might call "Bethunism," and continues today in the push to have China adopt Western concepts of human rights. Canada sent both Catholic and Protestant missionaries to China. Indeed, Canada sent them in numbers quite out of proportion to its population when compared to the efforts of other countries. Perhaps their greatest impact was in the fields of medicine and education. Canadian Methodists, however, utterly failed in their avowed pre-World War I ambition to convert the whole of Sichuan province (Deng's birthplace) to Christianity.

As an offshoot of the missionary effort, Canadians began to appreciate the depth and nature of Chinese culture. Artifacts sent home to Toronto from China by individual missionaries like Bishop William Charles White, Anglican bishop of Henan province, and James Menzies helped to spark the serious study of Chinese culture in Canada. Ironically, during the Cold War, after Canadian missionaries left China, it was a secular medical missionary, Norman Bethune, a Communist, who became the symbol of Canada–China relations. Canadian missionaries were among those who, in the first half of the twentieth century, were vocal in their criticism of Chinese society for its lack of emphasis upon individualism. The Confucian system of family values stifled the individual, it was argued, and held back progress and the modernization of society. Today, politicians, academics, human rights groups, and others have brought this earlier criticism up to date, arguing that without human rights based on the individual, democracy, and the rule of law, China cannot modernize its society. In this way Canada continues to missionize. Through the promotion of Chinese studies in Canada and Canadian studies in China, we strive for deeper understanding and appreciation of each other's culture.

The third thread, immigration, has been the most contentious inside Canada. Canada is a nation of immigrants, the majority of whom have come from Europe or the Americas. Canada was born in 1867 as a white dominion and that ambition remained strong until after World War II. In practice, it meant encouraging settlers who came across the Atlantic or the 49th parallel, and discouraging those who came across the Pacific. With regard to China, Canadian governments were torn. How to balance the need for cheap labour and the desire to keep Canada white? As was mentioned in earlier chapters, while arrangements to regulate immigrants, such as Gentleman's Agreements, were reached with Japan, there was no government in China prior to 1949 capable of regulating emigration effectively. Canada countered by first imposing a head tax to slow the influx of labourers and then by excluding them (1923–1947).

Despite the coming together of China and Canada in 1942 as wartime allies, the question of immigration remained outstanding until 1947 when restrictions were eased somewhat. But it was to be another twenty years before Chinese immigrants were put on an equal footing with those from other countries. And it was not until 1973 that the first agreements were signed to enable immigrants to enter Canada directly from the People's Republic. Currently, consistent with the past, Canada continues to limit the number of unskilled workers coming into the country, but it does welcome the well educated, skilled, and articulate.

A brief look, from a Canadian point of view, at these three threads in Canada–China relations indicates that while ideology has often kept the two countries apart, it has not been sufficient to dampen the desire for trade, and immigration has changed from exclusion to an open door. The view from Beijing of relations with Canada is different. For years, well into the latter part of the twentieth century, China's foreign ministry continued to look on Canada as an adjunct of Britain, a hangover from the nineteenth century. But by 1969, as China dedicated greater efforts toward replacing Taiwan at the United Nations, and ultimately toward gaining recognition by the United States, Canada was viewed as an American satellite, but more flexible and less ideological and anxious to improve international relations generally. As China's economy has grown and its international impact increased, Canada is seen primarily as a source of raw materials and investment, but with an annoying tendency to lecture China on the conduct of its internal affairs, while, at the same time, providing refuge for Chinese criminals.[15]

In short, Canada is no longer as important to China as we once were, and as we think we should be. We have less and less to teach China that it finds useful. Canadian views of China need to be revised. We need to appreciate that Chinese people are like us. They want to have as good and as secure a life as possible for their children and themselves. They do not like to be uprooted by natural or human-engineered disasters. They prefer order to chaos and will tolerate a great deal of discomfort to avoid disorder. Yet they are not afraid to risk their lives for a cause they believe to be just and right, or to protest against great injustice. Most importantly, and this most Westerners ignore, they view the world from a Chinese perspective and within the context of an unbroken history of over five thousand years. That is to say, to fulfill the dreams of the foreigner to get rich is not their prime purpose. Nor do they assume that foreign philosophies and modes of governing are necessarily the best or the most easily adapted to Chinese circumstances. Throughout their history, the Chinese have sought the way that best suits them. The Western human rights tradition stresses the rights of the individual over those of the collective, while the Chinese traditionally place the rights of the collective over those of the individual.

One of the most annoying aspects of relations with Canada, and indeed the West, for the Chinese is our obsession with telling them what to do. It seems that in order for us to feel secure, we have to make the Chinese into clones of ourselves. The Chinese are amazed at our lack of self-awareness and at our hypocrisy. What moral lessons do we have to teach the Chinese, or Asians in general, when it was the West that fought wars to force China to import opium and Christianity, when it was the West that dropped atomic bombs on the Japanese, and experimented with Agent Orange and napalm on the Vietnamese? Is this the same West that now badgers China over human rights, and interprets any growth in the Chinese defence budget as a threat? And is the America that criticizes China for its use of prisons the same America that, with one-quarter of China's population, has half a million or more people in jail? And is it the Canada of the great internationalist Norman Bethune that criticizes China for building a railway across Tibet to facilitate settlement and commerce, when the very same technique was used to open and settle the Canadian Prairies? And is it not interesting that the CPR and the new Tibetan railway both used Chinese workers and Canadian engineers? Is it the same Canada that says it cannot interfere with its own courts to respond to requests from China for the return of known criminals, while, at the same time, insisting that the Chinese government should override its legal system and release Canadians with dual citizenship charged under Chinese and international law? Why is the West always saying, "Do as I say, but not as I do, or have done"?

Then there are the repeated references in Canadian and Western media to the folly of the Three Gorges Dam, to the decline in the proportion of females in the Chinese population, and to the harvesting of human organs by gruesome means. In contrast, India, which is building very controversial dams on the Narmada River, which has a very similar male-female imbalance in its population, and which has major scandals over organ harvesting, receives little comment, let alone condemnation. And why is China always singled out as the country that, through outsourcing and cheap labour, is robbing North America of its economic strength, when Bangladesh, Indonesia, India, and other cheap-labour countries play a similar role? Moreover, why is China's global search for resources and sources of cleaner energy criticized as a thinly disguised threat, while the consumption by North Americans of many times their fair share of the world's resources is dismissed as something benign? And why is it that when China seeks more resources, it is to "hoard" them, while we only "stockpile" them?

Chinese regimes, up to now, have been rather serene in the face of their foreign critics, while holding to a policy of noninterference in the internal affairs of other countries. They know that public criticisms like those that come at times from Canadian governments are designed mainly for home rather than for foreign consumption. There are some indications, however, that younger Chinese, particularly those with experience of living in the West, are inclined to fight back. But this too is seen as a threat in the West where it is noted by some as a sign of a dangerous new nationalism in China.

SEEING THE FUTURE THROUGH THE PAST

One would be a fool to attempt to predict China's future, save to say that Canada, along with the West, is going to have to learn to live with a powerful China and not to overreact to everything the Chinese do. I align myself with those who are of the opinion that China and the West are destined to be friendly competitors. China has too many problems of its own to become involved in the affairs of others, except when there is a direct threat to China's security. Those who feel China is fated to be expansionist are invited to examine the historical record. In the early fifteenth century, China possessed sufficient ships and technology to found overseas colonies. Its fleets reached East Africa, but no effort was made to establish settlements. Australia was theirs for the taking, yet it was the British, from the faraway coasts of Europe, who colonized it centuries later. We have to be careful in attributing to others our own proclivities or faults: they just may not have them.

The current leaders of China are attempting to balance the forces of modernization unlocked by Deng prior to 1989 with the constraints of tradition and the ideological conservatives who cling to the socialist axioms of Marx and Mao. The next generation of leaders is expected to be made up of younger people more attuned to the world of globalization, along with its potential and its pitfalls, and to act accordingly. This will be a far cry from Mao's concept of self-reliance. Even so, the current regime has brought capitalists into the party and has moved to protect private property, much to the dismay of the old guard. Whichever generation is in charge, however, the leaders and the party have to learn how to renew themselves and to dilute their power gracefully. Otherwise they face the fate of the Soviet Communist Party, a lesson they have taken to heart. Moreover, they are reluctant to rush into democracy and run the risk of throwing up a leader like Boris Yeltsin or George W. Bush. To date, the Communist Party has provided the world's most populous country with over half a century of one-party rule, remarkable even by Alberta's standards.

Today, the Chinese are absorbing influences from all over the globe as they attempt to fashion their own way. So far they appear to adhere to one of the fundamental concepts of traditional Chinese philosophy: yin yang. Yin yang, expressed so beautifully in the circle divided in half by a lazy *S*, one side black and the other white with a large dot of the opposite colour in each half, is a perfect illustration of the balance between opposites: light and dark, male and female. It shows that inside darkness is some light and inside light is some darkness. A yin-yang symbol shows the perfect balance between the two. Good should not completely vanquish evil and vice versa. They are not in perpetual conflict, in a winner-take-all struggle, which so often has attracted Westerners. An example of yin yang comes with the economic downturn of the first decade of the twenty-first century. The Chinese, while maintaining that theirs is a socialist regime, practice capitalism without calling it such. The United States, which proclaims the triumph of capitalism, has indulged in nationalizing banks and car-makers while avoiding the word "socialism." It seems that these opposite systems each contain a dollop of the other. In my view, we should keep yin yang in mind as we watch China rising, while looking forward to a future that is fashioned through harmonious co-operation for the betterment of humankind. We should be mindful of the wisdom of Charles de Gaulle, who, in 1964, when bidding Godspeed to Andre Malraux, his first ambassador to Beijing, said: "Remember Mr. Ambassador that China is a very large country full of Chinese." With this phrase, he sums up my China.

AFTERWORD

The years following her retirement in 1982 my wife Margo devoted to her love of gardening and music. The results of her gardening efforts appear each summer like a French Impressionist painting. A pianist, she loved classical music, listening to it every evening as she sipped a glass of Harveys Bristol Cream Sherry after supper. As I prepared for my retirement in 1996, we expanded our house, nearly doubling its size by adding on a library-cum-gallery to contain the books, paintings, and *objets d'art* we had accumulated over the years. The work was completed by the spring of 1998, but these happy years ended too soon when Margo was diagnosed in October 1999 with an aggressive brain tumour. She passed away one week before Christmas. Suddenly, a friendship of half a century and a marriage of over forty-five years ended, leaving me devastated and alone in a very large house full of memories. Ours was a marriage free of acrimony, largely because of Margo's great tolerance and flexibility. She is the unsung hero of these memoirs. Never too tolerant of cats, Margo knew me well. Unbeknownst to me, she confided in a close friend that after her death I would get a cat. One year later, I brought home from Montreal a mature brown tabby called MOOKIE, and Margo's close friend has not yet stopped smiling.

And as for the person who launched me on my pursuit of China, my very first friend Herbert How, each year we manage to phone each other. Herbert now lives in British Columbia. In our annual chats, we talk about family matters and about the state of the world, much as we did seventy years ago in the playground of Taber Central School. As far as I know, he has never been to China.

ONE ★ *Prairie Roots*

1. Although the certificate filled in on their arrival to Canada, at Halifax, indicated that my father had $225 in his pocket, and my mother $25, together it was actually 250 pounds sterling (roughly $1,250). This was quite a lot of money at the time, but before arriving in Taber, my father had already been dealt the blow of a failed mining venture in Cardston, and before that a house robbery in Lethbridge, during which my mother's emerald engagement ring had been taken.

2. A *tipple* is a mining term for a structure at the top of which wagons of coal were tipped over to empty their contents into railcars or other conveyances.

3. As it turned out, I never did learn to drive. Driving was a matter of pride for my father, and being forty-seven years my senior, I did not want to push him to let me learn and take over driving his car. After leaving home, my life developed in a way that did not have me needing, or wanting, a car. At university I lived in residence and could not afford one anyway. Later, in England, I relied on public transport and once back home in Canada I lived close to my work. Never having children meant my wife and I were not required to shuttle anyone around.

4. "Git" was Herbert's family nickname, or Chinese *milk name* as they are called. Traditionally, a Chinese baby is not named until it is one month old. In the meantime, the baby is known by a pet, nick, or milk name, which often lingers well into childhood and sometimes beyond.

5. The word "families" is important because usually only Chinese merchants could afford to bring their wives to Canada, although some of the wives did not like Canada and returned to China. Members of merchant households were exempt from the head tax. Chinese workers who were admitted to the country only after paying the head tax rarely, if ever, earned enough to pay the fare and head tax for a spouse to join them. In any case, after the 1923 Exclusion Act, no Chinese women were allowed to immigrate to Canada. At that time, Chinese workers in Alberta were either single or "married bachelors," with wives and children in China. Japanese immigration to Canada was regulated by Gentlemen's Agreements signed between the governments of Canada and Japan. They regulated the number of Japanese immigrants allowed to enter Canada and allowed for single Japanese males to bring so-called picture brides into Canada, and thus to have families.

TWO ★ *Seeking a Path to China*

1. Margo was the eldest of the three children of Adam Proctor Burwash and Mary Isabel McLean. Her father was a son of Nathaniel Burwash, a rather

severe Methodist, who had been head of Victoria College in Toronto and the first chancellor of the newly assembled University of Toronto prior to World War I. Adam had broken free of the family's central Canadian base and travelled west, becoming a lay preacher and a general young man about the West prior to the turn of the century. In 1913, he married Mary McLean, who came from an "Ontario Scotch" (as used in the book by that name by Kenneth Galbraith) family that had settled in Alberta, and they took up residence in the city of Edmonton. During the war, they returned to Toronto where Adam worked in a munitions plant. Margo was born in Toronto on July 11, 1917. Hard times plagued Adam, with most of the stars to which he hitched his wagon failing to sparkle. Nevertheless, every sacrifice was made for the three children, two girls and a boy, to be well educated. Each of them graduated from the University of Alberta.

2. Fraternities had been banned at U of A until 1929 because up until that time, then university President Henry Marshall Tory considered both sororities and fraternities to be secret societies. After he left the university, fraternities were allowed, both men's and women's groups taking on the same name "fraternity," this being the case in the 1950s. The term "sorority" is now used at the University of Alberta.

3. I introduced him and chaired the meetings he addressed on campus in 1963 and 1974. We discussed the incident in 1953 that had given him so much local publicity. He was continuing to try to clear his name, still blackened by the germ warfare charge. He gave me a copy of his FBI file that he had wrestled from them after years of struggle. It had been redacted and consisted of pages of blacked-out text.

4. Hong Kong during the Korean War was a spot for rest and recuperation. It also received the fallout from the Communist victory in China as people sought refuge in the colony. Han Suyin, a beautiful Eurasian medical doctor and talented author, was having an affair with a married English newspaper correspondent based in Singapore. Hong Kong Anglo society was very small and rather claustrophobic; everyone knew everyone else. In a sense, it continues to be this way. Han's book caused a great sensation. It contained many devastating thumbnail sketches of English residents, most of whom were sure they were in the book somewhere. The book became the 1955 film *Love Is a Many-Splendored Thing*.

5. The third person was Bill Paranchych, a brilliant science student from Drumheller, who later became chair of the Department of Biological Sciences at the University of Alberta. His exceptional career was cut short by his early death from cancer in 1995.

6. Cameron was a student in commerce at U of A. He became a chartered accountant, going on to a distinguished career at Stelco, the Steel Company of Canada. Scrupulous and meticulous, he set a standard few could emulate. He passed away from cancer in 2005, shortly after he retired.

7. While the University of London and Cambridge were mostly on par as regarded expenses, part of the reason I chose London was because Cambridge made my acceptance conditional on getting into a college, something which my marriage to Margo would complicate.

8. The panda, called Chi-Chi, was taken to the London Zoo where she became a star attraction.

9. In 1964, I presented a copy of Mary Endicott's book to Harvard University, which did not have one.

10. Each of these scholars was later to pursue a distinguished career in the United States, Hong Kong, or Australia.

11. Margo and I never opened a bank account in the seven years we lived in London. We could not afford the charges involved in maintaining one. For example, cheques had to be purchased, each with a stamp embossed on it in accordance with an Act of Parliament.

12. She published her first books as Yan-kit Martin, but later under the name Yan-kit So, in order not to be confused with the popular television chef in the United States called Martin Yan.

THREE ★ *Rescued by NATO*

1. A detailed description of the founding of the organization is given in a pamphlet, *The North Atlantic Treaty Organization Parliamentarians' Conference 1955–1959* (London: Hansard Society for Parliamentary Government, 1960). The fifteen members of NATO were Belgium, Canada, Denmark, France, Germany, Greece, Iceland, Italy, Luxembourg, Netherlands, Norway, Portugal, Turkey, the United Kingdom, and the United States.

2. His comment was just as puzzling to me as the question posed to two graduate students from Hong Kong by a well-meaning spouse of a SOAS staff member: "Tell me, my dears, when did Hong Kong decide to join the British Empire?"

3. After Mao Zedong died in 1976, Jack was one of the first to travel to China as a teacher. He ran into contract disputes with the institutions that engaged him and he staged various pacifist strikes against them. We saw a lot of each other after I returned to Canada, meeting at least once a year at conferences. When I went to China in 1964, he convinced the University of Toronto librarian, although I was at the University of Alberta, to provide me with money and a list of books to buy for the U of T. I did not get them all, but I managed several parcels full. Jack was to grow more eccentric in later years. He fought his mandatory retirement from the University of Toronto, and for a while, I believe, lived in a trailer on a U of T parking lot.

4. In Japan, he stayed with a Japanese family of whom only the young son understood English. He asked John what his favourite foods were. John replied, bananas and beer. Each morning thereafter, John was served bananas and beer for breakfast. John loved England and returned to spend the rest of his days

there after a career at Boston College. He particularly loved British pubs and he was on their doorsteps the moment they opened in the late morning, for his first pint of Guinness for the day. Despite his time in pubs, he accomplished his research and became a scholar with a number of publications.

5. The flights to and from the conference marked a transition in air travel. The Lockheed Constellation was the last great propeller-driven airplane to fly the Atlantic. It needed to make stops in Shannon, Ireland, and Gander, Newfoundland, to refuel to accomplish the flights from London to New York or Washington. The Bristol Britannia we flew back on was one of the first turbo-prop passenger planes. Unfortunately, its time was limited as jet engines took over.

6. Through his seniority in Congress and his position on a couple of committees, Hays had travelled a great deal, inspecting State Department buildings overseas, earning himself the title "the Marco Polo of Congress." When it was proposed that the travels and expenses of all members of Congress be printed in the Congressional Record, Hays used his other committee position to attempt to limit the number of pages that the record could devote to such information. He was in the midst of such a fight when, as mentioned earlier in the chapter, it was revealed by the *Washington Post* on May 23, 1976, that he was keeping a woman named Elizabeth Ray on his payroll in a quiet and discreet office on Capitol Hill. Although Hays claimed he was happily married, the *Post* quoted Ray as saying she was being paid $14,000 a year to be his mistress: "I can't type, I can't file, I can't even answer the phone...Supposedly I am on the oversight committee. But I call it the Out-of-Sight Committee." After this revelation, Hays did not last long in Washington. He resigned his committee chairmanships in June and stepped down from Congress in September 1976 rather than face a judicial investigation. In 1978 he was elected to the Ohio House of Representatives for two years, but was not re-elected. He died in February 1989, aged seventy-seven.

7. The article by Jean Charpentier, published November 27, 1962, stated in part: "Always ill-prepared, often disinterested and sometimes without talent, Canadian parliamentarians make us feel ashamed of them at international conferences. The Canadian contribution at the NATO parliamentarians' conference recently held in Paris was no exception....A certain number of delegates were not seen during the whole of the conference: having spent their nights in Pigalle, they slept by day."

8. In 1964, the film *Ring of Spies*, based on the Lonsdale case, was released in Britain. In the United States it was later released under two titles: *Ring of Treason,* and *Shadow of Treason.*

9. I gathered this information from Christopher Andrew's *The Defence of the Realm: The Authorized History of MI5* (London: Penguin, 2009), 485–88.

10. Gordon Lonsdale, *Spy* (London: N. Spearman, 1965), 101.

11. See Helen Womack, "At last, the truth emerges about Gordon Lonsdale's shadowy life," *The Independent*, August 15, 1998.

1. East Asian Studies began to revive at McGill in the mid-1960s.

2. The institute was founded in 1925 and enjoyed tax-exempt status until it came under fire as a suspected haven for communists under its former director, Owen Lattimore. The institute and Lattimore fought their cases and won, but the IPR under Director William Holland lacked the funds to pay the costs of its defence, and it dissolved in 1959.

3. New staff members from the United States and Britain were given an income tax holiday for a couple of years as an incentive to come to a Canadian university. This policy was maintained for the next decade or more as rapidly expanding Canadian universities competed for competent staff. Universities were exploiting a loophole that really only applied to temporary workers, arguing that new appointees were temporary until they received tenure.

4. C.P. Fitzgerald was an extraordinary scholar and lecturer. He held a capacity audience spellbound on a frosty night in mid-February 1962 as he spoke for an hour without notes on the Sino-Soviet dispute. The author of numerous excellent works on Chinese history, he was very much in demand. His only degree was a first class BA in anthropology. Because of this, he was not appointed to a position in Britain but was recommended to Australia as "the sort of chap that would suit you."

5. In London, the group was called the Junior Sinologues and included students of Chinese culture from all over Europe. The term "junior" seemed strange since the membership included the most senior (and aged) academics from European and British institutions. It was, however, an indication of the monumental task facing any outsider in attempting to understand Chinese culture that the members refrained from calling themselves "senior."

6. This began to change in the mid-1960s when some heads gave up their positions and new appointees agreed to a three- or five-year term, but determined heads could stick to their contracts. Later, in 1969, the Faculty of Arts struck a committee, of which I was a member, to bring in reform within the faculty. We recommended a more open process of selection with committees, rather than the previous method of direct appointment by the dean.

7. Among them were John King Gordon, a former high official in the UN; James Barrington, former Burmese ambassador to the US, Canada, and the UN; professors Ivan Head and Leslie Green, both experts in international law; and professors Neville Linton, Christian Bay, and Grant Davy, political scientists specializing in international affairs.

8. Fairbank was burnt in the 1950s by the congressional hearings of the McCarran Un-American Activities Committee, which tried to implicate him in the "loss of China" to the United States. He was said to be "soft on communism." Suspected by his own government, criticized on both sides of the Taiwan Strait, Fairbank was later chastised by a younger generation of scholars for not doing enough

to push the study of the People's Republic of China. Fairbank, "JKF" as he was known, was very kind to me. He had a soft spot for Canadians stemming from his experience in Ontario as a member of Frontier College. He also found Canadians less blinkered in their public discussions of China policies and less inclined to join in witch hunts. Among other things, I was impressed with the way JKF handled his students. Each week, they were invited for tea at his house on the edge of Harvard Yard, when they were asked to report on their progress. Twenty years later, when I reviewed his autobiography for the journal *Pacific Affairs*, he was kind enough to send me a note to say that of all the reviews, mine came the closest to the truth about him.

9. The colony of Hong Kong was made up of three parts, each acquired by the British following wars or incidents with China: Hong Kong Island (1842), Kowloon (1860), and New Territories (1898). The border area is the site of the modern city of Shenzhen as a Special Economic Zone.

10. The Chinese completed a second bridge, without any outside assistance, over the Yangzi at Nanjing in 1968. It became a symbol of the Cultural Revolution's achievements.

11. One idea had been to build a new capital city to house the government and industry outside Beijing and to preserve the old city, but the new regime felt it had neither the time nor the resources to undertake such a plan.

12. All tourists were handled inside China by CITS, which had (and has) branches all over China. Hu informed the Tianjin office to receive me. When you arrived at a new city, you were sat down in order to "discuss your program," that is what they planned for you. You could make changes if you were familiar enough with the city to ask for them. It was a link to CITS that was (and still is) advertised in Edmonton in the spring of 1964. I took four of my nieces (all blondes) to China in the fall of 2009 and CITS routines were similar to what they had been in 1964, although now there are no politics and everything is done through the Internet.

13. The Treaty of Tientsin ended the war and opened China up to imports of opium and gave freedom of entry to missionaries. During the war, Anglo-French forces marched to Beijing where they sacked and destroyed the old Yuan Ming Yuan (Summer Palace), which was designed with the assistance of Jesuits.

14. Sun Yat-sen (Sun Zhongshan) is considered to be the father of modern China. He led a rebellion against the Qing Dynasty from abroad and temporarily became the first president of the new republic in 1912. He died in March 1925 before his dream of a united democratic and republican China could be realized.

15. There is a brief account of Bissell's trip in *University of Toronto Magazine*, Summer 2010, written by Bissell's daughter Deirdre Macdonald.

16. *Time* changed its policy once Richard Nixon went to China in 1972. In 1964, a colleague said to me, "Criticizing *Time* is as easy as standing in the sun."

17. On August 4, 1964, American ships and Vietnamese gunboats engaged in an action that the Americans said took place in international waters, but that claim

is open to dispute. President Johnson used the incident to get Congress to pass the Gulf of Tonkin Resolution, giving him the authority to wage war against North Vietnam.

18. I have since learned that the man's name was Murphy and the pagoda was known in those days as Murphy's pagoda.

19. All Chinese ambassadors except for a man named Huang Hua in Cairo were called home.

20. Intourist was the Soviet version of CITS, which was patterned after it. Intourist, however, was known for its inefficiency and general bloody mindedness.

21. They had some grounds for holding this opinion. When the Red Guards took the train into Russia, they defecated on the station platform and then caught the next train to China.

22. In the 1950s, the Soviet government designated a suburb of the city as a scientific research centre with fourteen research institutes and universities.

23. In my subsequent trips to Russia from the late 1970s to the early 1990s, drunkenness remained a major problem.

24. Milovan Djilas, a Yugoslavian author and official, published his book *The New Class* in 1957 in which he argued that Communist elites were behaving like the capitalists and landowners they had replaced.

25. I had no idea how terrifying tanks could be until years later in Kiev, when I heard Russian tanks in the streets, practising for the next day's celebrations of the anniversary of V-E Day. Even though that event was peaceful, the thunderous noise of the tanks was unnerving.

26. As a testament to Lee's talent, I put forward the example of his menu for the dinner on April 2, 1971. Appetizers: chicken rolls (shrimp, Chinese sausage, barbecued pork mushroom, abalone and green onions pressed into a tasty casing and deep fried); broiled whole boneless chicken, stuffed with water chestnut, minced duck meat, Chinese sausage, and ham. Soup: steamed whole winter melon soup with diced barbequed duck, chicken, ham, shrimp, bamboo shoots, mushrooms, water chestnuts, dry scallops, white pine nuts, and lotus nuts. Entrees: beef Canton (thick sliced sirloin beef fried in the chef's own sauce); walnut chicken (diced chicken with Chinese vegetables and mushrooms and fresh walnuts); Bamboo Palace special fried rice; Lobster Hong Kong; a Buddhist-style combination of vegetables (mushrooms, white nuts, soybean flakes, soybean dumplings, rice, vermicelli, and fine black seaweed); lemon chicken, fish Mandarin (crisp browned whole pickerel with an ingenious sweet and sour sauce containing finely silvered Chinese fruits); long life Chinese noodles in cane sugar syrup. Dessert: Chinese sweet donut pastry. Drinks: Chinese tea, sherry, and champagne.

27. Among those who took part in the committee were Hazel Jones, Stan Munro, David Young, David Bai, Al Forbes, Manobu Waida, Wally Cummings, Takashi Tsushima, and Carlo Caldorola.

28. See D.L.B. Hamlin, *International Studies in Canadian Universities* (Ottawa: Canadian Universities Foundation, 1964).

FIVE ★ *Old Dog, New Tricks*

1. Hurtig later found Trudeau wanting, specifically as a nationalist. Hurtig, along with others, founded the Council of Concerned Canadians in 1973, becoming a critic of successive Canadian governments' failures to preserve Canadian economic independence.
2. Nearly three decades later, I reminded him, then the federal minister for the environment, of the event. He laughed and said that he had since mellowed.
3. Canada, *Debates, House of Commons, 22nd session 28th Parliament,* Vol. I, Oct. 28–Nov. 21, 1969, Queen's Printer of Canada (Ottawa, 1970), 981.
4. A succinct account of the negotiations can be found in Mitchell Sharp, *Which Reminds Me...* (Toronto: University of Toronto Press, 1994), 203–07. See also Arthur Andrew, *The Rise and Fall of a Middle Power* (Toronto: James Lorimer, 1993).
5. The Shanghai Communiqué at the end of Nixon's visit called for the establishment of a liaison office in Beijing. Official recognition of China by the USA was announced by President Jimmy Carter on January 1, 1979.
6. The Great Revolution for the Establishment of a Proletarian Culture, generally known as the "Cultural Revolution," was officially sanctioned by Mao at a mass rally in Beijing on August 16, 1966. In effect, Mao called on the youth of China, well trained in his teachings, to attack all vestiges of tradition and old thinking in a drive to establish a worker, peasant, soldier culture. Mao was also using the young "Red Guards," as he called them, to restore him to a position of prominence in the Chinese Communist Party after his partial eclipse due to the failures of the Great Leap Forward. The movement took on the elements of a political purge, as well as a cultural cleansing. The protection against all-out chaos and disorder was the army led by Lin Biao, whose forces had already been indoctrinated through the introduction of the "Little Red Book" of Mao's sayings. Even prominent figures like Zhou Enlai and Chen Yi were subject to attack, until Mao placed them off limits as they struggled to keep the civil regime intact.
7. Meanwhile, in Ottawa, the Chinese were setting up their embassy, at first in the Juliana apartments and later in an abandoned nunnery fronting on St. Patrick Street and backing on the Rideau River. Their first ambassador, Huang Hua, a very high government official, assumed the position in July 1971, but very soon thereafter in November he was named China's ambassador to the United Nations, when the People's Republic of China filled the seat on the Security Council previously held by the Republic of China. His successor in Ottawa was another senior diplomat, Zhang Wenjin. Both Hua and Zhang were fluent in English.
8. "Mish kid" was a popular term used for children of missionaries, born in China.

9. When I returned to the university after my year in Beijing, I was again visited by the RCMP. This time it was a rather humourless sergeant who had learned that while I was in Beijing, Canada and China had signed a reunion of families agreement, enabling members of families, long separated by the Bamboo Curtain, to be united in Canada. The sergeant was worried about this. He had spoken to a member of the Mah family in downtown Edmonton, who had told him there were several million members of the Mah family in China. "What if they all come?" he asked.

10. Saywell was vice-provost at the University of Toronto. Later, he became president of Simon Fraser University and then head of the Asia Pacific Foundation. He was very active in APEC (Asia-Pacific Economic Cooperation).

11. Paynter was destined for a brilliant career, which was brought to a sad end with his sudden death just months after he was appointed ambassador in Beijing, on December 23, 1994.

12. Later, after my time in Beijing, Wang was overheard making a negative remark about Jiang Qing, Mao's wife, and was sent to drive a gravel truck on constructions sites, but after October 1976, when the Gang of Four was removed from all positions of power, he was allowed back and given a better position in the DSB that involved foreign travel. Eventually, he and his family were given compensation for property seized during the Maoist period. They received 10 per cent of the value. After Wang reached retirement age, he returned to teaching diplomats. He numbers among his students a host of ambassadors and former ambassadors from around the globe. While in Beijing, I looked forward each week to his visits and lessons and we became good friends. Our friendship endures to this day, and he continues to teach well into his eighties.

13. Copithorne and Waterfall each went on to serve as ambassadors in Europe before leaving the service for academia. Copithorne would later teach law at UBC and Waterfall would serve as a fellow at the Munk Centre and later as a philosophy professor at the University of Toronto.

14. In 1972, she rescued a small boy who had fallen through the ice when skating on the moat around the Forbidden City. Margaret, soaked to the bone, was rushed to the hospital. The ambulance drivers thought she was Russian, so they first took her to the anti-revisionist hospital, but upon discovering their error took her to the anti-imperialist one.

15. Ballard was a youth in Shanghai during this same period and his book is generally taken as being autobiographical. The film of the same name came out in 1987.

16. Walker was a veteran journalist. His beat was all of Asia, but he used Beijing as his base. Meanwhile, China was one of Burns's first overseas assignments. Burns was young, vigorous, and a first-rate newsman. He later left the *Globe* for the *New York Times*. He was expelled from China on his second assignment there in 1984–1986 but went on to report with distinction from the conflict in Serbia and later in Iraq. He is now the *New York Times* bureau chief in London.

17. Ted Pulleyblank, a graduate of the University of Alberta, had a gift for languages. He studied Chinese at the School of Oriental and African Languages (SOAS) in London and wrote a famous book on Tang Dynasty History. Later he was appointed Chair of Chinese at Cambridge University. He returned to Canada to lead the Department of Asian Studies at the University of British Columbia.

18. The Xinqiao hotel, where many foreigners stayed, and where I stayed in 1964, was built during the period of Soviet co-operation, which had come to a crashing halt by 1960, and still operated on the Soviet model. The hotel was the temporary home for some diplomats, like me, and journalists awaiting apartments, and of visiting delegations. In the evenings, several white Russian ladies came to the upper lounge to entertain and be entertained.

19. Norman Bethune (1890–1939) was a Canadian physician, a medical innovator, and a Communist, who is well known for his work in wartime medical units during the Spanish Civil War and with the People's Liberation Army during the second Sino-Japanese War. His name will be mentioned more than once in this chapter, but I will wait until the next chapter to explain his importance as a hero to the Chinese people and the uses to which his legacy was put in Canada–China relations.

20. The first Jesuit in China was Matteo Ricci, who entered the country in 1610. Once established in Beijing, the Jesuit fathers, most of them Italian and French products of the Renaissance, became advisors to Chinese emperors, teaching them Western science, and helping them to map the empire, design the Summer Palace, and design cannon and astronomical instruments. Their mission to Beijing ended in the eighteenth century.

21. Trudeau Is Coming.

22. The discussion then got down to details regarding how high a hill Mrs. Trudeau would be able to climb. In China, pregnant women rarely, if ever, went out in public then and even now, although more expectant mothers are seen in public nowadays. To be faced with making arrangements for the pregnant spouse of a foreign prime minister was a shock to the culturally conservative Chinese officials.

23. Trudeau and Ivan Head, in their book of memoirs, *The Canadian Way*, state incorrectly that the beaver were on the plane with them.

24. A few weeks after the arrival of the beaver, I applied formally for permission to see them. I was taken by a protocol officer to see them in their concrete pens, equipped with a small standpipe dripping with water. There was not a single maple leaf in sight. During the winter at the embassy, I offered a short course called The Beaver in Chinese History. The survey of the story of the Middle Kingdom took note that beaver could be found at the site of Beijing Man, but after that they appeared to have had little impact on the course of events. A year later, when I returned to the University of Alberta, I was disconcerted to learn that my dean had completely misconstrued what my duties as BLO had

entailed—a lewd interpretation later made popular by actor Leslie Nielsen in films like *Naked Gun*.

SIX ★ *Basic Diplomacy and the Many Uses of Norman Bethune*

1. Trudeau's arrival marked the first time a Canadian prime minister visited China while in office. Only Prime Minister Mackenzie King had visited China before him. William Lyon Mackenzie King travelled to China in 1909 as a Canadian representative to the International Opium Conference in Shanghai called by the United States. In September 1907, the Asiatic Exclusion League had sparked a riot against Japanese and Chinese in Vancouver. King, at that time a civil servant, investigated victims' claims. After his election to the House of Commons in 1908, King sponsored legislation banning opium imports into Canada. As mentioned in previous chapters, negative attitudes toward Chinese immigrants—and to Asians in general—hardened following World War I. Since 1885, Canada had sought to regulate the number of Chinese workers entering the country by imposing a head tax on each worker immigrant, but after the war there was a groundswell of support to exclude all Chinese immigrants. King's Liberal government prepared a revision to the Chinese Immigration Act of 1885 that passed in the spring of 1923, effectively halting all further Chinese immigration. King tried to take credit for having ended the head tax, but every Chinese Canadian knew there would no longer be any heads to tax.

2. Not everyone in the press corps was a regular. David C. McDonald, an Edmonton lawyer, Rhodes Scholar, and Liberal, after a drink one fine September afternoon in Ottawa with his old friend Ivan Head, offered to act as special correspondent for the *Lethbridge Herald*, a well-known Liberal paper, taking a spare seat on the PM's plane. McDonald was later appointed a justice of the Alberta Court of Queen's Bench. He was named by Trudeau in 1977 to head the Royal Commission of Enquiry into the Activities of the RCMP.

3. In addition to being the first to make a state visit to China, among Canadian prime ministers, Trudeau stands alone as a true sinophile. He was genuinely curious about China and its culture, travelling there in the 1950s. He had an appreciation for Chinese art, literature, philosophy, and was knowledgeable about China's history.

4. Anyone finding this far-fetched should be reminded of the criticism directed at Zhou Enlai for allowing the Italian filmmaker Michelangelo Antonioni to make a film called *Chung Kuo: China* in China in 1972. The great Yangzi River bridge pictured in the film to show China's achievements was said to have brought shame to the Chinese people because a pair of men's trousers was evident in the shot, hanging at one end of the bridge. And who was to blame for the humiliation? Zhou Enlai because he had approved the project. Early this century, when Antonioni's film was shown in Beijing in November 2004, the audience broke into laughter in disbelief of the China they saw.

5. There were a number of these rooms, each dedicated to one of the provinces.
6. Gossip in Beijing had it that there was a split between Mao and Zhou Enlai, but television and newspaper reports picturing the two of them smiling together as they spoke with various foreign visitors seemed to belie the rumours.
7. During Trudeau's chat with Mao, the subject of panda bears did not arise.
8. Much of what had been planned had to await the death of Mao and the reforms of Deng Xiaoping. In the 1980s, cultural agreements and exchanges flourished. May 1989 was set to be Canada Friendship month in China, with a host of Canadian cultural events to be staged in Beijing, but once again ideology asserted itself—this time with tanks.
9. The invitation was taken up four years later in May 1978 by the Toronto Symphony.
10. Strictly speaking, it was the Guangzhou Trade Fair, but at that time it was more popularly known as the Canton Fair.
11. The Chinese viewed it as an exchange of knowledge of the game that involved a Canadian team coming to China, with the coach staying on to help the Chinese national team.
12. The National Film Board short film, *Thunderbirds in China* (1974), covers the events of the tour.
13. A couple of years later in 1985, I received a card from Mr. Liu from Arizona where he had taken up permanent residence. Later that year, I was back in Beijing where I watched Karen Magnuson and other stars perform on the ice, in costumes that would have sent my old friend from the sports federation spinning in his grave, not to mention "Chairman Mou." I was amused, the next year, to see how snippets of this ice show were used as filler on Chinese TV. They appeared rather frequently.
14. Most Canadian ambassadors to China accepted the burden save for Michel Gauvin (1980–1984), who was said to have forbidden the Chinese from mentioning Bethune in his presence.
15. All of the items on display had been unearthed during the first six years of the Cultural Revolution. The Chinese government emphasized how the items reflected the skills of Chinese workers and the oppressiveness of the old imperial system and it was upset when the exhibition was displayed in the West in a way that emphasized the glories China's imperial past.
16. The exhibition travelled from Toronto to Washington, DC, which was to be its only stop in the US. However, following the death of Mao in September 1976 and the exchange of ambassadors between China and the USA, the exhibition went on to other centres as the Chinese looked for funding to get it back to China.
17. Zhou Enlai was suffering from cancer of the bladder, a condition that went untreated for too long, it is said, at Mao's orders. Zhou died in January 1976.
18. Ronning remembered the incident a little differently: "The sun was in my eyes,

so I threw away my script and finished in Chinese." Interview with the author, Camrose, Alberta, May 6, 1980.

SEVEN ⭐ *In the Hot Seat*

1. In fact, Zhou had been pushing for the four modernizations since 1963, but they were not carried out until after his death by Deng Xiaoping. Zhou called for modernization in Agriculture, Industry, National Defence, and Science and Technology.
2. Taken from the poem, "To a Mouse," (1785) by Robert Burns.
3. Unfortunately, my visit to Moscow had to wait until October 1978 when it became abundantly clear that the continuing ideological dispute between Moscow and Beijing was frustrating those sinophiles and sinologues, anxious to resume old friendships and cultural relations. Such was not to be the case until Deng and Gorbachev achieved reconciliation in 1989.
4. In Chinese cosmology, the Year of the Dragon is one when human affairs can expect to be placed in turmoil and major natural phenomena occur, as the dragon stirs to life.
5. And in the years since, they have not stopped, always interested at first in one's age, one's salary, and one's family.
6. A small bottle in Mandarin is called a *xiao ping*.
7. Qiao was highly regarded for his brilliance, but he chose the wrong side. When he arrived at the UN, he was pestered with the question: "Are you still the foreign minister of China?"
8. Their exchange received wide distribution and was issued as a book. Charles Bettelheim and Neil Burton, *China since Mao* (New York: Monthly Review Press, 1978).
9. Morris "Two-Gun" Cohen (1889–1970) was more famous in Edmonton than Bethune ever was. He had had a colourful career as a real estate developer and gambler in the city during the pre-World War I boom. Jewish, hailing from London's East End, Cohen had come to Canada as a teenager, living first in Saskatchewan, then Manitoba, and later Alberta. He joined the Edmonton Irish (a regiment made up largely of Ukrainians) to fight in World War I. Prior to the war, he had forged strong links with the Chinese community and through them, on his return, he was offered a job as Sun Yat-sen's bodyguard in Shanghai in 1922. Daniel Levy's book, *Two-Gun Cohen* (New York: Thomas Dunne Books, 1997) says about all there is to say about Cohen's career.
10. Details of the politics surrounding the exhibition are explained in the previous chapter.
11. Betkowski later ran for office and served in the provincial Cabinet before challenging Ralph Klein for the leadership of the Conservative Party in December 1992. She lost and later served in the Alberta legislature as leader of the Liberal Party.

12. The International Club in Beijing, which catered to diplomats, employed movie stars and directors as waiters and managers. They also served at the seaside resort of Beidaihe, where party members went for holidays and meetings and which was open to diplomats who wanted a break.

13. CAAC was unaffectionately known as "CAACK" to its foreign victims.

14. This slogan was particularly irksome for Shanghai, which had been an industrial leader in China before the war with Japan. Official China remained tight-lipped about this seeming slight and strictly followed the Maoist line. One night in early 1974, at the Peace Hotel on the Bund in Shanghai, I was the guest of the deputy mayor of Shanghai. As sometimes happened, we got into a Mao Tai toasting match. Each time I toasted Shanghai, the industrial capital of China, and each time he repeated the slogan about Daqing. As the game wore on, I kept asking him if it was not annoying to him as the deputy mayor to have Daqing placed before Shanghai. In the end he admitted that yes, it was an insult.

15. Then a town, Guilin is now a city, but it is also an area through which the Li River flows.

16. He remained as an ordinary member of the Central Committee until 2002, after which he was less involved and devoted himself to raising grapes. His death in August 2008 during the Beijing Olympics was little noted.

17. The formal agreement between Heilongjiang and Alberta was signed in 1981 when Premier Lougheed visited China.

18. A number of years later, Zhu was given a grant from an American foundation enabling him to live and carry out research in Washington, DC.

19. Russian jet fighters from the Mikoyan-and-Gurevich Design Bureau (MiG) were used during the Korean War and later by the Chinese air force.

20. Historically, it is a very interesting hospital. It was originally called the Peking Union Medical College (PUMC) and benefitted from Rockefeller money in the 1920s. When I was in it, it was called the Capital, but it has been further expanded and is known as the Xiehe (Union) hospital now. Sun Yat-sen died in this hospital on March 12, 1925. As for myself, it was my first stay ever in a hospital.

21. The year 1982 proved to be a turning point for Margo. On her mother's death, she inherited the family house and garden that she loved. At the same time, her place of work, the Alberta Correspondence School Branch, was moved by government fiat to Barrhead, the hometown of the deputy premier. Since the new location would entail either long daily car rides, or a move to that town, Margo, having reached the age of sixty-five, decided to retire. From then on, she was free to garden, read, listen to music, see friends, and enjoy herself. Together, we began to plan how we could modernize the old house and expand it to accommodate our collections of books, art, and artifacts.

22. Although China was becoming a lot more open, a love affair between an American woman and the son of a Chinese official led to a temporary ban.

The woman's flat had been searched and found to have classified documents, enough to have her expelled and a temporary ban on fraternizing with foreigners put in place. In those days, finding even a phone book, if stamped *nei bu* (internal use), was sufficient excuse for an arrest. I am not naming my old friend here because he had a rough Cultural Revolution and is best to remain anonymous.

23. I never learned my lawyer's name. I do not think I was ever given it. Lawyers were so new to China at that time they did not even have business cards.

24. I have been in correspondence with Robert Hurst, now president of CTV News, concerning the interview. He has a vague memory of it, but alas, it did not make it into the CTV archives.

25. To end the story, the provincial health plan paid my hospital bill and my doctor said that calamine lotion, peanut oil, and scalpels were about as good a treatment as you could get. One year later, I met Professor Zhu in Beijing and asked him what he had said to the visa officer. He answered, "Just that you were an old friend of China and that I had stayed in your apartment in Canada and had seen pictures of you with Premier Zhou Enlai and Deng Xiaoping." Zhu described me as an "old friend of China," a phrase I was happy to hear. To people who continue to think in Cold War terms, this may sound like "fellow-traveller," but the term does not mean this at all. It is used to describe someone who is comfortable in China and accepted by Chinese colleagues to whom he can be frank with both praise and criticism because they know he has a deep understanding of China and a respect for its past.

26. "South of the Clouds" is a literal translation of *Yunnan*.

27. Although he had sold the farm in Taber to settle in Sylvan Lake, he retained the subsurface mineral rights related to the old White Ash mine, which he had acquired for a pittance at the end of the Depression. He died still convinced that oil would be discovered there. In 1997, he was proven correct, much to the benefit of his descendants.

28. Dai Xianguang's older brother Dai Xianda had studied to be an engineer, but the Cultural Revolution interrupted his education. He was one of the first two students to come to U of A in 1980 to upgrade his credentials and we became friends. He returned to China and later accepted a position in western Australia at the university in Perth. Dai Xianguang was an interpreter and teacher at the Beijing School of Foreign Languages. Following his brother's advice, he applied to do graduate work at U of A, but his letter of acceptance to the master's program somehow went to Chile. He took up an offer from Arizona, re-applying to U of A for a PhD and entering the program in September 1984.

29. They sent three representatives carrying marble from Mount Dali, via Burma, to London to make their case to the British government. In essence, they were shown the city but they received no positive encouragement from the government. Shortly thereafter, the rebellion was crushed.

30. Ronning passed away on the last day of 1984, less than three months after my meeting with Huang Hua.

31. I was already being treated royally, thanks to Huang Hua, so I thought that acknowledging my links with Trudeau would be a bit like piling on the mayor.

32. The story behind the dish is of a wife whose young husband was studying for the civil service examinations. He was studying in seclusion, in a hut across a bridge from where the couple lived. Each noon hour, his wife brought him a bowl of noodles in broth, but each day they arrived cold, until she hit upon the idea of pouring a little sesame oil on top of them. The oil sealed the surface of the soup, keeping in the heat.

33. Deng's oldest son Deng Pufang was thrown out of a third-storey window by Red Guards at Beijing University. Later, the Canadian government arranged for him to come to Ottawa for an operation, which was moderately successful, but he remains confined to a wheelchair. In 1988, he founded the China Welfare Fund for the Disabled, and he is active in the organizing of the Paralympics and was executive president of the organizing committee for the Olympics in Beijing in 2008.

34. A key negotiator for Britain on the issue of Hong Kong was Richard Evans (now Sir), alongside whom I sat learning Chinese at SOAS in 1954–1955.

EIGHT ★ *Greet, Meet, and Eat*

1. It is customary to date U of A's international relations from the meeting of its founding President Henry Marshall Tory and a young Japanese student named Kurimoto on board a Pacific liner in the 1920s. As a result of that encounter, Tory persuaded Kurimoto to attend the University of Alberta, thus initiating the most abiding international connection in the history of the university. From that time onward, the U of A has had a lively interest in attracting international students, but the direct involvement of the university abroad only blossomed after World War II as Canada's role in the Commonwealth, through the Colombo Plan, expanded. In addition, Canada's active participation in United Nations programs provided opportunities. Individual members of the university staff were called upon to participate in projects. Among them were Fred and Helen Bentley of the agriculture and home economics faculties, respectively, who undertook assignments in India. The university also sent and received students under the Commonwealth Scholarship and Fellowship Plan.

2. By the time Horowitz stepped down as president, the university had projects in Brazil and Kenya (home economics); Thailand and China (agriculture and business); Japan, China, Korea, and Africa (pharmacy and medicine); Indonesia (rehabilitation medicine); Korea, China, the Caribbean, Africa, and Thailand (education); and Bangladesh (engineering). The university undertook a major management project in Africa, in collaboration with the World Bank. In addition, the university had scholarly exchange agreements with universities

in Europe, Asia, Africa, North and South America, and the Caribbean. Taking immediate advantage of Glasnost, the U of A became the first foreign institution to sign an agreement directly with a Soviet university (Ivan Franko University in Lviv) without having to go through Moscow's central authority.

3. Margo did not let matters go completely. When I was away in Bangladesh in the spring of 1987, she took advantage of a slump in the housing market to acquire, at a bargain price, the lot and house next door to her parents' house, thus solving the question of just where we would expand the old house.

4. In the spring of 1994, I received a letter from CIDA that stated I was being sued personally by the organization for a million dollars. The reason was an unresolved dispute over the Black Dragon River project, specifically over unspent funds. The director of the project felt that CIDA should pay money to the university according to the agreed budget, with any unspent funds accruing to the university. CIDA's view was that only actual expenditures should be reimbursed to the university, with unspent funds returned to the Canadian government, i.e., CIDA. With the discussions at an impasse, CIDA decided to get my attention with its letter. It did. I flew to Ottawa to meet with CIDA's vice-president. He was sympathetic to a compromise solution and the matter was put in the hands of the university comptroller to negotiate with CIDA. After a series of meetings, which blessedly did not involve me, the matter was resolved.

5. It was in the days when university administrators travelled in economy class. I took things one step further, using travel points for university business. I have not been able to find anyone to follow my example.

6. Myer Horowitz was the first U of A president to visit the People's Republic of China.

7. Ted Scott was later killed in a car crash in June 2004. John Harker is currently president of Cape Breton University.

8. Among the committee members were Iona Campanola, Flora MacDonald, Rosemary Brown, Jodi White, all women with great political experience.

9. When apartheid came to an end in 1994 so did SAETF. CIDA was now able to give assistance directly through the Canadian Embassy in South Africa.

10. Charles Burton has remained a close friend. He is currently at Brock University, but he served twice in the Canadian Embassy in Beijing in charge of cultural and educational affairs. He is superbly fluent in Chinese and a much sought after commentator on Chinese affairs.

11. At the time of this trip, the atmosphere between the two countries continued to be tense—Soviet scholars had interpreted the Cultural Revolution as primarily an anti-Soviet campaign. The only Chinese restaurant in Moscow was closed—it was made clear to me there would be no thaw in relations with China while Leonid Brezhnev was in power.

12. Krawchenko was a political scientist and an activist in Ukrainian affairs. After Ukraine broke from the Soviet Union, he pursued a career within the Ukraine

government. Currently, he is the director-general of Central Asia University in the Krygyz Republic.

13. Gorbachev introduced a policy in the 1980s of restructuring the Communist Party and the economy under the title Perestroika, which is now considered to have led to the collapse of the Soviet Union.

14. Canada granted refugee status on the assumption that a person faced severe punishment if they returned to their home country. Students who accepted the Canadian offer and then returned to China to find jobs brought their refugee status into question and could not expect services from the Canadian Embassy.

15. Meekison, in my opinion, was the best president the university never had. By employing a headhunter, a selection committee is automatically prejudiced against an internal candidate. The selection committee is aware of the reputation of the internal candidate but relies entirely on the headhunter's characterization of the outside candidate, who, it is often said, appears to walk on water in comparison. The headhunter process is not only confidential—it is secretive. The chair of the Board of Governors at the time of the Davenport selection was the chair in the final years I was on the Board. I wrote him an angry letter, not because Meekison had lost but because they had conducted the search in secret and had denied themselves the right to test the headhunter's suppositions against some other independent enquiry. Headhunters can bring in excellent external candidates, but the playing field should be levelled for the consideration of internal ones.

16. By 2006, most universities in Canada had abolished mandatory retirement at sixty-five.

17. During my years at the University of Alberta, I was fortunate to supervise a number of Chinese graduate students. My first, Chuang Chen-kuan, provided me with insights into Taiwan; Lawrence Lau and Kwok Choi Mung enlarged my appreciation of the geographical variations in Chinese culture; Chai Soon Joo gave me a better understanding of Singapore; P.K. Chiu and Ho Man Chan provided me with another side of Hong Kong life and history; while Zhao Yifeng and Dai Xianguang deepened my understanding of recent Chinese history.

NINE ★ *My China*

1. That she is a woman is worth noting, since traditionally few restaurant chefs are female.

2. Called *The Other Side of Gold Mountain*, the exhibit was displayed in the Bruce Peel Special Collections Library from June 9 to the end of August 2010. I curated the exhibit and wrote the historical text for the catalogue, which is now used in local schools.

3. The Democracy Project brought together scholars in the social sciences from China and Canada in joint seminars held in both countries (1992–1998). Funded mainly by CIDA, with assistance from the Department of Foreign Affairs and

International Trade and CASS, it enabled Canadian experts such as Alan Cairns, Jan Meisel, Craig Brown, Ramsay Cook, David Bercusson, and Stephan Dion to engage with Chinese counterparts on questions of Canada's history, and social, political, and economic structures. It was the first, and perhaps the only, intense and in-depth engagement between scholars of the two countries on the subject of Canada.

4. To someone like me, who visited China first in 1964 and at frequent intervals thereafter, the changes have been truly astonishing. Conversely, because I have observed China first-hand over a period of nearly five decades, Chinese interest in me has increased. I have been the subject of profiles in academic journals, and my observations on China, particularly in 1973–1974, have received public airing in journals, newspapers, and on television.

5. Among them were famous writers, historians, and thinkers. Mao Zedong worked in the Beida Library at age twenty-five (1918–1919). On May 4, 1919, students and professors from Beida marched in protest against the shoddy treatment China received at the Peace Conference at Versailles and the weak ministers of the Chinese government who accepted it. This demonstration and others at other universities in China sparked new movements in politics and culture. The Chinese Communist Party dates its birth to this event, four years before the party was formally founded.

6. Some of those who stayed were caught up in the Hundred Flowers and anti-Rightist campaigns of the mid-1950s and were put in prison or sent to the countryside for reform through labour, or both. Intellectuals had to understand the true meaning of the worker peasant state that Mao was shaping.

7. The goal of Gorbachev's scheduled visit was to formally recognize an end to the Sino-Soviet dispute. The visit was to be a triumph for Deng Xiaoping and his policies.

8. In 2006, I was made an honorary research member of the Chinese Academy of Social Sciences in the study of comparative civilizations.

9. Tiananmen is one of those events that everyone knows about but no one *knows* about. In the West, we are blocked from looking at its reality because our media have files in print and video that for them (and many of us) *are* the reality. The Chinese are blocked from looking at its reality because it strikes at the foundations of power of the current leaders. Not that the current leaders were personally involved in Tiananmen—they were not. But their positions, as heirs of Deng Xiaoping, are dependent on a certain interpretation of the events. (As a controversial event, it is not unlike October 1970 in Canada, except that the media of the world were not present in Quebec that October and Quebecers were not inclined to defy the proclamation of martial law.)

10. Li Peng is the adopted son of Zhou Enlai, but he is generally regarded as having very few of Zhou's qualities.

11. But the voices of those who want the matter fully aired remain strong. One

of those voices belonged to Paul Lin, who up to this time was noted more for explaining party policy than for challenging it. His voice fell silent in July 2004.

12. In China, it is known as Falun Dafa.

13. Westerners are always impressed by the numbers of people executed in China, many of them for property crimes and corruption. Yet in 1998, when looked at from the point of view of the number of executions per population, one was at greater risk of being executed in Texas under Governor George W. Bush than in China. Moreover, the United States continues to lead China in the total number of people in prison (roughly 2.3 to 1.6 million), even though the US has just under a quarter of the population of China. In 2008, China executed 1,178 people in contrast with India, with nearly the same population, where only one person has been executed since 1995. Iran reportedly executed 346 people in 2008, roughly 30 per cent of the Chinese total, but for a population of only seventy-three million.

14. The frustration of this attempt was illustrated by the fate of one Canadian company representative who went to China in the early 1970s to sell a certain process to the Chinese. On even days he lectured to Chinese technicians on the process and on odd days he was toured around the city. This went on for months, as he felt, and continued to assure his home office, that he was on the very cusp of clinching the deal. Unbeknown to him, the French were also pushing a similar process and on the odd days they were giving lectures and on the even ones they were being given tours. In the end, the Chinese opted for the French. The Canadian lost his job and his marriage broke up, but perhaps he ultimately enjoyed some wry satisfaction. It seems that both the French and Canadian processes depended on a key American component. Neither could get US permission to export it to China.

15. Currently, the most famous case is that of Lai Changxing of Xiamen, Fujian province, who fled to Canada in 1999 and is described as "China's most wanted fugitive." He is wanted on smuggling, bribery, and corruption charges, but to date he has succeeded in using the Canadian refugee and justice systems to evade deportation. He is but one of several such accused individuals. Before Hong Kong was returned to China, a number of members of the Hong Kong police force, both British and Chinese, found refuge in Canada for both themselves and their wealth acquired through bribes received while serving in Hong Kong.

INDEX

Bond, Mrs., 52, 57
Bordo, John, 126
Britnell, Sharon, 230
Brown, George, 81
Bumstead, Ivan, 201, 229
Burns, John, 145, 152, 160, 169, 179, 273n16
Burton, Charles, 230, 244, 281n10
Burton, Neil, 190–91

Cameo Café, 16–17, **26**, 27, 29, 37
Canada
　cultural relations with China, 151–54, 167–74, 176–77, 276n8
　and East Asian studies, 130
　history of relations with China, 134–37, 257–59
　and NATO Parliamentarians' Conference, 86–87
　and overseas development, 221–22, 223
　and Tiananmen Square protests, 236, 282n14
　and Trudeau policy on China, 137–39, 140–41
　and university boom of 1960s, 92–93, 269n3
　See also Canadian Embassy in China; CIDA
Canada Council, 87
Canadian Association for Asian Studies (CAAS), 98, 186
Canadian Embassy in China, 141–45, 147–49, 152–53, 208
Canadian Importers Association (CIA), 170–71
Canadian International Development Agency. See CIDA (Canadian International Development Agency)
Canadian Pacific Railway (CPR), 46–48
Canadian Wheat Board, 176
Cao Tejin, 245
Chai Soon Joo, 282n17
Chan Ho Man, 282n17

Chen Qineng, 245
Chen Yi, 272n6
Chen Yu-shih, 235, 236
Cheng, Daisy, 243
Chiang Kai-shek, 135, 138
Chiang Kai-shek, Madame (Soong Meiling), 135
China
　admitted to UN, 44
　BE as expert on, 133, 137–39, 249, 283n4, 283n8
　beaver trade with Canada, 155–60, 274n23, 274n24
　becomes People's Republic, 35, 135–36
　BE's early interest in, 20, 34, 35
　BE's travel in, 100–10, 112–13, 203–04, 213–19, 227–28
　break with Russia, 101, 103
　changes in under Deng, 195–96, 213–14, 220, 225, 227, 251–52
　criticism of Western attitudes about, 259–61, 284n13
　cuisine of, 241–42
　cultural relations with Canada, 151–54, 167–74, 176–77, 276n8
　early years under Mao, 63, 185
　embassy in Canada, 272n7
　fall of Gang of Four, 187–91
　future of, 261–62
　Great Leap Forward, 50, 106
　history of Canada's relations with, 134–37, 257–59
　history of universities in, 246–49, 250, 283n5
　and Lin Biao crisis, 161–62
　missionaries in, 257–58
　modern day problems of, 253–56
　and N. Bethune, 155, 159, 174–77, 183–84, 258, 276n14
　relations with Russia, 50, 234–35, 247, 255, 277n3, 281n11, 283n7
　Russian building in, 102, 106, 274n18, 278n19

University of Toronto, 91

Vancouver Symphony, 169

Wade-Giles system, 53–54
Waley, Arthur, 100
Walker, John R., 145, 179–80, 273n16
Wang, Chi, 244
Wang Benxu, 144, 273n12
Wang Bing, 246
Wang Hairong, 165, 166
Wang Hongwen, 162, 185
Wang Jun, 197, 198–99, 200–01
Warsaw, Poland, 123
Washington, DC, 81
Waterfall, Don, 144, 273n13
Watson, Patrick, 104, 211
White, Terry, 213
White, William C., 91, 258
White Ash, 2, 3–5, **6**
Wiedner, Donald L., 93, 98–99, 100
Willey, David, 110
Wiseman, June, 65
Wong, Sophie, 61, 100, 110
Wood, Patricia, 72
Wooding, Kathleen, 85
Wordie, Cameron, 48, 266n6
World Bank, 226
World War II, 17–18, 26, 134–35
Wright, Janet, 237
Wynne, Greville, 89

Xi'an, 228
Xinjiang, 255, 256
Xinqiao Hotel, 147, 274n18

Yakutsk, 233–34
Yao Wenyuan, 189
yin and yang, 262
Yom Kippur War, 164

Zelmer, Amy, 223, 224
Zhang Wenjin, 177, 272n7
Zhao Yifeng, 246, 282n17
Zhao Ziyang, 199, 220
Zhou Enlai
    criticism of, 172, 275n4
    and Cultural Revolution, 272n6
    death, 186
    and Deng, 220
    health, 179, 185, 276n17
    meets C. Bissell, 108
    and reform, 106, 124, 185, 277n1
    relations with Mao, 276n6
    and Trudeau visit, 162, **163**, **164**,
        165–67
    view of today, 249
Zhu De, 186
Zhu Guisheng
    background, 202–03
    and BE's injury, 207, 210–11
    and BE's visa expiry, 212, 213, 279n25
    research of, 278n18

Other Titles from
The University of Alberta Press

EMBLEMS OF EMPIRE

Selections from the Mactaggart Art Collection
John E. Vollmer & Jacqueline Simcox

368 pages | Full-colour throughout, colour photographs, map, index, glossary.
A copublication with University of Alberta Museums
978-0-88864-486-2 | 60.00 (T) cloth
Asian Art/Art History

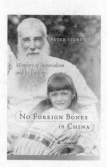

NO FOREIGN BONES IN CHINA

Memoirs of Imperialism and Its Ending
Peter Stursberg

240 pages | B&W photos
978-0-88864-387-2 | $24.95 (T) paper
Biography/History

THE LADY NAMED THUNDER

A Biography of Dr. Ethel Margaret Phillips (1876–1951)
Clifford H. Phillips
Brian L. Evans, Foreword

436 pages | B&W photos, index
978-0-88864-417-6 | $34.95 (T) paper
Biography /History